[澳大利亚] 米歇尔·巴德利 著   叶星 李井奎 译

牛津通识读本·

行为经济学

Behavioural Economics

A Very Short Introduction

译林出版社

图书在版编目（CIP）数据

行为经济学／（澳）米歇尔·巴德利（Michelle Baddeley）著；叶星，李井奎译. —南京：译林出版社，2024.7
（牛津通识读本）
书名原文：Behavioural Economics: A Very Short Introduction
ISBN 978-7-5753-0127-5

Ⅰ.①行… Ⅱ.①米… ②叶… ③李… Ⅲ.①行为经济学 Ⅳ.①F069.9

中国国家版本馆 CIP 数据核字（2024）第 095488 号

Behavioural Economics: A Very Short Introduction, First Edition
by Michelle Baddeley
Copyright © Michelle Baddeley 2017
Behavioural Economics: A Very Short Introduction was originally published in English in 2017. This licensed edition is published by arrangement with Oxford University Press. Yilin Press, Ltd is solely responsible for this bilingual edition from the original work and Oxford University Press shall have no liability for any errors, omissions or inaccuracies or ambiguities in such bilingual edition or for any losses caused by reliance thereon.
Chinese and English edition copyright © 2024 by Yilin Press, Ltd
All rights reserved.

著作权合同登记号　图字：10-2020-535 号

行为经济学　［澳大利亚］米歇尔·巴德利　／著　叶　星　李井奎　／译

责任编辑	陈　锐
装帧设计	景秋萍
校　　对	施雨嘉
责任印制	董　虎

原文出版	Oxford University Press, 2017
出版发行	译林出版社
地　　址	南京市湖南路 1 号 A 楼
邮　　箱	yilin@yilin.com
网　　址	www.yilin.com
市场热线	025-86633278
排　　版	南京展望文化发展有限公司
印　　刷	江苏凤凰通达印刷有限公司
开　　本	890 毫米 ×1260 毫米　1/32
印　　张	9.625
插　　页	4
版　　次	2024 年 7 月第 1 版
印　　次	2024 年 7 月第 1 次印刷
书　　号	ISBN 978-7-5753-0127-5
定　　价	39.00 元

版权所有·侵权必究

译林版图书若有印装错误可向出版社调换。质量热线：025-83658316

序　言

王湘红

在这个快速变化的时代,经济学作为一门科学,其理论和实践都面临着前所未有的挑战和机遇。传统经济学的理性人假设,虽然在理论上具有简洁之美,但在解释现实世界中人们的经济行为时却显得力不从心。正是在这样的背景下,行为经济学应运而生,它为我们理解人类决策提供了新的视角和工具。

"牛津通识读本"丛书的《行为经济学》是澳大利亚著名经济学者米歇尔·巴德利撰写的一本介绍行为经济学基础的图书。这本书以浅显易懂的方式向读者介绍了行为经济学的基本概念、理论、实验和应用,以及它对传统经济学的挑战和影响。本书在国际上已经广受好评,我很高兴将这本书介绍给中国的读者,并相信它将深远影响对经济决策感兴趣的广大读者。

在这篇序言中,我想强调几个关键点:

- **跨学科的融合**

行为经济学是心理学与经济学交叉融合的产物。它突破了传统经济学的局限，将人类行为的复杂性纳入考量，为我们提供了一个更为全面和真实的经济决策模型。

- **深入浅出的阐述**

本书以通俗易懂的语言，向读者介绍了行为经济学的核心概念和理论。即使是没有经济学背景的读者，也能够轻松地理解和掌握书中的内容。

- **启发性的思考**

本书鼓励读者对传统经济学的假设进行批判性思考，并探索人类行为背后的深层原因。这种启发性的思考，有利于培养读者的独立思考能力和创新精神。

- **理论与实践的结合**

米歇尔·巴德利教授不仅介绍了行为经济学的理论基础，还展示了这些理论是如何在市场营销、储蓄决策、政策制定等领域得到应用的。这使得本书不仅具有学术价值，也具有实践指导意义。

- **丰富的案例分析**

通过大量的实证研究和案例分析，米歇尔·巴德利教授生动地展示了行为经济学理论的实际应用，使读者能够直观地感受到行为经济学理论的力量。读者可以重点关注一下行为助推机制：在个人决策中，行为助推可以帮助解决自我控制问题；在公共政策中，行为助推可以通过非强制的政策手段优化团体和社会的福利。

我希望本书的出版能够帮助中国读者了解和学习行为经济学。同时，我也期待读者能够通过阅读本书，对经济决策有更深刻的理解，对行为经济学有更大的兴趣，并在各自的领域中应用行为经济学的原理。

最后,感谢译林社邀请我为本书作序,愿它能够激发读者的更多思考,为中国的行为经济学研究和实践贡献力量。

谨以此书献给我的祖母艾琳·巴德利（1916—2009），

纪念她百年诞辰。

怀念她的生活智慧和对孙女们的慷慨支持！

要是一年四季,全是游戏的假日,
那么游戏也会变得像工作一般令人烦厌;
惟其因为它们是不常有的,
人们才会盼望它们的到来。

——威廉·莎士比亚《亨利四世》第一部
（第一幕第二场,173—195）

目 录

致　谢　1
第一章　经济学与行为　1
第二章　动机与激励　8
第三章　社会生活　19
第四章　快速思考　34
第五章　风险选择　49
第六章　如何看待时间　67
第七章　性格、心境和情绪　82
第八章　宏观经济中的行为　100
第九章　经济行为与公共政策　115
索　引　126
英文原文　143

致　谢

我要感谢我的文字编辑乔伊·梅勒尔，她对手稿做了热情、细致的工作，并提出了许多良好建议；感谢多萝西·麦卡锡，她通校了全书，对本书的内容颇为赞许。我还要感谢牛津大学出版社所有同人的帮助，包括：安德莉亚·基根，感谢她所提出的明智建议，以及在本书早期阶段所给予的指导；杰妮·纳吉，她异常高效地指导了本书的出版工作；黛博拉·普罗瑟罗，感谢她在插图方面给予的帮助和建议；以及鲁比·康斯特布尔、克洛伊·穆森和玛莎·坎尼恩在编辑工作上的帮助；还要感谢萨拉斯瓦蒂·伊斯拉贾对本书制作过程的监督。本书样章和初稿的匿名审稿人也贡献了一些很好的想法和建议，所以我也要感谢他们。当然，一如既往，全书的错漏之责，悉由本人担负。

我还要感谢所有读过本书书稿的我的家人、朋友、学生和同事。我特别感谢彼得·卢恩，他通读了本书手稿，并提出了一些很好的建议；感谢尼西·桑巴特朗对本书初稿的热情反馈，也感谢她提出了第二章中泰国的例子。我还要特别提一下我以前在伦敦大学学院的学生约瑟芬·普赖茨,她认为"牛津通识读本"系列是一个极好的项目,建议我优先考虑这本书的写作。

最后感谢我的丈夫克里斯,感谢他的慷慨、热情和对我所做一切的耐心支持。

第一章

经济学与行为

行为经济学是一个热门话题。行为经济学研究经常出现在经济学和科学领域的顶级学术期刊上。它在社交媒体上也有很高的知名度，新闻记者们经常就这一领域出现的新书和新的研究撰写文章。世界各地的政府和其他决策者正将来自行为经济学的洞见融入他们的政策设计中，同样，越来越多的主流经济学家在设计他们的模型时也在不断增添行为经济学的因素。

什么是行为经济学？为什么人们对它如此感兴趣？通过承认我们的决策在成本和收益的理性计算之外还受社会和心理因素的影响，行为经济学扩展了经济学原理。它还拓宽了经济学的研究领域，让更多的人更容易理解经济学。不可否认，经济学是一门极其重要的学科，因为无论从个人层面、国家层面还是国际层面，它都关乎我们以及我们子孙后代的福祉。但也有许多人认为，经济学是一门深奥的技术统治论学科，缺乏经济学专业训练的很难理解其中的关键概念。行为经济学有可能改变这一点，因为它让许多人觉得更有趣。它为我们的决策提供了更

1 直观、更少数学的解释。

行为经济学之所以有趣的另一个原因，是其基本原理的多元性和多样性。行为经济学家将经济学与其他诸多学科的见解结合在了一起，例如心理学（尤其是社会心理学）、社会学、神经科学和演化生物学。行为经济学家利用这种多学科思想的融合，在丰富我们对经济和金融行为理解的同时，又不必放弃那种通常与传统经济学相联系的分析能力。

为什么行为经济学如此不同？

大多数经济学家将人描述为数学计算器，他们能够轻松而准确地以英镑和便士、美元和美分的形式，将他们所做选择的货币成本和收益相加，而不用在意周围的人在做什么。大多数经济学家的出发点都是这样一个假设，即经济问题的出现，不是因为作为个体的人容易犯错，而是因为市场及其配套制度的失灵。行业进入壁垒阻止小公司加入市场竞争，从而使资金雄厚的大型垄断企业主导了市场，抬高了价格，并限制了产量。信息可能会被扭曲。可能存在市场的缺失——例如，由于不存在香烟烟雾和污染的自然形成的市场，所以价格不能完全平衡吸烟或污染的收益和成本。

行为经济学中的理性

虽然传统经济学家不关注理性的诸多局限，但行为经济学家不会假设人是超理性的生物。相反，他们更为关注理性决策所面临的一些局限。许多行为经济学家都会援引赫伯特·西蒙的一些观点。西蒙不仅是一位心理学家和计算机科学家，还是一位诺贝尔经济学奖得主。他以提出了**有限理性**这一概念而闻名，这个概念表明，在我们做出决策时，我们是被各种各样的约束所限制的。认知的约束可能会限制我们选择最佳策略的能力。我们在记忆或数字处理能力上的局限，意味着有时我们不得不选择某个特定的选项，因为我们没有信息，或者缺乏处理认知的时间或能力来考虑其他选项。

行为经济学家还发展了理性的其他概念。另一位诺贝尔经济学奖得主弗农·L.史密斯发展了**生态理性**的概念。他假设理性是可塑的，因为它是由我们所处的情境和环境所决定的。同样，格尔德·吉仁泽认为，我们受实践理性的驱动——在现实世界中，我们必须快速而"节约"地做决定——我们没有时间去搜集大量的信息或是应用复杂的决策规则。我们的决定迅速而简单。这种方法通常很有效，但有时会导致我们产生系统性的行为偏差。

另一位对理性的含义有着有趣见解的经济学家是哈维·莱本斯坦，他提出了**选择性理性**的概念——类似于弗农·L.史密斯的生态理性。我们会选择何时变得超级理性，有时我们会充分考虑所有可用的信息。然而，在其他时候，我们可能会决定维持现状，停留在莱本斯坦所描述的**惰性区域**。这让我们的选择变得"有黏性"。我们并不总是能有效地使自己的行为适应新环境。莱本斯坦认为，当我们的行为变得有黏性的时候，这里有两种解释：要么是我们认为改变选择的成本太高；要么是我们太懒、太缺乏兴趣，从而不愿做出改变。

因此，行为经济学家对于理性意味着什么有着复杂的看法。大多数情况下，他们承认我们的理性是可变的，并且取决于我们所处的环境。当我们无法获得好的信息，当我们匆匆忙忙，当我们面临认知约束或社会影响时，我们可能就会遽下决策，而在一个时间和信息均充裕的完美世界，我们是本可以改善这些决策的。

数据约束

虽然这种形式的经济学有很大的潜力，但对行为经济学家来说，一个关键的制约因素是寻找相关和可靠的数据。行为经济学家经常利用实验来搜集数据，这与经济学中传统的经验主义方法形成了鲜明对比，即用计量和统计方法来分析政府和国际统计机构搜集的公开历史数据。

通常，行为经济学家试图推断出人们的思维和感受过程，但尚不清楚到底是什么在推动人们的选择。标准的经济数据来源在这方面没有太大帮助，因为传统的经济数据是关于观察到的选择和结果（例如宏观经济背景下的就业和失业统计数据）的数据。行为经济学家可以依赖调查数据，例如，关于人们对自己幸福和福祉的看法的问题正在被纳入家庭调查。但调查数据有其局限性。研究人员如何识别具有代表性的样本？研究人员如何应对调查问题的不真实或不了解情况的答案？这些都是问题所在。

实验数据

实验室实验可能是行为经济学家最常用的数据来源。许多实验室实验的问题在于，它们是在大学里进行的，通常是由大学生作为实验参与者。学生在实验中的选择可能与现实世界的选择不太相关,在这种情况下,实验数据会缺乏**外部有效性**,实验结果将无法很好地转化为现实世界中的结果。例如,如果一名学生参与交易实验,那么所观察到的他们的选择可能与真正交易者的行为方式几乎没有联系,因为学生的知识和经验有限,他们可能没有那么强烈的谋求成功的动机。

获得可靠实验数据的另一个重要障碍是实验设计。实验人员会发现,很难在经济学中构建一个"干净的"受控实验。一些经济学家批评了行为经济学家的早期发现,理由是实验参与者的反应表明他们对自己应该做什么感到困惑,并且所发现的异常行为并非真正的系统性偏差。其中也有道德权衡。我们应该允许实验人员让他或她的参与者经历什么样的实验干预措施?比如说,如果他们是脆弱的医院患者的话。欺骗实验参与者是否合法?有没有可能设计一个完全不涉及欺骗的人为实验?

通过"顽童调查"(Survey Monkey)、"高产学术"(Prolific Academic)和"猎兔任务"(Task Rabbit)等网络工具以及越来越多的移动应用程序可以进行在线实验。这些方法成本低廉,并且是获得大量实验数据的快速简便的方法。但研究人员如何确保他们使用的是具有代表性的样本呢?他们如何处理无动机参与者的问题?这些人可能只是随意地敲击计算机键盘,最感兴趣的只是从这种操作中赚钱。激励实验参与者在实验中真实地表现,是行为经济学家面临的一个重要问题,尤其是在学术研究预算往往有限的情况下。

神经科学数据和神经经济学

结合实验数据,神经科学数据可以帮助阐明一些关键的影响。神经科学技术是多种多样的。脑损伤患者所做的选择可以帮助我们了解哪些大脑区域与经济决策有关。同样，脑成像技术（例如，功能性磁共振成像）可以捕捉到我们的经济决策与特定大脑区域的神经反应之间的关系。另一种越来越流行的技术是经颅磁刺激（TMS），它涉及大脑的特定区域，并可以观察人们的选择如何因这种暂时干扰而发生变化。还有其他更简单、更便宜的神经科学工具，包括监测生理反应（心率、脉搏率等），或测量激素水平（例如，信任研究中的催产素水平，金融风险研究中的睾酮水平）。

神经科学数据的主要优点是它相对客观。就调查的情况而言，受访者可能表达了不可靠的主观意见，或者他们可能有理由撒谎或操纵自己的反应。对于实验参与者来说，对使用神经科学工具所测量的生理反应加以控制，即使有可能，也要困难得多，尽管这并不能消除他们实验设计中的实验者偏差。

自然实验和随机对照试验（RCT）

如前所述，标准实验的一个问题是，它们可能缺乏外部有效性。**自然实验**——如果我们能找到的话——是一种解决方案，自然实验数据是从真实世界的事件和行为中偶然产生的。一个例子是经济学家德拉维尼亚和马尔门迪尔对健身房会员和出勤数据的研究，如第六章所述，这项研究表明，许多人为很少使用的健身房会员身份支付了大笔的费用。但是，来自自然实验的优良数据是很罕见的，如果仅仅依靠这些数据来源，我们不会走得太远。还有一种解决方案是使用随机对照试验。这些是临床试验中常用的实验方法，用于识别处理效应：对接受试验处理的实验参与者的影响与对仅接受安慰剂的对照组的实验参与者的影响进行比较。

行为经济学家借用这些方法来比较对照组与处理组的反应。然而,由于实验者会发现很难设计出安慰剂的社会经济等效物,因此这些研究中的对照组根本没有接受任何处理。这意味着,对于行为经济学的随机对照试验,我们不可能确定干预本身是否改变了行为,抑或仅仅是对任何干预都会做出积极反应的人们得到安慰剂的某种经济等效物后所产生的效应,而不管这种干预真的多么有效。尽管如此,行为发展经济学家现在广泛使用随机对照试验,来研究发展干预措施对社会经济成果的影响。

关键主题

行为经济学的文献可谓汗牛充栋。在这个非常简短的介绍中,我们将重点关注几个关键主题,每个主题都在以下章节中进行了探讨:是什么激励了我们;我们如何受到社会的影响;我们犯错误的方式和原因是什么;我们如何判断和误判风险;我们的短期主义倾向;以及性格、心境和情绪如何驱使我们做出选择和决定。一旦这些关键的行为微观经济学原理被探索出来,我们就可以探讨如何在行为宏观经济学中把它们结合起来。然后,我们将转向公共政策制定者所采纳政策的含义和教训,运用基于行为经济学洞见的一些具有影响力的政策研究案例加以说明。

第二章

动机与激励

如果你去看一群经济学家聚在一起谈话——例如在一场会议上——你就会发现，不消多长时间，一定会有经济学家提到"激励"这个词。激励是经济分析的基本驱动力。激励措施鼓励人们更努力、更好地工作。它们支持企业提供更多、更好的产品。经济学家通常认为，金钱是主要的激励因素，并且无疑可以提供客观（尽管不一定准确或公平）的价值衡量标准。在日常生活中，金钱激励着我们。它决定了我们为购买的商品和服务所支付的价格，以及我们所挣得的工资。价格越高，工资待遇越好，决策就越富有成效。金钱激励是市场的基础，而市场协调了许多不同的人和企业的选择。

作为一名行为经济学家，我不会反对价格和金钱是激励我们更努力、更好地工作的强大动力的观点，而是认为还有一系列复杂的其他社会经济和心理因素也在驱动我们的决策。我们的动机远远不只是金钱。作为一名学者，我的薪水可能不如我在私营部门的薪水高。如果纵观我一生的收入，我有丰厚的养老金和更高的工作保障这一事实，也许解释了为什么我今天没有最大化我的收入。但还有其他的东西在起作用，因为我的工作中有一些我真正喜欢的部分——它们利用了我的其他非金钱动机。有时，我想，即便我中了彩票，此生再也不必担心是否有足够的钱来生活，我还是不会放弃我的工作。我的工作除了带给我一份薪水，它本身还时常带给我一份快乐。

内在和外在动机与激励

我们每天都在工作和生活中看到这一点——在工作中，我们受到各种不同的金钱和非金钱奖励的激励。大多数人都希望自己所做的工作能得到报酬，但有些人不仅仅为了钱而工作。有些人之所以去工作，也可能是受到来自努力工作和拥有一份受人尊敬工作的社会奖励的激励，例如社会认可。有些人则是受到道德激励的驱使，例如那些为慈善机构工作的人。其他人也许只是喜欢他们所做的事情，所以即使报酬不高也会去做，例如许多艺术家就是这样。

行为经济学家通过将激励和动机分为两大类——**内在的**和**外在的**——来体现它们对我们决策和选择的更广泛影响。

外在动机

外在动机包含了我们作为个体所受到的激励和奖励，例如，当这个世界和我们周围的人鼓励我们去做一些我们本来不愿意做的事情时就是这样。此时，我们的行为一定受到自身之外某种事物的驱动：我们需要以激励形式存在的外在动机。一个常见而有力的激励因素是金钱：我们工作是因为我们拿到了工资或薪水。更强力的外在激励是身体威胁。但外在动机也可以来自非金钱激励,例如,像社会认可和社会成就这类社会奖励。更高的工资,更好的考试成绩,奖项以及社会认可,这些都是外在奖励。

内在动机

内在动机反映了我们的内在目标和态度的影响。内心的反应有时会鼓励我们努力——这是为了我们自己,而不是因为我们被某种外在奖励所驱使。当我们被自己内心的某种东西内在地激励时——无论是职业自豪感、责任感、对事业的忠诚、解决谜题的乐趣,还是使身体保持活跃所带来的愉悦——我们就不需要外在激励了。当我们下棋、玩牌或打电脑游戏时,我们享受这种挑战,并且这种享受是由我们自身内在驱动的。许多工匠和手工艺人喜欢他们的工作,并为此感到自豪。虽然他们和他们的家庭需要钱来生活,他们的工资并不是无关紧要的,但金钱只是诸多激励因素之一。

挤出效应

外在动机和内在动机不是相互独立的。外在动机会**挤出**我们的内在动机。当我们的内在动机被外在奖励所抑制时,就会发生这种情况。一些实验已经表明了这是如何发生的。在一组研究中,实验人员要求大学生解决一系列的谜题,以表明内在动机被挤出的现象。学生被随机分为两组:第一组有报酬,第二组则没有。令人惊讶的是,第二组的一些学生比第一组的学生做得更好。没有报酬的学生享受着智力上的挑战,有报酬的学生可能是因为报酬相对较低而失去了积极性。当学生有报酬时，他们的注意力从享受任务的智力挑战（内在动机）转移到了是否得到足够的报酬上（外在动机）。其他研究也表明，小额报酬可能会使人失去动力，导致比完全没有报酬时更糟糕的表现，因为小额报酬挤出了内在动机，又没有提供足够的外在激励来充分发展外在动机。

正如经济学家乌里·格尼兹和奥尔多·鲁斯蒂奇尼对托儿所的一项研究所显示的那样，外在的奖惩也会影响我们的日常生活，而且往往是以令人讶异的方式。以色列的一家托儿所出现了家长接孩子迟到的问题。老师们常常被迫在下班时间过后还要留下来照顾孩子，直到孩子的父母来到托儿所接走他们。这对托儿所和它的老师来说是要付出高昂代价的，而且不胜其烦，所以托儿所管理人员决定引入罚款作为一种威慑。

效果令人惊讶：引入罚款后，迟到的家长越来越多，而不是越来越少。研究人员推测，这可能是因为父母没有把罚款理解为一种威慑。他们把它理解为一种价格。托儿所提供了一项额外的服务——在正常上学时间以外照顾孩子。一些家长愿意为这项额外的服务付费，因为家长们认为这是一种互惠的安排（毕竟托儿所得到了更多的钱），他们不再感受到以前那种阻止他们经常迟到的罪恶感。这可能再次反映了内在动机的挤出现象。在罚款之前，许多父母可能在本质上都是出于合作和体谅的考虑，尽可能准时到场。引入罚款后，他们对事态的看法发生了变化——他们只是在为迟到付费。罚款的金钱不利因素挤出了成为乐于配合的父母的内在动机。

献血是外在动机何时以及如何挤出内在动机的另一个重要

例子。在许多国家和地区,献血水平低是一个大问题,一些经济学家探索了鼓励更多人献血的新方法。显而易见的经济解决方案是给捐赠者支付报酬。然而,当研究人员尝试引入为献血支付报酬以鼓励更多人献血时,他们发现这产生了一种反常和意想不到的效果:它降低了而不是提高了人们的献血意愿。一种可能的解释是,来自金钱报酬的外在动机削弱了捐赠者成为好公民的内在动机。

亲社会选择和形象动机

慈善捐赠是外在动机和内在动机之间相互复杂作用的另一个例子。有些人做慈善是因为他们觉得有道德或宗教义务去这样做。另一些人做慈善是因为这能让他们看起来更加善良。很多人这么做可能是出于各种各样的原因。当马克·扎克伯格和他的妻子为庆祝他们第一个孩子的出生而捐赠了大部分财产时,这一选择是否与对世界有所帮助这样的内在道德动机有关呢?也许,他们的选择是为了让别人钦佩他们是慷慨的慈善家,从而提高他们的社会声誉?

行为经济学家更深入地研究了这些慈善动机,探究外在奖励何时以及如何"破坏"亲社会行为(如慷慨和慈善)的声誉价值。他们发现,当人们从他们的"慷慨"中获得了个人利益,而且有关这些利益的信息被公开时,人们就不太可能表现出慷慨的意向了。我们的一位年轻研究人员告诉我,在泰国,节日或葬礼期间人们会把他们想捐的钱放在一个信封里,信封上写有他们的名字。或者,他们直接把钱交给收集者,收集者会记下捐赠者的详细信息和捐赠金额。然后,组织者通过安装在村里的扩音器，公开、大声地宣布捐赠者的姓名和捐赠金额。很显然，方圆一公里内的村民都能听到广播，孩子们则被告知要关注那些名字。

这些类型的行为表明，我们的社会声誉对我们很重要，特别是在慷慨和慈善的情境下，它们说明了一种社会类型的外在动机：**形象动机**。我们的一些选择反映了这样一个事实：我们想要提高我们的声誉并改善我们的形象。

为了探索形象动机的影响，丹·艾瑞里和他的同事们探索了当外在奖励对其他人可见时，人们的亲社会选择是如何受到影响的。他和他的团队最开始的前提假设是，对慈善事业的捐款是由形象动机驱动的，是向别人表明你是一个好人的一种方式。然而，如果额外的利益可以作为慈善的奖励，如果每个人都能看到我们的慈善选择以其他方式得到回报，那么形象动机就会减弱。当我们给慈善机构的捐赠被公众知晓时，我们就在向别人发出信号，表明我们是好人。但如果别人看到我们从慷慨中获得了个人利益，那么我们慷慨的社会信号价值就被稀释了。

为了验证这些想法，丹·艾瑞里和他的团队设计了一个"点击慈善"实验。在他们的实验中，人们被随机地分配到两个慈善机构中的一个：一个是"好的"慈善机构——美国红十字会，还有一个是"糟糕的"慈善机构——美国步枪协会。然后，实验参与者被要求完成一项不费多大力气的任务，例如在键盘上按下"x"或"z"。对于所有的实验参与者来说，在这个简单按键任务中的表现会得到向他们的慈善机构捐款的奖励。为了测试额外私人利益的影响，实验参与者被分为两组：如果表现良好，其中一些人可以为自己赚到钱；其他人则完全不会得到额外的报酬。

13 根据他们在"点击慈善"任务中的表现是向实验组的其他成员公开，还是保持隐私状态而只有参与者个人和实验者知道，这两组人再次被分成两个子群。

艾瑞里和他的团队毫不意外地发现，通过按键盘次数来衡量，最努力的组是那些为"好的"慈善机构（红十字会）完成任务的人。更令人惊讶的是，在金钱动机和形象动机方面，参与者表现出了一些外在动机的复杂相互作用。表现最好的组没有奖金，但他们的努力是公开的。形象动机是他们卓越表现的最可能的解释——他们努力表现以提高他们的社会声誉，因为他们的努力将被公开。表现最差的组也没有得到额外的金钱激励，但他们的努力只有他们自己和实验者知道。他们什么也没有得到：既没有额外的收入，也没有社会价值，因为没有人知道他们是否付出了努力。事实上，鉴于他们既没有社会奖励也没有金钱奖励，后一组人又有什么理由付出努力呢？

最有趣的发现出现在那些通过努力获得额外私人收入的人身上。他们的努力程度不如表现最好的那一组（即那些没有私人收入，但他们的努力是公开的）。从这项研究来看，至少在慈善捐赠的情况下，形象动机似乎比金钱报酬更具有激励作用。但是，形象动机并不能完全挤出传统的金钱激励：对于两组获得报酬的人来说，那些努力的情况被公开的人仍然比那些努力的情况不被公开的人表现得更好。形象动机和金钱报酬都在对努力的激励中发挥着作用。

14 总的来说，这项研究和其他研究的结果证实了大多数经济学家可能的预测：金钱激励可以鼓励匿名捐赠。也许，这就是对慈善捐赠予以减税——例如英国的捐赠补助——在现实世界中运作良好的原因所在。但在某些情况下，金钱激励是不起作用的。许多人在慈善捐赠时并没有享受到税收优惠，但这可能反映了申报税收返还和/或递延所涉及的交易成本的影响——这是第六章讨论的主题。这些研究还提供了另一个可能更有力的政策经验：如果人们的慈善冲动能够更容易地公开，那么他们的慈善倾向就会增强，并且这种影响可能比税收减免等传统的金钱激励更有力。在一个被社交媒体主导的世界里，我们有机会宣传我们的良好品质和慷慨品格，就会让慈善捐赠变得更为可能。

这些发现也与有关慈善部门高管薪酬的辩论相联系。向慈善机构的首席执行官支付高额的商业化薪水，可能会对慈善机构产生适得其反的影响——无论是就被这些工作吸引来的人，还是就潜在捐赠者的负面看法而言，都是如此。如果一个慈善机构的首席执行官明显是受到金钱激励的强烈驱动，那么这与慈善工作的预期风气是背道而驰的，因此慈善机构的声誉可能会受损——像我这样的潜在捐赠者可能就会认为，这不是我们希望支持的那种慈善机构。

对工作的激励

内在和外在的激励和动机对我们的工作也有很大的影响。大多数员工的动力来自内部和外部影响的相互作用。外在的激励和动机包括我们所挣的工资或薪水，以及当我们被雇用时所获得的社会认可——特别是当我们从事的工作（如医疗或教育）被认为有价值的时候。工作也反映了内在动机，例如：我们喜欢挑战，做某事是令人满意的，或者我们被个人抱负所驱使。

这些来自行为经济学的关于激励和动机的见解,可以与理解工资和员工努力及生产率的最有力和最有影响的方法——**效率工资理论**——相联系。效率工资理论揭示了经济和社会心理因素如何激励工作上的努力。效率工资理论家解释了什么是有效工资——定义为使企业的劳动力成本最小化的工资。如果提高工人的工资会导致工人的生产率成比例地增加,那么公司的利润就会上升,而不是下降。例如,如果一名工人的工资增加了1%,但更高的工资激励他们更加努力地工作,从而使产出增加2%,那么单位产出的劳动力成本就下降了。在其他条件不变的情况下,利润将会上升。

　　工资和利润同时增长可以用标准的经济学概念部分地予以解释。如果一个员工的报酬高,那么他就会更加珍惜自己的工作,不想失去它,所以他会更努力地工作。在非常贫穷的经济体中,提高工资可能会帮助工人买得起更好的食物、住房、医疗保健和衣服——因此,他们的身体会更加强壮,能工作得更久、更卖力,并减少因病请假的时间。支付更高的工资还可能会阻止工会工人的罢工活动。

　　然而,更高的工资能驱动员工努力工作,不仅是因为金钱上的好处,还因为社会和心理上的奖励和激励,包括良好的待遇对员工的信任和忠诚的影响。当你的老板对你比你预期的要好,你就会想要做一个更好的员工来回报他。雇主与雇员的关系不仅仅是金钱交换,它还涉及社会、心理激励和驱动力,包括忠诚、信任和互惠。乔治·阿克洛夫和他的同事们将这称为一种"礼物交换"的形式。我的老板对我很好,给我的薪水也很高,所以我会更努力地工作来回报他。

我们当中的许多人在工作中可能都经历过这种情况。我们一生中所做的工作，以及我们最好的和最差的工作之间的对比，可以说明员工的动机是多么复杂。想象一下，你在一家商店里工作，商店里摆满了你通常喜欢买的东西——运动器材、美味的食物或漂亮的鞋子。从一开始，你就更有可能喜欢你的工作并努力工作。如果你的老板再对你很好，你的工作内在地也令人满意，那么你很可能在没有密切监督的情况下也会努力工作，这节省了老板的监督成本——你和老板彼此信任，所以你表现出了努力工作的主动性。你也可以在你的朋友和其他网络中传播这个消息，这将帮助你的老板吸引优秀的新员工，而不需要大做广告。这将节省你的老板寻找劳动力的成本，也降低了他们雇用一个偷懒者的风险。

因此，将非金钱激励纳入劳动力市场分析，不仅仅关乎我们的慈善冲动，这对企业和政策制定者也有重要意义。降低工资并不一定会增加企业利润，但支付**更高的**工资可能会增加利润。效率工资理论还为有关最低工资和维生工资（使工人能够满足当地基本生活成本的工资）的政策辩论带来了深刻见解。更高、更公平的工资对每个人都有好处——对雇主和雇员都是如此。如果支付更高的工资能激励员工在公司内外更努力地工作，那么提高工资的理由就更容易得到辩护。

这一章展示了行为经济学家如何提出基本的经济学见解——例如，人们对激励的反应——并更为宽泛地定义这些概念（在本例中是激励和动机），从而让社会心理因素也发挥作用。一旦我们接受了选择和行为会受到更广泛的社会、经济和心理动机的影响，就会极大地改变提高绩效的标准经济处方。

我们如何思考我们自己和他人的形象以及社会声誉,会影响我们对慈善机构的捐款和我们对罚款的反应。我们与他人的社交互动推动着我们的工作表现和公司利润。市场体现了人们之间的互动,虽然人们显然会对金钱激励做出反应,但也有一系列其他的强大影响因素。作为个人、雇员、雇主、政策制定者和公民,行为经济学的见解可以帮助我们对驱动我们做出选择和努力的复杂动机及其后果有更丰富的理解。

  本章探讨了影响我们的选择和决策的一些因素,其中包括了社会影响,它会给驱动我们的一些外在动机带来影响。在第三章中,我们将看到人们是如何受到更广泛的社会因素影响的,其中包括对不平等结果的厌恶,信任和互惠,社会学习和同伴压力。

第三章

社会生活

在第二章中,我们探讨了我们的经济和金融决策是如何由一系列金钱以外的因素决定的。大多数经济理论一开始都假设我们是独立的、自私自利的家伙,在决定做什么时不会考虑他人。在其他条件不变的情况下,匿名的市场是最优的方式,它可以协调经济活动,并确保消费者和生产者获得最佳、最互利的交易可能。

经济学的标准假设是,我们所有人的行为都好像其他人作为个体并不存在一样。我们只是间接地受到其他人的影响,因为他们关于供求的决策决定了市场价格。这忽略了人们经济生活的一个重要方面。价格是没有人情味的,如果在经济分析中只关注价格,经济学家很容易忘记人际关系和社会互动在经济决策中的重要性;而我们周围的人会在很多方面影响我们的经济选择。来自社会心理学和社会学的文献揭示了这种情况发生的方式和原因。在本章中,我们将探讨社会影响驱动行为的一些主要方式。

信任、互惠和不平等厌恶

我们关心身边的人，也或者对他们漠然视之；他们关心我们，也或者对我们漠不关心。我们担忧公平问题，倾向于选择公平的结果而非不公平的结果。我们也倾向于在某些情况下信任他人，而他们有时也会反过来信任我们。当别人值得信任，对我们很好时，我们更有可能以信任和值得信任作为回报。例如，如果我的同事帮助我完成讲课和行政工作，那么我就会更愿意帮助他们完成讲课和行政工作。这种信任和互惠之间的相互作用，是我们每天进行的许多合作和协作活动中的关键因素——从我们工作或学习时的团队合作，到我们向慈善机构捐款时的利他主义，以及家庭生活、社区项目和政治运动要取得成功所必需的合作，莫不有所体现。

行为经济学中对信任和互惠的分析，始于人们通常不喜欢看到不平等的结果这一洞察。人们不喜欢受到不公平的对待，也不喜欢看到别人受到不公平的对待。如果我们觉得自己受到了不公平的对待，那么我们就不太可能去信任和回报他人。在我们的社会互动中，这一关键因素将我们对公平的偏好与我们对涉及他人的自己的所做所为感受如何联系了起来。我们不喜欢别人做得总比我们更好或更差，因为我们不喜欢不公平的结果。行为经济学家称这种偏好为**不平等厌恶**。

不平等厌恶主要有两种类型，想一想银行家在伦敦街头遇到无家可归者的情景，就能察知这两种类型。银行家可能会因看到有人遭受贫困而苦恼——他宁愿生活水平更加平等——如果是这样，那他正在感受**有利地位**的**不公平厌恶**。银行家处于有利地位，但也许他不希望看到其他人的生活水平低那么多，而希望看到无家可归者能得到更公平的结果。无家可归者也不想遭受不公平的待遇。她更想有足够的钱来负担一个安全舒适的居住之地——她的困境是不公平的，她会经历一种所谓的**不利地位的不平等厌恶**；从她的不利地位来看，她不想比周围的人过得更差。

尽管两者都对不平等结果产生了类似的厌恶，但无家可归者很可能比银行家更关心自己的不平等地位：人们更容易受到不利地位的不平等厌恶的影响，而不是有利地位的不平等厌恶的影响。银行家在街上看到一个无家可归者可能会感到轻微的不适；然而，无家可归者会对这种不公平感到更不高兴。

我们对公平的偏好也可以解释利他主义，例如，我们做志愿者，或为慈善机构捐款。我们这样做可能是因为我们喜欢表现得慷慨，有时我们从慷慨中可以得到一种温暖的感觉。一些实验表明，这并不总是纯粹的利他主义，有时它是在向他人发出信号，表明我们是善良和慷慨的人。正如在第二章中提到的，当人们的慷慨表现被公开时，他们更有可能给予更多。

许多实验研究已经证实，不平等厌恶是一种强烈的倾向，不仅在大多数国家和文化的人类中如此，在我们的灵长类表亲中也是如此。用来测试不平等厌恶的基本实验博弈是**最后通牒博弈**。在最简单的形式中，这个博弈由两名玩家参与。参与人A是提议者，她有一笔钱，比如说100英镑，她可以给作为回应者的参与人B任意她想给的金额。

如果回应者拒绝提议者的提议，那么两个参与人都得不到任何东西，提议者必须将100英镑归还给实验者。非行为经济学家可能会预测,考虑到人们对其他参与人策略的看法,他们会非常自私地玩这个博弈,并以尽可能多地获取收入为目标。参与人A会认为参与人B更喜欢1英镑而不是0英镑,因为有总比没有好。所以参与人A会出1英镑的价格,因为她认为参与人B可能会接受。如果参与人B不关心参与人A的想法或行为,他会更喜欢1英镑而不是0英镑,因此他会接受参与人A的出价。参与人A推断出参与人B会有这样的反应,因此出1英镑,自己留99英镑。

最后通牒博弈是行为经济学中使用最多的实验之一,它已被用于测试人们对不同数额金钱的反应,并探索不同国家和文化之间的差异。该实验甚至被用于动物实验。黑猩猩以果汁和水果玩这个游戏,表现出与人类相似的行为。在所有这些不同的研究中,一个有力的发现是,现实世界的行为与大多数经济学家可能预期的非常不同:提议者通常非常慷慨——出的钱远远超过1英镑或其对等物,而回应者经常会拒绝提议者的提议,即使给了他们总金额的40%乃至更多。

一些行为经济学家将不平等厌恶解释为一种情绪——一种社会情绪。我们的社交环境会让我们产生特定的情绪,比如羡慕、嫉妒和怨恨,当人们在最后通牒博弈中受到不公平对待时,可能就会产生情绪上的因素。例如,如果回应者(参与人B)对提议者(参与人A)提出的小气条件感到不满,那么他可能准备支付四十多英镑来惩罚提议者。神经科学家利用脑成像研究来揭示我们的大脑可能发生了什么。其中一项研究是对回应者角色的实验参与者的大脑进行成像。他们的大脑反应表明,在人们对难闻的气味感到厌恶时被激活的神经区域,也会在人们于最后通牒博弈中受到不公平对待时被激活。一些神经科学家和神经经济学家将这些发现解释为，当别人对我们不公平时，我们会经历某种形式的社会厌恶。

合作、惩罚和社会规范

社会规范是驱动我们行为的另一组社会影响因素，而这些因素通常通过同伴压力得到加强。鉴于我们的社交天性，我们通常会奖励（也会因此被奖励）亲社会行为——如果青少年模仿同龄人的选择和习惯，那么他们或许更有可能被邀请参加最"酷"的派对。从众有很强的影响力，它驱动着我们的习俗、传统和宗教生活。当被盲目的从众所驱动时，社会影响因素并不总是有益的——例如，当邪教形成时就会产生有害的结果。邪教是破坏性社会行为的一个极端例子，但从众在更普遍的情况下也有其作用。我们经常将自己的行为与他人的行为进行比较，而他人的行为则为我们提供了行为经济学家所说的**社会参照点**：我们根据自己认为的群体平均决策来做出自己的决定。从政府决策者到市场营销人员，许多组织都利用我们关于社会参照点的信息（例如，更多的利润）来推动更有建设性的行为。

社会规范有助于解释我们是如何以及为什么进化成一个合作物种的，但我们如何确保没有人搭别人慷慨的便车呢？那些研究**公共品博弈**的行为经济学家探讨了这个问题。公共品博弈是一个实验工具，不仅可以研究我们的合作倾向，还可以研究社会制裁和惩罚在维持合作行为方面的作用。公共品博弈是由公共品的经济学概念发展而来的。

就其最纯粹的形式而言，公共品是指每个人都可以自由和轻易获得的东西——没有人会被阻止消费这种产品，因此它不容易为私人所占有。公共品的典型例子是灯塔——每个路过灯塔的人都可以得到灯塔照明所带来的好处，但要向任何一个人收取灯塔照明**费用**却极为困难。因此，任何想要从私营企业中赚钱的人都不太可能投资灯塔，因为它很难赚到钱。这就需要一些其他的动机来确保提供像灯塔这样的公共品。经济学家发现，地方社区在确保公共品的提供和维护方面表现极为出色。

行为经济学家通过使用公共品博弈，揭示了影响我们关于公共品的行为的一些因素。在一个这样的博弈中，一组实验参与者被召集在一起，并被要求向一个公共的钱罐贡献一笔钱，然后在小组成员之间平分。这有点像一个社区需要一大笔钱来建造一个社区公园。许多经济学家会预测，大多数人将什么都不捐，因为他们的理由是，无论他们捐献与否，这笔钱都会被平均分配。因此，个人实现净收益最大化的最佳方式是，在自己无需做出贡献的情况下，同时从别人的贡献中分得一份钱。这种推理的问题在于，如果每个人都这么想，并且每个人都计划免费搭乘其他捐款人的便车，那么就不会有人贡献出钱来供大家分享，也就没有公共品了。在这种情况下，自私的个人会产生对整个群体不利的结果。

幸运的是，行为经济学家和实验经济学家发现，在公共品博弈实验中，人们出人意料地慷慨——这与人们在最后通牒博弈中的慷慨程度大致相同。大多数参与者会付出很多，而不是分文不给。公共品博弈实验的各种变体表明，当第三方在公共品实验中观察到他人的刻薄行为时，他就愿意花钱惩罚不合作的参与者——这种现象被称为**利他惩罚**。人们愿意放弃自己的某些东西，以惩罚那些违反慷慨与合作的社会规范的人。这本身就是一种合作形式，因为利他惩罚强化了那些慷慨施与的人的合作行为，并阻止了那些不慷慨施与的人的自私行为。神经经济学家和神经科学家研究了公共品博弈中的利他惩罚。他们发现，参与利他惩罚的实验参与者感受到了大脑奖赏中枢的神经激活——这表明，当我们惩罚违反社会规范的人时，我们会感到快乐。

利他惩罚是合作演化过程中的一个重要现象。在现代世界，利他惩罚有助于解释为什么我们会迅速公开谴责那些社会所不能接受的行为。社交媒体让这一切变得容易多了，但也带来了负面后果——例如，推特上的恶意发帖人。更普遍地说，这些合作和强化社会规范的倾向，也可以解释为什么社会信息是操纵行为的一个如此强大的工具。一个例子是关于能源消费的证据——当能源消费者被告知他们邻居的消费情况时，他们很可能会根据朋友和邻居能源消费的社会参照点来调整自己的消费。类似地，英国税务机构——英国税务与海关总署（HMRC）——写信给逾期缴税者，在信中包含一些关于他人行为的社会信息，并告知这位不服从指令的人，她的行为在社会上是不正常的，因为她的大多数同龄人都按时支付了税单，这会促使许多（不是所有！）逾期缴税者比未收到他人缴税决定社交信息的逾期缴税者支付得更快。

身　份

身份是我们社会本性的另一种表现形式，在很多方面，就像一种非常具体的社会信号形式，在这个意义上类似于第二章讨论的形象动机在慈善捐赠中所扮演的角色。我们对某些群体的认同感高于对其他群体的认同感，这可以追溯到社会心理学家亨利·泰弗尔早期对偏见和歧视的分析。泰弗尔想要了解的是，为什么那么多的普通人会如此受制于希特勒和纳粹党。他关注的是群体间的关系，在这种关系中，我们认同一个特定的**内群体**，我们准备着对**外群体**发起挑战和冲突，在某种意义上，我们把外群体视为我们的对立面。泰弗尔还指出，一群人很容易就能相互认同，并决定维持一种互爱关系。对特定艺术类型的简单偏好，甚至是简单的掷硬币，都可以将一个群体与另一个群体区分开来。我们愿意付出代价去认同一个特定的群体——例如，流行歌星凯蒂·佩里的粉丝会在一年内花费数千英镑或美元，因为他们认同其他凯蒂·佩里的粉丝。泰弗尔关于群体的见解与行为经济学家对身份的分析息息相关。乔治·阿克洛夫和雷切尔·克兰顿对身份进行了分析，观察到一些看似反常的行为，包括以文身和穿孔的形式进行自残，都是在试图向我们的内群体发出信号，表明我们和他们是在一起的。

　　身份认同在政治中发挥着特别强大的作用。我们大多数人都有一种强烈的需求，想在社会、政治和文化上认同他人。在2016年6月英国公投脱欧之后，评论人士观察到，许多投"脱欧"票的人是出于这样一种感觉，即他们的身份已经因欧盟移民的增长而失去或稀释。具有讽刺意味的是，除了几个显著的例外（例如林肯郡的波士顿），公众中最狂热的"脱欧派"，就是那些觉得自己最害怕移民而住在低移民率地区的人。也许，他们只是基于几乎从未有过的直接经验而判定移民属于外群体的，这种现象不会让泰弗尔感到惊讶。

羊群效应和社会学习

我们社会本性的一个重要方面是我们倾向于模仿、随大流，表现得像羊群一样。社会学家将羊群效应解释为两种影响的反映：**规范性影响**和**信息性影响**。规范性影响是驱动我们决策的社会规范——我们中的许多人经常想要融入并去做别人在做的事。它们可能反映了进化的本能反应。我们的许多决策，包括经济和金融决策，都与跟随他人有关，这也许是因为我们自认为可以向他们学习，也可能是因为有一些更原始的本能过程在发挥作用。

社会心理学家所罗门·阿希发现，即使是在非常简单的决策任务中——比如判断队伍的相对长度——别人也能轻易地操纵我们。阿希发现，当一个单独的、真诚的实验参与者被纳入一个由十九个对非常简单的问题给出明显错误答案的实验伙伴组成的小组中时，真诚的实验参与者经常会改变主意，从明显正确的答案切换到错误的答案，因为这是小组所做的决定。这并不一定是非理性行为，如果这个人的判断是：不可能其他十九个人都错而只有自己对。

关于我们如何以及为什么模仿他人行为的有趣的新研究正在不断涌现，对经济学家来说，一个很有前途的研究领域是**镜像神经元**的神经经济学分析。镜像神经元存在于人类和灵长类动物的大脑中，也存在于其他一些动物的大脑中。科学家们认为，当我们模仿他人时，它们可能会发挥作用。神经科学家已经对猴子进行过单神经元实验，包括监测单个神经元的发射速率。当一只猴子以某种方式移动时，镜像神经元不仅在所观察的猴子移动时被激活,而且在这只猴子看到另一只猴子移动时也会被激活。在我们的灵长类祖先身上也发现了类似的反应,这可能表明羊群效应是无意识的、"天生的",或许反映了我们更原始的、包括冲动在内的情感。在经济和金融情境中,类似的神经过程有可能也会使我们产生羊群效应。

羊群效应的经济分析中有一个重要的因素,是建立在社会学家对信息性影响的洞察之上。信息性影响是指从他人的行为中学习。当难以找到替代信息时,这些行为很容易被观察到,它们可以成为有用的指南。其他人可能知道一些我们不知道的事情,所以模仿他们可能是有意义的——随大流或许是一种理性的社会学习手段。然而,有时随大流只是一种冲动,我们不加思考就这么做了,这也许反映了进化后的羊群效应本能。

在日常生活中有很多这样的例子。当我急需现金时,看到一台自动取款机前面排着长队,而另一台却没有人,我就会假设人们没有使用第二台自动取款机是有原因的——它可能坏了,或者银行收取了过高的费用——如此思考可以节省时间。我从群体的决定中学习。这既不错也不对——羊群有时选择了正确的策略,有时选择了错误的策略。我随大流是否明智,要视情况而定。当我们选择一家餐馆时,其他人的选择也提供了信息。隔壁餐馆人多的时候,我通常不会去空无一人的餐馆。我更喜欢人多的餐馆,即使我不得不排队,因为人们可能知道一些我不知道的事情:人少的餐馆酒质低劣,食物难以下咽;人多的餐馆食物味道极美。羊群效应到底是好是坏?这取决于那些群体的判断和决定是对还是错。

羊群效应也会产生负向溢出效应。如果我要在空荡荡的餐馆和拥挤的餐馆之间做选择,为什么要选拥挤的餐馆呢?如果我跟随别人进入一家拥挤的餐馆,我是在使用关于群体决策的社会信息,但如果我拥有其他有价值但他人无法直接观察到的私人信息呢?假设我有两条信息:一条是一位从悉尼来拜访我的朋友的推荐,他告诉我这家空荡荡的餐馆是伦敦最好的尚未被人们发现的餐馆;一条是我从观察别人对餐馆的偏好中推断出的信息。

我可能会决定随大流去一家受欢迎的餐馆——忽视我的私人信息(我朋友的推荐),而任何观察到我行为的人就无法获得我的这条私人信息。他们会从我选择的餐馆推断出,这家空荡荡的餐馆根本没有什么值得推荐的地方——他们看不到或不知道我有私人信息,该信息表明这家空荡荡的餐馆实际上可能非常好。因此,他们可能也会在不那么好而且拥挤的餐馆排队就餐,其他人也会跟在他们后面。通过这种方式,关于他人选择的社会信息就会通过群体传播。当羊群效应导致有价值的私人信息被忽视,因为人们被羊群效应所误导,它会对其他人产生负面影响——消极的**羊群效应外部性**。羊群效应提供安全保障;在某些假设下,集体决策可以导致更好的决策。集体信息可以更准确。但羊群效应也可能意味着有价值的私人信息会丢失或被忽视。

羊群效应的另一个原因是,别人关于我们的看法对我们很重要。我们的声誉是有价值的,我们试图小心地保护它,这也与第二章中讨论的形象动机因素有关。如果我们只在别人犯错的时候犯错,我们的声誉通常会更好——套用经济学家约翰·梅纳德·凯恩斯的话:我们墨守成规时犯错会比我们推陈出新时正确带来更好的声誉。流氓交易员是建立在逆向选择基础上的声誉脆弱的一个例子。当交易者违背金融市场惯例出价时,可以获得惊人的收益。但当大众是对的,而反向操作者是错的,如果她不能用"这是一个常见的错误"来为自己辩护,那么她的声誉就无法轻易挽回。

进化很可能扮演着重要的角色,因为许多其他物种分享着我们的社会学习行为。南极的阿德利企鹅表现出强烈的群居倾向。它们处于食物链的中间——以磷虾为食,被豹斑海豹吃掉。在寻找食物时,它们面临着两难的境地——如果它们潜到海里,可能会找到一些磷虾来享用,也可能会被豹斑海豹攻击并吃掉。它们最好的策略是运用某种社会学习,在决定做什么之前观察它们的同伴。最勇敢和/或最饥饿的企鹅会冒险,如果其他企鹅看到没有豹斑海豹攻击它,那么其他的企鹅就会跟随它蜂拥入海。现代的人们也有类似的表现——我们使用消费者的反馈和评论来指导我们的购买行为——随着互联网和网上购物的发展,这样做变得更加容易了。我们会对名人使用特定产品的信息做出反应。我们在选择买什么东西时关注他人的所有这些方式,都反映了我们对社会信息的敏感性。

类似的,人类的羊群效应往往与群体中的安全感有关。人多会提供安全感。想象一下在雅加达穿过一条挤满汽车和摩托车的繁忙道路。穿过这条路的唯一方法就是和一群当地人一起走过去——向他们学习当地行人的习惯,但也享受人群所带来的安全和庇护。汽车撞到一个行人的可能性,要比撞到一群人的可能性大得多。在我们的公民生活中有这样一些推论:集体诉讼依赖于这样一个事实,即群体比个体拥有更多的权力和影响力,它也可以保护我们免受不公正的待遇——例如,如果我们联合起来采取法律行动，就可以做到这一点。芬芬减肥药的集体诉讼就是一个例子。美国食品和药物管理局发现，使用芬芬减肥药与心脏病发病存在关联。超过12.5万名减肥药用户对制造商惠氏公司提起了集体诉讼，最终让该公司以近1660万美元的代价达成庭外和解。孤立无援的个体聚集在一起，为他们的集体伸张了正义。

虽然其中很多都是现代的例子，但我们的羊群效应本能是古老的、根深蒂固的，历史极其悠久。我们的群居本能被许多其他物种所共享——例如，前面提到的企鹅。羊群效应与动物行为密切相关。奶牛的羊群行为是一种本能，是为了抵御捕食者而进化出来的。对于人类和其他许多动物来说，跟随他人的行为是一种进化出来的生存策略，它使我们的祖先能够找到食物、住所和生育伴侣。这些根深蒂固的本能是如何在现代的人为环境中发挥作用的呢？在现代的人为环境中，（当我们在易贝网进行买卖时，用猫途鹰、爱彼迎和优步预订我们的假期酒店和出租车时）互联网和移动端技术影响我们的社会关系和互动吗？在这个快速发展的电脑化世界里，群居和社会影响的优点和缺点都被放大了。今天的金融危机是由投机者追随其他投机者以寻求利润所驱动的，从郁金香狂热（17世纪荷兰人对买卖郁金香球茎的投机狂热）时期及之前的几个世纪以来一直如此。

金融羊群效应是一种直接或间接地深刻影响我们所有人的羊群效应类型。我们生活在一个全球化、电脑化、相互依赖的金融体系中。资金流动的速度和规模可能非常之惊人——纳温德·辛格·萨劳案就是一个例子，此人被指控在他父母位于伦敦郊区的家中通过电脑进行欺诈交易，导致了2010年华尔街数万亿美元的"闪电崩盘"。羊群效应会破坏市场和金融体系的稳定。它也有能力破坏我们的购买模式、投票习惯、宗教观点和习俗以及文化偏好。它会扭曲我们的社会关系和互动。

在福利和福祉方面,羊群效应也有更广泛的含义。从伦理上讲,如果企业和政府利用社会信息来操纵决策,将我们带向《1984》那种集体思维和老大哥的世界,这可能就是有问题的。如果操纵社会决策具有商业价值,那么企业和政府就有强大的动机来侵犯个人隐私和挖掘个人信息,从而导致现代高科技企业对他人的剥削。它还会影响我们未来的财务状况——例如,如果群体思维主导了养老基金受托人的决策过程,使撒谎的个人和团体能够吸走资金,那么大量的人将面临晚景凄凉的脆弱财务状况。不幸的是,养老基金欺诈并不罕见——从罗伯特·麦克斯韦开始,就有很多这样的故事——最近在英国发生的故事,则是人们对英国家居商店前雇员养老基金管理的担忧。好消息是,监管机构意识到了这些影响,并正在制定政策,以限制风险,确保养老基金能够得到妥善管理。

本章探讨了社会因素影响我们广泛的经济和金融决策的诸多方式。我们会对社会影响做出反应,因为它们反映了我们对某些事情的观念,即如何看待涉及他人的自己的所做所为和涉及我们的他人的所做所为。许多人更希望看到平等的结果,不喜欢不平等,尤其是当这种不平等影响到他们个人的时候。我们信任他人并互惠地回报他人,许多经济关系依赖于这种社会行为。我们向别人学习,我们模仿别人。各种羊群效应和社会学习影响着我们的经济和金融决策。在所有这些方面,行为经济学汇集了社会心理学、社会学、神经科学和进化生物学的见解，以解释社会影响如何以及为什么对我们的经济和金融行为具有如此强大的拉力。

对羊群效应的一种解释是，它是一种快速决策工具——行为经济学家称之为**启发式**——使我们能够在从零开始做所有决定时节省时间和认知努力。例如，假设你需要买一台新冰箱，你知道你的邻居刚刚花了很多时间调查最好的冰箱品牌。如果你可以让他给你推荐一下的话，你为什么还要费这么大的劲呢？你的启发式是去询问你的邻居，这样做将节省你大量的时间和精力。但启发式的问题在于，尽管它们快捷方便，通常也足够有效，但它们与系统性行为偏差有关。当我们关注我们的邻居和朋友时，我们可能利用了有价值的社会信息，也可能只是在重复他们的错误。此外，羊群效应只是启发式的一种——关于启发式的行为经济学文献非常丰富，在第四章中，我们将介绍其中的一些关键洞见。

第四章

快速思考

在第三章中,我们讨论了决策是如何受到社会因素以及他人的行为和态度影响的。羊群效应就是一个重要的例子——我们跟随他人的行为,因为模仿他们的做法是决定下一步要做什么的快速方法。在我们的日常选择中,我们会使用这些快速规则,本章将探讨一些主要的启发式和使用它们所产生的后果,特别是在行为偏差方面。

传统上,经济学家关注的是市场在协调许多消费者和企业的决策和选择方面的作用。在市场中,价格通过传递有关生产成本和供求平衡的信息,发挥着关键作用。尽管市场发挥着非常重要的作用,但价格机制却容易出错,市场中的各种失灵意味着价格不能有效地涵盖供求的所有方面。经济学家比任何人都更清楚这一点,许多经济学家穷尽一生分析市场失灵的方式和原因——主要关注市场和制度失灵。

行为经济学家引入了一个新的维度,不是通过考察市场及其配套制度(如政府和法律体系),而是通过考察构成市场的个体决策者的行为。在这方面,行为经济学家抛开了标准的经济学假设,即人们在决定做什么、买什么、卖什么以及如何努力工作时会使用相对复杂的数学决策规则。

传统上,经济学家认为,尽管市场失灵,但使用市场的人是超理性的存在。有时,这些超理性的生物在事后诸葛亮和更好信息的帮助下,是可以改善决策的。但是,根据当时可获得的信息,他们尽了最大努力,而且没有重复他们的错误。这些理性个体的选择是他们潜在偏好的稳定反映——例如,如果一个理性个体喜欢书胜过巧克力,喜欢巧克力胜过鞋子,那么他们也会喜欢书胜过鞋子。他们的偏好是稳定和一致的。他们处理所有最新的信息,并使用数学推理得出最好、最优的解决方案。对于当这些信息不可靠或在某种程度上不完美时会发生什么,有着大量的经济分析,但大多数经济学家并不关注其他不那么数学化的选择和决策方法。这就是行为经济学的作用所在——它对理性的看法较为软化。

对于行为经济学家来说,传统经济学的问题在于,这些关于人们决策工具的假设是不完整和/或不现实的。事实上,我们每天做许多决定都很快,根本没有经过过多的思考。这并不是愚蠢或不理性,而是恰恰相反。如果我们花几个小时搜集信息,为一些对我们的生活只有短暂影响的日常决定仔细谋划计算,那将是更加愚蠢和非理性的。有时我们想要或需要迅速做出决定。这并不意味着快速思考是一件好事。当我们决定得太快时,我们会犯错误。当我们回顾这一天的时候可能会认为,如果我们花更多的时间做决定,可能会做出更好的选择。本章探讨了其中的一些主题,聚焦于我们在日常决策中的快速思考规则和相关的错误。

使用启发式快速决策

当我们被信息淹没时，我们会面临**信息过载**，迅速做出决定是很困难的。当我们面临**选择过载**时，也很难快速准确地做出决定。传统上，经济学家认为有选择是一件好事，更多选择总比更少选择好。更多的选择意味着我们每个人都能更容易地找到完全符合我们需求和期待的产品和服务，从而提高我们的福利。然而，在现实世界中，拥有非常广泛的选择似乎并不能改善结果。

研究选择的专家希娜·艾扬格和马克·莱珀探讨了选择如何以及为什么会让购物者和学生失去动力。在一组实验中，他们让杂货店的购物者浏览出售果酱的摊位：一个摊位出售二十四种果酱，另一个只有五种。虽然购物者花了更多的时间在有很多果酱的摊位上浏览，但他们在品种较少的摊位上买得更多。也许是购物者被琳琅满目的选择压垮了，失去了动力，他们做出任何选择的能力都受到了损害。在另一项选择实验中，两组学生被设置了不同的评估任务。其中一组学生被要求从三十篇文章中选择一篇，另一组学生被要求从六篇文章中选择一篇。就像购物场景一样，面对更有限选择的学生表现更好，动力也更足。选择范围更窄一些的学生写出了更长、更好的文章。

在现代世界，选择过载的问题尤其严重，信息过载也加剧了这一问题。当面对选择过载时，消费者会快速做出决定，例如，他们可能会选择清单上的第一个项目，而不是充分考虑提供给他们的所有选项。如果选择太复杂，特别是涉及没有切实和直接利益的"无聊"决策时（例如选择养老金计划），我们可能会放弃任何选择的尝试。关于选择过载的后续证据有多种，但亚历山大·切尔内夫和他的同事们最近的一项研究表明，情境是很重要的：所提供选择的复杂性、任务的难度、参与者对自己偏好的不确定性，以及他们想要尽量减少努力的愿望——所有这些都与选择过载的敏感性增加有关。

我们在购买从果酱、面包到复杂金融产品的各种商品时，面临着各种各样的选择，与之平行的是，在线上和线下都有大量复杂的信息，这些信息不一定能快速和轻易地浏览。与经济学的标准观点相反，行为经济学家发现，信息越多并不一定越好。在许多日常情况下，我们不想在复杂的计算上浪费时间和精力，而是使用简单的经验法则来帮助我们快速做出决定。行为经济学家称这些简单的决策规则为**启发式**。有时启发式很有效，但并非总是如此。其他时候，它们会把我们引向差错和错误。

使用启发式通常是明智的。只有愚蠢的人才会在决定购买一种特定类型的汽车、电视、冰箱或电话之前，花好几天时间在各种不同的线上和线下销售点上寻找，目的只是希望能省下几英镑。对于较小的日常选择来说尤其如此。我不会每次买面包的时候都做一个全面的调查研究。我不会浪费时间比较伦敦所有超市的面包价格，因为虽然我可以在面包上省下五十便士，但我必须花五英镑去最便宜的超市，而且还必须考虑到我所浪费的时间的价值。这一洞察与对交易成本的标准经济学分析是一致的。大多数经济学家都会同意，我们不仅在决定买什么时节俭，而且在交易、讨价还价和搜集信息的过程中也同样节俭。

但是，行为经济学家将这一洞察进一步加以深化，他们认为,我们甚至也没有对这些交易成本进行计算。我们使用启发式,这样我们就不会浪费时间过于深入地思考不同选择的**任何**直接和间接成本。回到我对面包做出选择的情况,我可能会使用一系列的启发式。我可能会买上次买的那个牌子,因为我记得它很好吃。如果我想变得健康,我可能会选择一个从包装上看显得健康的品牌——它用纸多,用塑料少,还配有绿色植物和种子的图样。如果我在家,而且很懒,就会去附近的便利店,即使我知道它们的价格比那些大超市要高得多。但这些过程几乎是无意识地进行的。我不会以任何分析深度来考虑面包师和供应商提供的信息,我也不会太深入地考虑不同选择的相对交易成本。

使用启发式的问题是,它们通常会导致我们犯错误和产生偏差。心理学家丹尼尔·卡尼曼和阿莫斯·特沃斯基是分析启发式的先驱,这项工作在卡尼曼2011年出版的《思考,快与慢》一书中得到推广。通过一系列的实验和洞察,卡尼曼和特沃斯基展示了一小组启发式是如何导致我们犯系统性、可预测的错误的。当我们快速做出决定时,有时我们的选择会被扭曲而偏离对我们来说最优的选项。

卡尼曼和特沃斯基探讨了三种主要类型的启发式和与之相关的行为偏差:可得性、代表性和锚定/调整。

使用可得信息

当我们在做决定时,特别是在我们很匆忙的时候,我们不会仔细考虑我们所拥有的所有信息。相反,我们将使用易于访问、检索和回忆的信息。使用我们的知识,就像我们赶着去开会时在文件柜里翻找一样。我们倾向于去找我们能找到的第一个相关的文件夹，但我们没有时间和精力仔细浏览每个文件夹，以寻找最相关的信息。这意味着有时我们会错过重要的信息并犯下错误。

当我们依赖于容易检索的信息，而不是全面、仔细地查看所有相关信息时，卡尼曼和特沃斯基称之为**可得性启发式**。可得性还与心理学中的下述概念有关：**首因效应和近因效应**。我们更容易记住我们遇到的第一个和最后一个信息，而中间的信息更容易忘记。

可得性启发式可以解释我们的习惯性行为。我和我丈夫喜欢旅行，通常是我订机票和酒店。我知道线上和线下的旅行社种类繁多，但我每次都倾向于找同一家旅行社，因为我很容易记住如何使用。我记得我的上一段经历有多好（或多坏）——在线网站通过让我储存我过去经历的信息来帮助我回忆上一段经历。在线供应商频繁的邮件提醒，强化了这些记忆。我可能会错过各种各样的便宜机会，因为我没有做到货比三家。但我也不想上当，所以我偶尔会在其他网站上看看，但通常酒店和机票的价格相差不大——这到底是反映了旅行社串通起来收取了过高的要价，还是反映了竞争性的价格水平，还是两者兼有，我并不清楚。不管怎样，当我仔细思考时，我感到放心的是，我对现有信息的快速利用并没有导致我犯重大的错误，尽管我可能是错的。

有时我们更有意识地使用可得性启发式（例如，当我们选择密码时就会这样做），这增加了我们在黑客、垃圾邮件发送者和钓鱼者侵犯网络隐私和安全方面的脆弱性。一个上佳的密码很难记住。我们可以使用可得性启发式为自己设计一个容易记住的密码，但一个容易记住的密码也很容易被破解。安全公司"飞溅数据"（SplashData）编制了一份年度最糟糕密码榜单。最常见、最持久的密码是"123456"（它连续几年在该公司的密码列表中名列前茅）。第二常见的是"password"。这两个密码都可以使用可得性启发式轻松地检索到，而且任何黑客都知道这些密码是常用的。

政策制定者和竞争监管机构对我们如何使用启发式很感兴趣，特别是在消费者"转换"行为的情境下——我们在转换能源、手机和金融服务供应商方面非常缓慢，即使我们可以在其他地方获得更好的交易。为什么不经常转换到更好的交易呢？也许是因为懒惰和拖延，但也可能是"可得性启发式"在起作用。除非我们有过令人难忘的糟糕经历，否则我们倾向于坚持我们所知道的，因为我们知道我们所知道的。政策制定者越来越担心企业会利用消费者的惰性。如果企业没有受到来自消费者的竞争压力的约束（例如，消费者决定去别处买更便宜的东西），那么企业就没有动力改进它们提供的交易。解决方案是什么？比价网站可以帮助我们更快地获取更好的信息。政府也在努力使我们更容易地转换供应商，这将在第九章"经济行为与公共政策"中加以更详细的探讨。

使用代表

特沃斯基和卡尼曼指出的另一个引导我们产生偏差的启发式是**代表性启发式**。我们经常通过类比来做决定——我们与其他表面上相似的事件进行比较，有时这种相似不过是一种虚假的相似罢了。行为经济学家和心理学家使用了大量的实验来证明,我们是如何草率地得出情景相似的结论的。我们对他人的看法也符合我们已有的刻板印象。

特沃斯基和卡尼曼用一系列实验阐明了代表性启发式。在一项实验中,他们要求实验参与者判断一个人可能从事的职业。有些人得到了对史蒂夫的描述。他们被告知史蒂夫害羞、孤僻,对细节很有眼光。有了这些信息,参与者更有可能预测史蒂夫是一名图书管理员,即使有关他是一名图书管理员的相对可能性的客观信息并不支持他们的判断。

特沃斯基和卡尼曼在探究"琳达问题"的实验中捕捉到了类似的现象。他们要求另一组实验参与者阅读一些关于一位名叫琳达的女性的信息。参与者被告知琳达三十多岁了。她聪明,单身,直言不讳。她关心社会正义和歧视问题,一直是一名反核抗议者。然后问实验参与者:

"以下哪种判断可能性更大?"

1. 琳达是一名银行出纳。
2. 琳达是一名银行出纳,在女权运动中很活跃。"

许多人选择选项2:琳达是一位在女权运动中很活跃的银行出纳,尽管这一类别是选项1的一个子集,选项1包括所有的银行出纳。选项2和选项1的可能性至多是一样大。这是极有可能的。这个错误被称为"联合谬误":它是关于概率理论家所说的"联合事件"的概率,即事件一起发生的概率,如图1所示。

首先,琳达是一名银行出纳;其次,她也是一名女权主义者。这两件事的结合却被许多人判断为比单一事件更有可能——无论她是否为女权主义者,琳达都是一名银行出纳,琳达作为银行

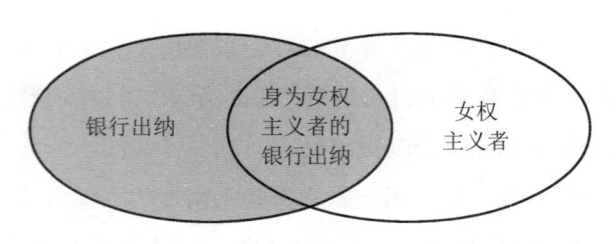

图1 琳达问题——联合谬误

出纳涵盖了更大的一组可能性。考虑到所提供的信息，琳达有可能不是一个女权主义者，那么，如果人们正确地应用了概率规则，他们就应该判定选项1的可能性更大。

为什么这么多人忽视简单的概率规则呢？这个想法就是，我们不会纯粹根据数学和统计学规则来做决定。相反，我们在脑海中形成叙事。故事对我们的想象力有强大的吸引力。运用代表性启发式，我们将我们的判断与我们对先前情景和刻板印象的认识相匹配。琳达的故事让我们认为她更可能是一个女权主义者，所以我们选择了明确包含她是一个女权主义者的可能性的选项。即使我们知道统计和概率的规则，这种概率规则的知识似乎也与我们无关，我们抛弃了它，转而支持一个连贯的叙事——一个似乎体现了琳达是谁和她做了什么的故事。

如果我们慢于调整之前的信念以适应新的信息，那么代表性启发式就会扭曲我们的判断，这与**确认偏差**和**认知失调**的问题有关。

当我们把自己的判断严格地固定在先前的信念之上时，就会发生确认偏差。这在政治辩论和左右两派的争论中是一种普遍现象。马丁·帕利特在2014年出版的《妖魔化总统：巴拉克·奥巴马的异化》一书中，探讨了人们对巴拉克·奥巴马在

2011年4月击毙奥萨马·本·拉登中所扮演角色的反应。从表面上看,很难想象巴拉克·奥巴马在本·拉登之死中所扮演的角色会被解释为支持恐怖主义的行为,然而保守派报纸《华盛顿时报》认为,奥巴马允许本·拉登有一个传统的穆斯林葬礼,是对他的敬意。保守派认为奥巴马是恐怖分子的同情者,因此奥巴马的任何行为,甚至是杀死恐怖分子头目,都被保守派解读为支持恐怖主义。

在2015年的英国,杰里米·科尔宾意外当选反对党工党的领袖也体现了确认偏差。在第一次参加首相问答时,他把选民提出的问题也包括在内,而通常这些问题都是由反对党领袖所领导的英国国会的议员提出的。他的支持者认为,这极好地说明了他值得称赞的民主倾向;他的批评者则将其解释为他不知道自己在做什么,也想不出任何自己的问题的证据。不管怎样,杰里米·科尔宾的行为基本上没有改变人们对他的看法;他的行为只是证实了那些人们已经相信的东西。

确认偏差是指根据我们现有的信念来解释新的证据,而认知失调是指我们的信念和行动之间的冲突。我们可能相信自己是善良、仁慈的人,却经常在面对无家可归者向我们讨钱时漠然置之。我们的行为与我们对自己的信念相冲突,所以我们要为自己的行为找借口。我们可能会决定让无家可归者去卖《大志杂志》①——如果他们在卖杂志,我们就从他们那里买一本。或者我们可能会得出结论,这个无家可归者是一个骗子,他真的只是想偷我们的钱包。或者我们可能会认为,给他们钱并不能

---

① 这是一本于1991年创办于英国伦敦的杂志,该杂志以非营利组织的形式存在,以帮助解决无家可归者的生活问题,让他们重新取得生活的主控权。——译注

真正帮助他们,因为他们只会把钱花在毒品上。在上述任何一种情况下,我们都操纵了自己对情况的感知,从而使我们先前的信念——在这种情况下就是指对我们慷慨大度的肯定——不受挑战。

乔治·阿克洛夫和威廉·狄更斯通过一些行为实验证实了这一趋势。他们让学生们互相侮辱,比如说:"你很肤浅,不值得信任,而且很无趣。"阿克洛夫和狄更斯发现,侮辱他人的学生通过更加真诚地批评被侮辱者,调整了对被侮辱者的态度。说侮辱话的学生并不想挑战他们对自己是个"好人"的信念,而解决这种不和谐的唯一方法就是调整他们对他人的看法。阿克洛夫和狄更斯的结论是,学生的反应可能与人们更普遍地为暴力和攻击性行为辩护的方式相似。

锚定与调整

第三种偏差发生在我们围绕一个参照点做决定,并根据这个参照点调整我们的选择之时。特沃斯基和卡尼曼再次用一系列实验证据说明了这一观点。在一项研究中,他们要求在校儿童对算术作业进行快速猜测。一组儿童被要求估计8×7×6×5×4×3×2×1的结果;第二组儿童被要求估计1×2×3×4×5×6×7×8的结果。这些猜测应该是相似的,但是被要求从8×7×…开始的孩子给出了比要求计算1×2×…的孩子更高的估计。对此有一种解释是,第一组孩子把他们的估计固定在他们看到的第一个数字"8"上,得到的答案比第二组孩子的答案高;第二组孩子则把他们的估计固定在"1"上。孩子们的回答说明了一个更普遍的问题,当我们围绕一个最初的锚点调整时,我们会得到不充分的调整。我们的决策和选择会被我们的初始位置所扭曲。

关于锚定和调整的日常例子可以用悉尼的房地产市场来说明。在澳大利亚，许多房子都是通过拍卖出售的，这为学者们提供了一个丰富的研究数据库。拍卖清仓率是悉尼住房市场繁荣的一个重要信号，2015年是房价上涨的丰收之年，悉尼房价平均上涨了20%左右。这个泡沫在2015年年底（暂时）破裂，拍卖清仓率从高达90%（即90%的挂牌拍卖的房子成功售出）暴跌至50%以下（见www.abs.gov.au/ausstats/abs@.nsf/mf/6416.0）。到2016年年初，潜在的房屋卖家已经对经济低迷做出了反应，拍卖清仓率再次上升，但这只是因为卖家拍卖的房屋数量降得太快所致——挂牌拍卖的房屋数量从2015年年底的数百套下降到2016年年初可怜的几套。一种可能的解释是，潜在的卖家将他们的预期锚定在了特定的销售价格上。一旦他们意识到不可能达到这个价格，他们就决定不再出售，而不是让市场力量为他们确定结果。

在某种意义上，锚定和调整启发式的锚定要素与前面描述的可得性启发式有所重叠。我们的参照点通常比其他信息更容易被认知。例如，我们经常以现状作为参照点——我们倾向于避免脱离现状的改变。有时这会导致**现状偏差**和**熟悉偏差**——人们抗拒改变，或者他们根据事件与当前情况有多不一样来判断事件。在我们的日常生活中，我们的许多判断都是基于我们的决策能在多大程度上让我们脱离现状。当我们找新工作或卖房子时，我们对公平工资或公平房价的看法是基于我们今天的收入，或是我们买房子时支付的价格，或是我们的邻居卖房子时得到了多少钱。问题是，这些判断可能与市场供求关系不大。这些判断也可能阻碍市场的平稳运行。

企业和政策制定者可以利用我们的现状偏差来操纵我们的决策，例如，通过默认选项来设置现状。提供给我们的默认选项代表了现状，我们必须有意识地努力才能脱离这些默认选项。企业经常利用这种趋势，设计复杂的默认选项来迷惑我们，如图2所示。

然而，政策制定者可以更有建设性的方式使用现状偏差和默认选项，以解决我们的惰性可能产生的问题。一个重要的例子与养老金有关。在人口老龄化和预期寿命延长的情况下，为人们的退休提供资金是许多发达经济体面临的一个日益严重的政策问题。行为经济学家什洛莫·贝纳茨和理查德·塞勒设计了一个养老金方案，其基础是现状偏差以及人们倾向于坚持默认选项（默认代表现状）的相关思想。他们的计划被称为"多为明天储蓄"，旨在将未来工资上涨的一部分存入工人的养老金账户。因此，除非工人们选择退出，否则当他们获得加薪时，其中的一部分将会进入他们的"多为明天储蓄"养老基金账户。这一方案还意味着，相对于目前的工资，工人们不会觉得他们失去了什么，因为只有工资**涨幅的一部分**被纳入进"多为明天储蓄"基金。工人们仍然有一个选择。自动缴纳一定比例的工资涨幅是默认选项，但如果工人不想失去工资涨幅的任何一部分，那么他们可以选择退出。贝纳茨和塞勒发现，仅仅通过这种方式操纵默认选项，养老金缴纳额就显著增加了——这一洞察带来了许多国家对养老金计划和政策的重新设计。

自从卡尼曼和特沃斯基在20世纪70年代进行了开创性的

图2　令人费解的默认选项

研究以来，经济学家和心理学家所识别出的启发式和偏差的范围迅速扩大。维基百科上关于"认知偏差"的条目目前列出了一百多种不同类型的偏差。为这些洞察建立一个分析结构，将会帮助我们更深入地理解这些偏差是如何以及为什么影响我们的选择的。许多行为经济学家一直在研究这个问题，希望发展出理论来，以体现这些重要的洞察。**前景理论**是这一领域最具影响力的理论发展之一。在构建这一理论的过程中,卡尼曼和特沃斯基将他们早期关于启发式和偏差的想法发展为对决策的更丰富、更系统的分析,特别应用于我们在风险情况下如何做出决定。我们将在第五章探讨前景理论,以及一些关于风险决策的其他竞争性理论。

第五章

风险选择

在第四章中，我们探讨了快速决策可能导致我们犯错误的一系列方式，尤其是当我们面临风险和不确定性时。当我们决定过马路、买彩票、投资或申请发薪日贷款时，所有这些决定都包含着风险和不确定性。经济学家通常认为风险是可以量化的——如果我们能算出我们在过马路时被公交车撞到的概率是八千分之一，那么我们就可以决定是否要冒这个险，这取决于我们如何评估后果。

经济学家通常还假设，我们在风险选项之间的选择取决于我们有多喜欢冒险，或者多不喜欢冒险。我们的风险偏好不会因为我们面临的一个选择以不同的方式呈现和使用不同的框架呈现而改变。如果我买彩票，我中一百万英镑的概率是一千四百万分之一，所以我不太可能中奖，但我会权衡这些关于中大奖前景的低可能性，并根据我的风险偏好做出决定。我喜欢冒险吗？或者在可能的情况下，我更愿意规避风险？又或者，我是一个风险中性的人，对这两种情况到底是哪一种都不太在意？如果我喜欢规避风险，我就不会买这张彩票；如果我喜欢冒险，我就会买这张彩票。

行为经济学家质疑这种对风险的理解。他们关注的是我们对风险的认知在不同情况下的变化。一个例子是，我们判断风险的方式取决于我们回忆起信息的容易程度，这与第四章探讨的可得性启发式有关。我们的选择，不是基于我们能找到的所有信息，而是基于我们能迅速获得的信息——那些我们能快速、容易地回忆或检索的信息。关于飞机失事的头条新闻就是一个例子：我们经常读到飞机失事的新闻，这些新闻通常伴随着触目惊心的断体残骸和极度不安的亲属的画面。这导致我们产生一种误解，认为飞机失事比马路上行走遭遇死亡事故的可能性要大得多。我们更有可能在过马路时被撞死，但马路上的死亡事故很少出现在当地报纸的报道之外。当我们决定要坐飞机的时候，我们可能会更加谨慎，也更加担心，而事实上，当我们过马路的时候，我们才真应该更加小心谨慎。

我们在做风险决策时犯的另一个错误是，我们夸大了损失相对于收益的影响。许多行为实验表明，人们从损失中遭受的痛苦要比从同等收益中获得的快乐更甚——例如，我们往往更关心失去十英镑而不是赢得十英镑。这种现象被称为"**损失厌恶**"——它被发现适用于人们广泛的决策。

一个影响房地产市场的例子是：当房主看到房价下跌时，他们不愿意再出售房屋，因为如果出售，他们可能不得不经历房价下跌带来的损失。因此，房主推迟了他们的出售决定，直到突然间，更多的房主被迫同时出售房屋——也许是因为经济状况恶化，或抵押贷款利率上升。此时的房地产市场到处充斥着待售房产,讽刺的是,如此一来房主的损失可能会被放大,这一切都是因损失厌恶使人们推迟了出售的决定所致。

行为经济学家正在发展一些理论,这些理论抓住了承担风险的人类心理方面的一些因素,以与标准经济学假设相竞争——标准经济学假设认为人们会仔细地、始终如一地、用数学方法去平衡有关风险的信息。

前景理论与期望效用理论

行为经济学中关于风险的关键模型,是由丹尼尔·卡尼曼和阿莫斯·特沃斯基提出的,在某种程度上,它将第四章中所探讨的他们的启发式和偏差分析中的一些关键概念给形式化了。前景理论是关于未来的风险前景的:例如,当我们买房子时,我们可能有两个前景可供选择。想象一下,一个第一次买房的人,不确定是要在一个便利但昂贵的城区买下一套公寓,还是要在不太方便但价格便宜的郊区或乡村买一栋大房子。另一个人可能在权衡两种就业前景。想象一下,一名年轻的毕业生面临着这样两种前景:她可以选择一份无薪实习,这可能会给她带来一份未来更有趣和/或更高收入的工作;或者,她也可以选择一份稳定的、收入相当高的工作,为她带来稳定的收入。每天我们都在权衡不同的风险前景。

作为前景理论发展的起点,卡尼曼和特沃斯基批判了风险的标准经济学分析方法——**期望效用理论**——的一些关键要素。什么是期望效用理论?"效用"是经济学家用来表示幸福和满足的词,而期望效用理论探究了我们如何根据我们对未来的期望——从我们未来效用的角度——来决定不同的选择。但我们并不是完美的预测者，有时这些预期可能被证明是错误的。

期望效用理论建立在一系列关于行为的限制性假设之上。期望效用理论家认为，人们会充分利用所有相关的、可得的信息。他们还假设我们使用相对复杂的数学工具来确保最大化我们的效用——他们假设我们正在尽己所能做到最好，因此，给定做决定时我们拥有的信息，我们所选择的选项能给我们带来我们所能希望得到的预期最高水平的幸福和满足。一旦我们确定了这个最佳选择，我们就不会改变主意。我们的选择也不会矛盾。如果我们喜欢苹果胜过橘子，喜欢橘子胜过香蕉，那么我们也会喜欢苹果胜过香蕉。

行为悖论

根据卡尼曼和特沃斯基的说法，期望效用理论的问题在于，它不能轻易解释一些常见的行为悖论，包括（其中的）阿莱悖论和埃尔斯伯格悖论。

20世纪法国经济学家莫里斯·阿莱证明了人们在风险情境下的选择往往不一致，这个著名的行为悖论——**阿莱悖论**——就是以他的名字命名的。它表明人们对不同的风险结果并没有稳定的反应。具体来说，如果某人在面对一系列风险选项的同时，也面对一个确定结果的选项，那么他就会倾向于选择确定的结果，即使面对不同的前景他准备承担风险，情况亦是如此。卡尼曼和特沃斯基称这种效应为**确定性效应**，并用自己的实验证实了这种效应的存在。他们想看看人们是否愿意为增加1美元的收益而冒一点额外的小风险。如果人们对风险承担有一致的偏好，那么喜欢风险的人会冒险，而厌恶风险的人则不会。卡内曼和特沃斯基通过加入一个有确定性保证的选项来检验阿莱悖论，这样他们就可以看到这会否扭曲人们的选择，尤其是会否扭曲那些通常更倾向于承担风险的人的选择。

卡尼曼和特沃斯基的实验参与者被要求在两场博弈（博弈1和博弈2）中评估不同的前景。如果你是他们的参与者之一，你会被要求在每个博弈中从两个选项里选择一个。对于博弈1，你有两个选择。你要么确定可得24美元（即有100%的机会可得24美元），要么进行一场赌博，有1%的机会一无所获，但存在赢得超过24美元的可能性——33%的机会可得25美元，66%的机会可得24美元，总体上你有99%的机会至少可得24美元。这些选项在表1中进行了概括。

表1　阿莱悖论博弈

	选择一个选项	
	博弈1	博弈2
选项1	确定可得24美元	34%的机会可得24美元 66%的机会可得0美元
选项2	1%的机会可得0美元 33%的机会可得25美元 66%的机会可得24美元	33%的机会可得25美元 67%的机会可得0美元

就其本身而言，博弈1的前景并不能揭示任何信息。一个厌恶风险的人可能会选择选项1，因为它提供了24美元的确定性收益。一个喜欢冒险的赌徒可能会选择选项2，有机会赢得25美元，从而多赚1美元，即使这个选项会使他有很小的机会一无所获。两种选择都符合期望效用理论。但我们可以通过比较参

与人的这些选择与博弈2中参与人的选择（博弈2包含另外一组选项）来判断是否存在**不一致**。

博弈1和博弈2之间的关键区别是，博弈2不提供任何确定性结果：选项1是有34%的机会可得24美元，66%的机会一无所获。与博弈1一样，选项2提供了稍微低一点的机会赢得多一点的钱——33%的机会可得25美元，但博弈2也稍稍更有可能一无所获——67%的机会可得0美元。所以博弈2在很多方面与博弈1相似，**只是**它不包含任何确定性选项。

期望效用理论预测，结果将由一个人的风险偏好决定，在风险和回报之间会有权衡。如果有两种人——厌恶风险的谨慎的人和爱冒险的赌徒——谨慎的人总是选择安全的选项，赌徒总是选择有风险的选项。在博弈1中，赌徒会多冒一点险，希望得到25美元——他们用略高的会一无所获的风险换取略高的回报。在博弈2中，他们也会冒险押宝在获得25美元上——在这两种情况下，他们都会选择选项2，因为他们喜欢冒险。

而谨慎的人则应恰恰相反——在这两种情况下，他们都会选择选项1，因为在博弈1和博弈2中，这都是最安全的选项，而且什么都得不到的可能性更小。在博弈1中，选择选项1意味着不会一无所获。在博弈2中，选项1一无所获的风险为66%，比选项2一无所获的可能性略低，后者是67%。

真实世界中的人们会怎样进行这个博弈呢？卡尼曼和特沃斯基确证了之前的实验研究，他们发现人们的选择并不一致：赌徒并不总是风险承担者。许多人会在博弈1中选择选项1（确定的、安全的选项），但在博弈2中选择选项2（更有风险的选项）。卡尼曼和特沃斯基将这一证据解释为确证了确定性效应的存在。许多人乐于冒险和赌博，但当他们可以得到确定的结果时，这就会扭曲他们的选择，使他们不再为了更高的回报而冒额外的风险。

这是如何与日常选择联系在一起的呢？也许它影响了我们如何在比赛中获得奖品。卡尼曼和特沃斯基还设计了一个假日游戏版本的确定性效应博弈。在一场博弈中，参与者被要求在以下两个选项中做出选择：一个是50%的机会去英国、法国和意大利旅游三周；另一个是确定的（100%保证的）结果，即去英国旅游一周。请注意，英国假期过得不太好的概率是欧洲假期过得好的概率的两倍。大多数人（100名参与者中有78人）选择了过得好的概率较低但确定的选项——有保证的一周英国之旅。

然而，在第二场博弈中，参与者在争夺假期奖品时准备冒更大的风险。相对概率和第一场博弈一样——英国假期的概率是欧洲假期的两倍——但没有确定性选项，即没有包括概率100%的选项。预计有5%的机会享受为期三周的欧洲假期，10%的机会享受为期一周的英国假期。当有5%的机会去欧洲度假时，100名参与者中有67人选择了去欧洲度假，而不是去英国度假。尽管概率的相对平衡是一样的，参与者已经从更有可能（实际上是肯定的）但更少的奖品，切换到更好但更不可能的奖品。因此，确定性效应似乎也在推动参与者在假期博弈中的决策。卡尼曼和特沃斯基将其归因于**权重**：我们并没有对所有的可能性一视同仁，而是倾向于赋予某些结果比不那么确定的结果更多的权重。确定性分散了我们的注意力。

卡尼曼和特沃斯基描述的另一个著名的行为悖论是埃尔斯伯格悖论，以经济学家和军事分析师丹尼尔·埃尔斯伯格的名字命名,他曾受雇于兰德公司。他也可能是像爱德华·斯诺登和朱利安·阿桑奇这样的现代"吹哨人"和新闻记者的早期榜样:埃尔斯伯格在1971年向《纽约时报》透露了一份"五角大楼文件",这份文件记录了美国政府在越南战争期间所做出的富有争议的决定。

埃尔斯伯格的博士论文是一项关于风险决策的研究。在他给出的一个实验中,他告诉实验参与者,他在一个瓮里装满了90个球,其中30个是红球,60个不是黑球就是黄球,但实验参与者并没有关于这60个球中有多少是黑球、多少是黄球的精确信息。接着,埃尔斯伯格问他的实验参与者,如果就从瓮中随机抽取的球的颜色打赌,会选择供他们挑选的哪组选项。这组博弈的选项在表2中列了出来。

表2　埃尔斯伯格悖论博弈

	你会赌哪一个?	
	博弈1	博弈2
选项1	红球	红球或黄球
选项2	黑球	黑球或黄球

注意,这两组选项本质上是相似的。在博弈1中,选项1是选择"红球",选项2是"黑球"。在博弈2中,除了"或黄球"以相同的方式添加到两个选项中这一点之外,其选项与博弈1的情况相同。期望效用理论家可能会预测,如果有人在博弈1中选择选项1(红球),他们也会在博弈2中选择选项1(红球或黄球),因为从博弈1到博弈2抽到红球的概率不会改变。同样的,如果

他们选择博弈1中的选项2（黑球）和博弈2中的选项2（黑球或黄球），他们的选择将是一致的。

一种解释是，人们可以精确计算出"红球"和"黑球或黄球"的概率，因为他们已经得到了事先计算它们所需要的信息。但是，根据先前的信息，他们无法准确地知道得到黑球或黄球的概率（他们只知道得到黑球或黄球的总体概率）。所以对于博弈1来说，选项2是模糊的；而对于博弈2来说，选项1是模糊的。大多数人会避免模糊的选项——他们感受到了**模糊性厌恶**。当我们避免模糊的结果时，我们并不完全是非理性的，但卡尼曼和特沃斯基认为，用期望效用理论来解释模糊性厌恶很困难，他们旨在发展他们的前景理论，使其与模糊性厌恶**相一致**。

不一致的选择

在发展前景理论的过程中，卡尼曼和特沃斯基热衷于发展一种替代期望效用理论的方法，该方法可以把阿莱和埃尔斯伯格实验中发现的异常行为，以及卡尼曼和特沃斯基在他们自己的实验中注意到的一些新效应，纳入到理论的范围之中。

这些效应是什么呢？卡尼曼和特沃斯基还发现，如果人们想要避免损失，就会愿意承担更多的风险，而如果他们为了收益而赌博，则只愿意承担更少的风险。卡尼曼和特沃斯基认为，面对损失时的冒险偏好是收益背景下冒险偏好的镜像，因此他们称这种效应为**反射效应**。

卡尼曼和特沃斯基用表3中给出的一组博弈表明了反射效应。

这两个博弈的收益是相似的。在这两个博弈中，参与者都要在一个有风险的选项（选项1）和一个确定的结果（选项2）之间做出选择。唯一的区别是，博弈1涉及收益，而博弈2涉及损失。期望效用理论家会预测，追求风险的参与人会在两种情况下都选择选项1，规避风险的参与人会在两种情况下都选择选项2，但卡尼曼和特沃斯基发现，人们的行为并未遵循期望效用理论所预测的模式。大多数博弈1的参与者（80/100）选择了确定的结果，但大多数博弈2的参与者（92/100）选择了有风险的选项。他们愿意承担风险以避免损失，但在给他们提供有收益的前景时，他们更喜欢确定的结果。有了这个证据，卡尼曼和特沃斯基就确证了反射效应的存在——人们愿意承担更多的风险以避免损失。

表3　反射效应博弈

	你会选择哪一个？	
	博弈1	博弈2
选项1	80%的机会赢得4000美元，20%的机会赢得0美元	80%的机会赢得4000美元，20%的机会损失0美元
选项2	3000美元的确定性损失	3000美元的确定性收益

　　卡尼曼和特沃斯基认为，这可以解释为什么人们更喜欢**或有保险**（即保险赔付取决于特定事件，如火灾、毁损或盗窃），而不是**概率保险**（即没有可保证的保险，赔付根据偶然性确定）。

　　概率保险交易可以将投保人的常规保费减半，条件是他们愿意冒险自己承担所有损失的费用。因此，如果发生了损失或损害，就抛硬币决定下一步怎么做——要么是50%的可能性由投保人支付剩下的一半保费,保险公司支付所有损失的费用;要么是50%的可能性由投保人自己支付所有损失的费用,保险公司返还他们的保费支付。卡尼曼和特沃斯基认为,从本质上讲,购买防盗报警器与此是相似的——人们为降低损失风险而付费,而不是为完全消除损失而付费。然而,当提供概率保险时,大多数人会避开购买它。如果他们的风险偏好是一致的,追求风险的人可能更偏爱概率保险才对。

卡尼曼和特沃斯基还发现了第三种效应——**孤立效应**。这是关于我们何时会忽略我们所面临的选项中重要元素的效应。我们分离出特定的信息片段,而不是完整地查看所有相关信息。卡尼曼和特沃斯基从另一组实验博弈中发现了孤立效应。其中一个博弈包含一系列概率选项,如表4所示。

这些博弈都是精心设计的,以便参与人能够从这两个博弈中获得相同的收益。为了表明这一点,我们需要考虑不同选择范围的可能性。

表4　孤立效应博弈

	博弈1:序贯博弈	博弈2:一阶段博弈
	阶段1:你有25%的机会走到阶段2(75%的机会走不到阶段2);如果你走到了阶段2,你会选哪一个选项?	选择一个选项
选项1	80%的机会赢得4000美元,20%的机会赢得0美元	20%的机会赢得4000美元,80%的机会赢得0美元
选项2	3000美元的确定性收益	25%的机会赢得3000美元,75%的机会赢得0美元

在博弈1中，参与人只有25%的机会走到阶段2，所以他们有75%的机会什么都赢不到，因为这是他们甚至都无法走到阶段2的可能性。在计算收益时，参与人应该考虑到这样一个事实：他们只有25%的机会走到一个真正能赢得任何东西的阶段。

因此，对于博弈1的选项1，不同选项的期望值将是25%（走到阶段2的机会）乘以80%获得4000美元的机会和20%一无所有的机会：

$$25\% \times [(80\% \times 4000) + (20\% \times 0)] = 800$$

对于博弈1的选项2，如果参与人有25%的机会走到阶段2，即保证可以获得3000美元，那么期望值将是750美元，即：

$$25\% \times (100\% \times 3000) = 750$$

在博弈2中，卡尼曼和特沃斯基构建了与博弈1相同的选项期望值，但没有第一阶段，即参与人直接选择两个列出的选项——这更容易计算收益，因为即使是最聪明的数学家也只需要考虑一组选项：

选项1：
$$20\% \times 4000 = 800$$
选项2：
$$25\% \times 3000 = 750$$

注意，就选项的期望值而言，这些博弈是相同的。在两个博弈中，选项1的期望值都是800美元。在两个博弈中，选项2的期望值都是750美元。所以我们可以做一些比较。如果期望效用理论是正确的,那么,在博弈1中选择选项2的人应该在博弈2中也选择选项2。然而,卡尼曼和特沃斯基发现,大多数参与人(78/100)在博弈1中选择选项2,但在博弈2中大多数参与人(65/100)则选择选项1。卡尼曼和特沃斯基认为,也许人们忘记了博弈1的第一阶段。他们一开始就忘记了他们只有25%的机会走到阶段2。卡尼曼和特沃斯基的解释是,人们在计算博弈1的期望值时,没有包括走到阶段2的这25%的机会。通过选择性地将注意力集中在博弈1的阶段2上,人们将所面对的不同选项孤立开来。

构建前景理论

卡尼曼和特沃斯基认为,任何决策理论都应该能够解释前面概述的三种效应:**确定性效应**、**反射效应**和**孤立效应**。他们对期望效用理论的批判,围绕着期望效用不能解释这些效应的事实展开,他们决定发展一种可以解释这些效应的理论,即**前景理论**。他们认为,前景理论比期望效用理论在现实世界中具有更强的解释力。

前景理论的基础是,我们以特定的方式对不同选择的价值做出判断,这与期望效用理论所体现的标准经济学方法不一致。第一个洞见是关于我们在做选择和决定时所做的相对比较。我们不会只根据我们所获得的关于特定手机和其他新产品的所有信息来决定购买一部新手机——我们会将我们已有的可供交易的手机选项进行比较,然后决定新的交易是否需要改进。当我们做出选择时,我们并不会完全重来一遍。我们会把各种选项与一个起点——**参照点**——来进行比较。其中一个含义是，我们的决策是由相对于参照点的**变化**驱动的，而不是由我们拥有的所有信息驱动的。

参照点的思想发展了卡尼曼和特沃斯基早期关于锚定和调整启发式的见解，这些洞见在第四章中讨论过：我们围绕参照点锚定我们的选择，并相应地调整我们的选择。正如我们在第四章中看到的，现状通常是我们的参照点。卡尼曼和特沃斯基将此与内稳态的生理概念联系起来。内稳态是关于生理上我们如何有一个设定值，而我们的身体反应是由这个设定值决定的。同样的事件会对我们的生理产生不同的影响，这取决于我们的起点是什么，例如：如果我们太热了，一阵冷风吹来，我们会感到愉快；但如果我们太冷了，同时又有一阵冷风吹来，那就会感到不舒服了。我们对参照点的选择是有黏性的，不太可能改变。我们在日常行为中表现出大量的惯性。这可能是因为改变所需的努力太大了，所以我们表现出拖延和懒惰——可能有一系列复杂的社会经济和心理原因可以用来解释我们对改变的抗拒。

前景理论的第二个关键特征源于本章前面提到的卡尼曼和特沃斯基关于反射效应的见解，这与损失厌恶的概念有关——我们更关心损失而不是收益。根据许多行为经济学家的说法，损失厌恶和现状偏差的表现之一是**禀赋效应**。我们更在意那些我们拥有而可能失去的东西，而不是那些我们没有但能买到的东西。丹尼尔·卡尼曼、杰克·克内奇和理查德·塞勒，在一些学生作为被试的实验中阐述了禀赋效应。学生们被随机分为不同的组，包括"买家"和"卖家"。卖家拿到了杯子，他们可以把杯子卖掉。买家得到了购买马克杯的机会。卖家被问他们是否准备以不同的价格出售杯子。买家被问是否准备以不同的价格购买。卖方和买方价格存在巨大的差异：卖方愿意接受的中位数价格是7.12美元，买家愿意支付的中位数价格是3.12美元。

仅根据这些证据，我们很难认为这肯定是禀赋效应在起作用。你可能会认为利润最大化的卖家会以不成比例的高价开始，以防他们错过更高的收益。在讨价还价的过程中，卖方降低接受的意愿，而买方提高支付的意愿，直到找到一个均衡。尽管如此，有证据表明，支付意愿和接受意愿之间的差异在其他选择中也很明显。

基普·维斯库西和同事们就人们对化学中毒的态度进行了一些实验，在更广泛的背景下证明了类似的分歧。他们向消费者展示了杀虫剂和马桶清洁剂的金属罐，并询问人们愿意为一种更安全、中毒风险更低的产品支付多少钱。然后，人们被问是否愿意接受一种价格下降但中毒风险增加的产品。大多数经济学家可能会预测，消费者对这些问题的反应应该是对称的：他们愿意为更安全产品支付的金额，应该与他们期望从相对不安全产品中获得的降价补偿金额相似，但维斯库西和同事们的实验结果并不支持这一结论。人们对降低风险的反应表现出了经济学理论预测的标准模式：为更高水平的风险降低付费的意愿是递减的。但是，人们非常不愿意接受以补偿换取**任何**形式的中毒风险增加。

卡尼曼和特沃斯基通过描绘**前景理论的价值函数**来表明我们对价值的主观感知，从而将他们的见解结合在一起，如图3所示。

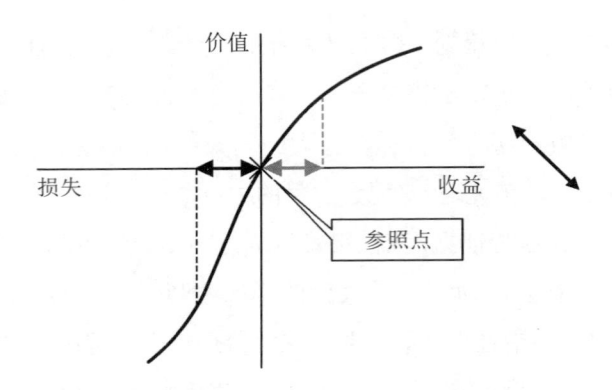

图3　前景理论的价值函数

本章所确定的许多现象都可以在前景理论的价值函数中看到。它被锚定在一个参照点周围（不一定是零）。价值函数具有S形状，并且在参照点周围不是对称的，反映了损失对价值的影响大于收益的事实。通过更仔细地查看图3，我们可以看到损失对我们的价值评估产生了不成比例的影响。黑色双头箭头表示损失。灰色双头箭头表示与损失大小相等的收益。虚线垂直向下延伸到价值函数，以说明损失与收益对价值的影响。黑色虚线比灰色虚线要长得多：一定规模的损失对我们价值感知的侵蚀，远远大于同等规模的收益对我们价值感知的增强。通过这种方式，损失厌恶被体现到价值函数中，以显示人们如何更关心损失而不是等价的收益。当我们失去100英镑时，我们的沮丧感远远大于赢得100英镑时的喜悦感。

后悔理论

尽管前景理论（及其变体）在行为经济学中影响很大，但它只是行为经济学家使用的理论之一。除了他们的这个理论，还有理查德·塞勒的心理账户模型和后悔理论。心理账户建立在前景理论中关于框架和情境的一些想法之上,但它也涉及对未来的规划——我们将在第六章中更详细地探讨这个模型。

格雷姆·鲁姆斯和罗伯特·萨格登发展了后悔理论,作为前景理论的替代性理论。他们认为,后悔理论给我们提供了一种比前景理论更简单、更直观的方法,以解决与期望效用理论相关的一些行为悖论和不一致。

后悔理论的本质是什么呢?后悔理论允许世界存在着不同的状态——这些状态我们无法知道,因为我们无法预测明天会发生什么。我们今天的选择和未知的未来之间的相互作用,最终决定了我们的选择能给我们带来多少快乐(或不快乐)。我们对一些决定感到后悔;我们对其他一些决定感到"高兴"——但我们是后悔还是高兴由世界的未来状态决定,而这可能完全不受我们的控制。这是后悔理论相对于前景理论的一个重要区别。前景理论只假设世界的一种可能状态,而后悔理论则允许存在两种(或更多)状态,我们对自己幸福的评价取决于世界最终出现的状态,也取决于我们对未来后悔的预期。

例如,想象一下,你正在决定是否带把雨伞去上班。你不知道今天的天气情况(比如你住在英国)。带雨伞会遇到一些麻烦——它可能不容易放进你的包里;如果你有点健忘,雨伞可能是你经常丢失的物品之一。然而,如果下雨了,这点麻烦也就是值得的。所以你的幸福/满足感是由你完全无法控制的东西决定的:英国的天气。如果下雨了,你会为你带雨伞这种行为所体现出来的未雨绸缪而高兴。如果天气晴朗,你会后悔费心把它打包,尤其是如果你把它还弄丢了的话,就更加后悔了。幸福不仅仅取决于我们的感知、喜好和选择,它还取决于我们如何回顾过去的选择,并给定我们做出选择**后**世界的状态——这时改变主意已经太晚了。我们无法控制世界的这些状态,但我们的幸福却在很大程度上依赖于它们。

经济学家研究了更重要的例子,包括核电站的选址。如果核电站建在一个意外发生地震和海啸的地区(就像2011年的日本),规划者会后悔他们的选择。如果没有发生地震,他们会为自己明智的核电站选址而高兴。结果不仅由我们自己的选择决定,也由我们周围发生的事件决定。

在本章和第四章中,我们重点讨论了启发式、偏差、行为悖论以及用来解释它们的行为理论。到目前为止,研究的重点主要聚焦与我们在风险情况下的决策和选择有关的偏差。行为经济学家已经发展了一整套的额外文献来研究我们做决策时所出现的偏差类型。时间和风险当然是相互作用的,但出于本书的目的,我们将在比较简单的情况下讨论它;在第六章中,我们将聚焦随着时间的推移而出现的偏差。

第六章

如何看待时间

在第四章和第五章中,我们关注的是风险选择。我们做决定的另一个重要维度是我们对待时间的态度。我们有耐心吗?我们无耐心吗?还是视情况而定?我们每天的许多决策都是随着时间的推移而发生的,我们今天想要的和明天可能想要的并不总是一致的。现实中的人们如何处理时间,如何处理对未来有重要影响的当前决策呢?我们并不总是善于为未来的养老金进行储蓄。我们可能会努力应对水电等账单,因为当感觉有点太冷或太热时我们太喜欢打开暖气或空调,而没有认真考虑未来电费账单的后果。在保持健康的同时,我们并不总是善于为未来做规划:由于不健康的生活习惯和生活方式,我们经常累积出一些将在未来暴发的健康问题。

标准的经济学理论确实承认人们对时间的偏好是不同的,或者说他们有耐心和无耐心的程度是不同的。对大多数经济学家来说,人们的**时间偏好**可能**因人而异**,但在**个人内在**应该是稳定的。在标准经济学中,如果有人缺乏耐心,急于在今天得到某样东西而不能等到明天，那么如果他们在相同的时间间隔（一天）但向前推到未来进行选择，他们也会表现出同样的无耐心。这是所谓的**时间一致性**——我们有耐心和无耐心的水平不会随着时间的推移而改变；它们是稳定的。例如，如果让我在今天的巧克力蛋糕和明天的巧克力蛋糕之间做出选择，我选择了今天的巧克力蛋糕，那么，如果我是时间一致的，即使这组选择向前推一年，我的偏好也应该不会改变。我也应该更喜欢一年后的巧克力蛋糕，而不是一年零一天后的巧克力蛋糕。当我在为近期的未来和遥远的未来做决策时，我的选择不会改变。

标准方法并不排除**不同的**人会做出不同的选择——例如，一个人决定早一点吃蛋糕而不是晚一点，另一个人决定晚一点而不是早一点。同样，这并不一定是不一致的。在很短的时间内进行消费和支出的决策可能是严格理性和一致的，特别是当你面临迫在眉睫的财务问题和/或你的预期寿命很低的时候。对大多数经济学家来说，如果人们始终倾向于尽早获得较小的奖励，而不是稍后获得较大的奖励，那么他们仍然是严格理性的。

在一项关于军人及其养老金选择的研究中，经济学家沃伦和普利特发现了显著的个体差异。军人有两种选择：他们可以接受大额的一次性支付；也可以接受小额年度支付（一种"年金"），但持续终生。沃伦和普利特发现，大约51%的军官选择了一次性支付，但更大比例的入伍人员（92%）选择了一次性支付。沃伦和普利特分析了数据，发现不同群体之间存在显著差异：白人、女性和受过大学教育的群体更有可能领取年金。这一证据表明人与人之间存在差异——这本身并不是时间不一致的标志,因为标准经济理论并不排除不同的人有不同程度的耐心和无耐心。那么,行为经济学还能补充些什么呢?

何为时间不一致性?

行为经济学利用心理学的证据表明,标准经济学方法所假设的时间偏好一致性并不适用于人类(以及其他动物)。在短期,我们**格外**没有耐心(我们今天就想要巧克力蛋糕),但在规划未来时,我们更有耐心(我们准备为巧克力蛋糕等待一年零一天)。这就是**时间不一致性**——我们对延迟结果的偏好随着时间的推移而改变。我们的时间偏好是不稳定的。我们会困扰于**当前偏差**——我们对较小的即时回报和延迟的较大回报有着不成比例的偏好,这反映了潜在的时间不一致性。我们的忍耐能力会随着时间的推移而变化。我们在某些情况下有耐心,但在另一些情况下却无耐心。例如,如果我们有10英镑,我们要决定今天花掉它还是把它存到下周,那我们更有可能今天花掉它。而当我们考虑更长远的决定时,我们可能会更有耐心——如果我们考虑一年花10英镑还是把它存起来供一年零一周花,那么我们的选择可能会改变,我们会计划为那额外的一周存钱。当我们今天的无耐心意味着我们在一年、十年或退休后没有什么东西可以花或存时,麻烦就出现了。

动物模型

一些关于时间不一致性的早期证据来自**动物模型**——这些模型比较了人类行为与其他动物行为之间的相似之处。精神病学家和心理学家乔治·安斯利,在鸽子的冲动控制研究中观察到了时间不一致性。鸽子被关在一个房间里。它们可以通过在红灯或绿灯亮时啄按键来获得食物。如果它们在红灯亮时啄按键,奖励的食物较小但来得更快。如果在绿灯亮时,奖励的食物会更大,但鸽子必须学会等待。鸽子很快就懂得了啄红灯和绿灯按键所得奖励之间的区别,但它们也很冲动,喜欢在红灯亮时啄按键,以便更快地得到食物。不过,其他动物行为学家已经确定了动物中更具建设性的长期计划行为。生物学家马尔卡希和考尔观察到倭黑猩猩和猩猩会选择并保存工具以备日后使用,这表明它们正在计划未来的行动。丛林松鸦和其他动物也会保存和储存食物。

为什么我们在规划遥远的未来时更有耐心?斯科特·瑞克和乔治·洛温斯坦用收益与成本的相对有形性来解释这一点。今天的诱惑很难抗拒。抵制诱惑需要有形的短期成本,这些会阻碍我们实现未来的目标。节食、去健身房和戒烟的例子都属于这类。我们必须放弃一种即时的、有形的快乐,比如吃巧克力或吸烟。或者我们必然马上感到不适(例如去健身房锻炼)。而未来的目标可能看起来遥不可及,也不那么切实可行,这使得今天的自我控制更加困难。当人们无法控制眼前的诱惑时,它会导致严重问题,如肥胖、吸毒和赌博成瘾,所有这些都会对个人、家庭和公共卫生系统产生严重影响。

心理学家沃尔特·米舍尔和他的团队进行了著名的**棉花糖实验**,说明了儿童选择中的这种现象。沃尔特·米舍尔和他的团队为孩子们提供了一系列甜食(包括棉花糖)。如果孩子们能够抵制住马上享受甜食的诱惑,那么他们以后会在第二轮实验中得到奖励。如果孩子们被分散了注意力，并且他们也会使用自己的方式来分散注意力，他们就可以等待更长的时间。这也与孩子们未来的生活际遇息息相关。那些更能抵制诱惑的孩子在青少年时期表现出了优越的情感和认知功能，成年后的社交和学业能力也更强。棉花糖实验激发好莱坞编剧创作了一个虚构的例子。在电影《五年婚约》中，心理学家维奥莱特（艾米莉·布朗特饰）认为她的副主厨未婚夫汤姆（杰森·西格尔饰）很软弱，因为他无法抗拒吃不新鲜甜甜圈的诱惑，而不愿等待新鲜的甜甜圈。（电影快结束了，当汤姆发现维奥莱特这样评价他时，他为自己的行为辩称，可能还有其他各种各样的理由让他吃不新鲜的甜甜圈。）

跨期斗争

棉花糖实验和其他类似研究的证据表明，我们的诱惑会引发内部冲突。就好像我们在与自己斗争，好像我们有两种性格：有耐心的自我和无耐心的自我，而这两个自我处于冲突之中。经济学家罗伯特·斯特罗茨利用安斯利的证据，结合这种个人冲突的观点，发展了早期关于时间不一致性的经济学见解。他假设我们面临着有耐心的自我和无耐心的自我之间的**跨期斗争**。虽然斯特罗茨用大量的技术细节阐述了他的想法，但这也只是一个有很强直觉力的想法。我们大多数人都会拖延；我们中的许多人可能会拖延去健身房的时间。有耐心的自我担心未来——以及缺乏锻炼对我们未来健康的影响；而无耐心的自我喜欢现在舒适的生活，喜欢坐在沙发上吃巧克力和薯条。净影响将取决于哪种自我占据了上风。

即时奖励与延迟奖励的神经经济学分析

神经科学工具可以用来捕捉我们在面对延迟和即时奖励时的某些神经反应。山姆·麦克卢尔和他的同事们使用了功能性磁共振成像,这是一种监测大脑和底层神经区域含氧血液流动的技术。他们受到伊索关于蚂蚁和蚱蜢的寓言的启发,建立了一个多重自我模型。有耐心的蚂蚁在夏天努力工作,收集食物。无耐心的蚱蜢以唱歌来消磨夏天。结局谁都猜得到——冬天来了,蚱蜢乞求蚂蚁给他食物,因为他快要饿死了;蚂蚁让他滚开,自己则唱着歌来打发冬天,就像蚱蜢唱着歌打发夏天一样。

当我们就即时奖励还是延迟奖励进行决策时,我们心中的蚂蚁和蚱蜢之间会有一场跨期斗争吗?为了找出答案,麦克卢尔和同事们要求实验参与者在脑部扫描过程中对即时奖励和延迟奖励进行估值。他们根据奖励的时间来识别不同的神经激活情况。与高级认知功能相关的神经区域因延迟奖励而被更强烈地激活。与更原始的、冲动本能相关的神经区域则因即时奖励而被更强烈地激活。他们得出的结论是,当我们面对即时的较小奖励与延迟的较大奖励之间的选择时,不同的神经过程是相互作用的,这可能反映出多重自我之间的内在冲突——有耐心的计划者和无耐心的短期分子之间的冲突。

然而,神经经济学证据喜忧参半。保罗·格莱姆彻和同事们检验了麦克卢尔团队的一些结论。格莱姆彻的团队调整了实验,**所有**的选择都被推迟了。最早的奖励只有在延迟60天后才可获得。他们发现了与麦克卢尔的即时奖励研究相同的模式。格莱姆彻的团队得出结论,他们的证据表明,时间不一致性并不是多重自我间冲动和跨期斗争的反映。它只是普通的诱惑,并且可以用有着连贯信念和目标的单一自我来解释。

预先承诺策略和自我控制

这些自我控制问题的解决方案是什么?这在一定程度上取决于我们的自我意识。泰德·奥多诺霍和马修·拉宾认为,有些人比其他人更了解自己的行为,他们区分了两大类:天真的和老练的决策者,分别称之为**天真汉**和**老油条**。这些不同类型的人会以不同的方式对时间不一致性做出反应。这两类人都会困扰于当前偏差,但老油条会意识到他们的自我控制能力是有限的,并且愿意采取策略以迫使自己走上一条更具建设性的道路。

奥多诺霍和拉宾举了一个学生们选择看电影的例子——学生们喜欢在周六晚上去看电影,但他们必须在四周里的某一个周末工作,因为他们有一篇重要的论文要在一个月内完成。他们必须决定哪一个周六工作,而不是去看电影。奥多诺霍和拉宾为这个问题所作的设定,使得四周里并不是所有的电影都是一样的——第一周的电影很普通,第二周的还不错,第三周的很好看,第四周的电影则是最好的,是一部约翰尼·德普主演的优秀影片。最优的选择是在第一周完成文章,然后在接下来的几周去看所有更好的电影,包括第四周的优秀影片。

问题是,学生们可能没有所需的自控能力来确保这一点,但老油条可能在权衡方面做得更好。天真汉则会完全低估他们未来的自我控制问题,并且会拖延到最后一个周六,因为他们还有一篇文章要写,所以他们会错过约翰尼·德普主演的那部最好的电影。老油条也会遇到自我控制问题,会有点拖延(他们可能会在第一周去看一部普通的电影),但他们也意识到自己可能会拖延太多而错过最好的电影。因此,他们在第二周完成论文,为自己做好准备,因为他们意识到,如果把文章留到后面去完成,他们可能会错过约翰尼·德普的电影。这与行为经济学家所称的**预先承诺策略**是联系在一起的:老油条为了实现长期目标,限制了他们未来的选择范围。

约束自己以确保我们走上建设性道路的想法,是古典文学中的一个古老现象。在荷马的《奥德赛》中,奥德修斯(又称尤利西斯)驾船驶过塞壬身旁,这些神秘动物会用歌声引诱水手走向毁灭。奥德修斯的船员们被塞进耳朵里的蜡弄聋了,所以他们能够过去,而奥德修斯则把自己绑在船的桅杆上,让自己既听到塞壬的甜美歌声,又不会被引诱而把他的船弄沉没。J.W.沃特豪斯在他的名画《尤利西斯与塞壬》(如图4所示)中讲述了这一经典故事。尤利西斯的前瞻性自我,约束住了他无耐心的短期自我,以求逃过这道难关。

柯勒律治是另一个例子,他很清楚地意识到了鸦片成瘾的毁灭性后果,因此他雇了个用人让他远离鸦片店,这是一种有远见的尝试,旨在约束他纵欲吸毒的即时渴望。

自然实验也说明了这些自我承诺的行为。正如第一章所解释的,自然实验研究的是真实的选择和行为,而不是许多实验者被迫做的人为的、假设的选择。德拉维尼亚和马尔门迪尔研究了一组关于健身房会员的真实数据。出勤记录显示,人们每年支付数千美元的会员费,然后只去健身房几次,尽管他们可以通过使用健身房提供的更便宜的即付即用选项而省下许多钱。表

图 4 尤利西斯预先承诺自己以抵抗塞壬的召唤

面上，我们可能认为只有愚蠢的人才会花很多钱购买他们很少使用的健身房会员资格，但我们中的许多人确实表现出这种行为，也许这并不那么愚蠢。一些行为经济学家将其解释为一种预先承诺策略：通过在健身房会员上花费大量金钱，我们试图迫使无耐心的自我在短期内更加负责。我们有耐心的自我这样解释说，如果我们花了很多钱，即使是我们的短期自我也不会想浪费它。

现代企业今天提供的服务，都是围绕着人们的自控能力并不完美这一观点而设计的。抵制短期奖励的诱惑是很难的，我们中的许多人都准备通过买东西来摆脱诱惑。节食圈子里有许多这样的例子，戒烟的辅助手段——近期风行的是电子烟——也有很多这样的例子。对于那些早上起床有困难的人，他们可以给自己买一个漫游闹钟。原创产品"落跑闹钟"会在房间里跑来跑去，所以你必须追着它把它关掉，希望到那个时候你会真正醒来。

在线服务的增长也提供了一些预先承诺服务，包括"毕曼得"（Bee Minder）和"斯提客"（Stikk）。后者提供一种服务，帮助人们利用财务激励来管理他们有限的自我控制问题。Stikk 用户在线定义他们的目标。这构成了**承诺合同**的基础：如果用户没有实现他们的承诺，那么将被收取费用，资金将流向他们选择的受益人。用户可以让他们最不喜欢的慈善机构成为受益人。如果他们未能实现目标，民主党选民可能会承诺向共和党捐款。Stikk 确实依赖于诚实的参与者，但不诚实本身往往是一种短期策略，假如 Stikk 发现要检查自己用户的诚实性是非常困难和昂贵的，那么他们如何才能设计出一个无懈可击的合同呢？

BeeMinder是一个类似的服务，但具有不同的基本业务模式。BeeMinder提供"面对面"的目标跟踪，以实现"灵活的自我控制"。与Stikk一样，它们的客户为自己设定目标，以形成与BeeMinder签订的承诺合同的基础。如果他们未能实现目标，BeeMinder就会向他们收费。这些服务可以产生强大的影响，特别是如果它们利用现代技术解决了Stikk所面临的不诚实问题的话。一个真正诚实的BeeMinder客户可以将他们的锻炼目标与个人健身监控设备的输出连接起来。技术，提供了监视者。

行为生命周期模型

如果我们不善于储蓄，如果我们的养老金不足以让我们在退休后照顾自己，那么这将对政府预算和债务具有重大影响。行为生命周期模型探索了这些模式，发展了戴维·莱布森的洞见，即我们照看**金蛋**（大多数人以养老金和住房财富的形式持有的非流动性财富存储）的能力，是如何超过我们管理信用卡账单的能力的。

行为生命周期模型将关于时间不一致性的行为洞见，与假定时间一致性的标准生命周期模型相结合，以研究我们的储蓄、投资和支出模式在我们一生中是如何演变的。乔治-马里奥斯·安杰雷托斯和他的同事们，用这些模型来解释为什么人们可能同时拥有大量的信用卡债务和大量以住房或养老金形式存储的非流动性财富。

交易成本是部分原因。卖房子来支付信用卡账单，是一个复杂而昂贵的过程。人们用信用卡作为对意外账单的缓冲，但对安杰雷托斯和他的同事们来说，这不足以解释这一现象。他们通过做一些假设来模拟消费和储蓄模式,以匹配当今人们的平均经历。例如,一个人最多能活九十年,平均工作四十三年,随着人们离开父母的家、结婚、成家和退休,家庭规模在一生中不断变化。然后,安杰雷托斯和他的同事们使用利率和就业率等关键变量的实际数据,将他们的模拟与有关消费和储蓄模式的真实数据进行匹配。他们的发现与时间不一致性的行为理论是一致的:假设时间不一致性的模拟模式,比基于时间一致性标准经济学假设的模型的模拟模式更符合真实的宏观经济趋势。

选择托架、框架和心理账户

在决定今天消费还是明天消费时,我们的决策情境起着至关重要的作用。如第五章所述,如果一个决策被框定为损失,那么最终的选择可能不同于一个决策被框定为收益时所做的选择。我们的选择如何组合在一起,影响着我们的最终决定。这就形成了另一种可能对看起来不一致的选择加以解释的基础:**选择托架**。当我们面对许多复杂但相关的决策时,我们可以把我们的选择放在一起来简化我们的任务。

理查德·塞勒在他的**心理账户**模型中发展了其中的一些见解。心理账户有助于解释为什么我们可能并不总是尽可能多地储蓄。框架、参照点和损失厌恶,都会决定我们对潜在花费和储蓄决策的看法。塞勒将心理账户定义为我们用来组织、评估和跟踪财务决策的一系列认知操作。塞勒认为,我们并没有把所有的金钱都一视同仁。金钱是**非同质的**——无论我们在何时何地花钱,我们都不会认为它是完全一样的东西。我们如何看待我们的金钱以及我们如何花掉它,取决于我们赢得或挣得它的情境。我们有一套独立的心理账户，在我们的头脑中，我们给不同的账户分配不同的选择。有一个意外之财账户，它是指我们通过幸运事件（彩票和其他偶然事件）获得的钱；有一个为我们所挣的钱设置的收入账户；还有一个非流动性财富账户，用来储存我们省下的钱。

我们对金钱的决策取决于我们认为哪个心理账户是最相关的。如果我们买彩票赢了钱，我们可能会大肆挥霍。如果我们通过努力工作赚到同样的钱，我们更可能会把它存起来。如果我们用我们的信用卡在网上购物花了大量的钱，我们会觉得在某种意义上比付现金更便宜。我们对待信用卡购物和现金购物的态度非常不同，这可能部分反映了贫乏的远期计划。

心理账户意味着我们对经济决策的评估取决于情境。我们会把我们的选择放在一起，并在我们的头脑中对选择进行组合。我们对便宜货的看法并不完全取决于我们买的是什么——有时购物或找到便宜货的过程本身就有价值。塞勒用一个女人买被子的例子来说明：所有的被子不管大小都是一样的，但她会买最大的被子，即使对她的床来说它太大了。

科林·凯莫勒和他的同事们探索了"托架"的另一种表现形式：纽约市出租车司机的收入托架和目标定位。凯莫勒和他的团队获得了一家出租车公司的出租车司机的每日行程记录，因此能够研究其工作模式和收入。标准的经济理论预测，出租车司机应该最大化他们的每日收入，在繁忙的日子赚更多，在清闲的日子赚更少。然而，他们发现了一些令人惊讶的事情：出租车司机在繁忙的日子里并没有赚更多的钱。他们不是在最大化自己的收入，而是在朝着一个目标而努力，在繁忙的日子里他们让自己提前收工了。凯莫勒和他的同事们也给出了另一种解释——也许出租车司机把收入目标作为一种预先承诺的形式。如果一个出租车司机预先承诺，随着时间的推移，她将获得稳定的收入，那么她就不会在繁忙的日子里额外工作，因为她无耐心的自我可能会把额外的收入挥霍在琐碎的消费和去酒吧这样的事情上去。相反，如果她每天都朝着一个稳定的目标努力，在清闲的日子里工作更长时间，在繁忙的日子里工作更短时间，那么偶尔就可以早点回家，而不是被诱惑着去过度花费。

行为发展经济学

关于时间不一致性的洞见也被应用于发展中国家。埃斯特·迪弗洛和她的团队使用了一系列随机对照试验（RTC）来提高贫困农村农民的农业产出。如第一章所述，随机对照试验是一种借鉴自医学科学的技术，在临床试验中用于测试药物和其他医疗干预措施的疗效。随机对照试验将参与者分为两个或两个以上的组：处理组和对照组。对照组的参与者不接受干预。处理组接受政策干预，为了检验干预是否产生了影响，我们可以将处理组的结果与对照组的结果进行比较。

在他们的一项实验中，迪弗洛和她的团队关注的是购买化肥的肯尼亚农民。化肥在贫穷的农村社区相对昂贵，但如果农民能够储蓄，通常就可以负担得起购买化肥的较小固定成本。发展中世界许多贫穷农村地区的问题是，不存在实现储蓄所需的金融基础设施（即银行和建房互助会）。如果没有储蓄能力，农民可能就没有钱购买化肥，因为他们必须等到收获季到来才能有钱（这是一个标准的经济学问题），而且无法使用以前收成收入的储蓄。另一个问题可能是农民的当前偏差：他们可能会拖延和推迟购买化肥。不管怎样，他们的农业产出都会大大低于他们之前购买化肥时的产出。然而，如果为农民提供少量的、有时间限制的化肥折扣，以克服当前偏差，并且是在庄稼刚刚收获之后，他们有钱购买化肥时这么做，那么他们就更有可能购买所需的化肥，从而使他们的农业生产力和年收入获得显著提高。

心理学家、神经科学家、进化生物学家以及行为经济学家和经济心理学家，对时间不一致性和当前偏差的研究是行为经济学中一些最重要的研究。我们大多数人都知道，我们很难抵制诱惑，标准经济学模型并没有真正帮助我们太多，因为它不切实际地假设我们总是能够聪明地做出促进我们长期福利的决定。理解为什么许多人的行为不符合他们自己的长期最佳利益，以及如何应对这类现象，是行为经济学家和政策制定者面临的一个关键挑战，而时间不一致性研究为这些辩论增添了许多内容。

第七章

性格、心境和情绪

　　经济学家经常假设所有的人都超级聪明,能够很容易地做出正确的选择。然而,正如前几章所解释的,心理偏差导致我们比标准经济学所预测的更经常地犯错。到目前为止,我们还没有强烈关注潜在的心理原因。在本章中,我们将解释诸如性格、心境和情绪等心理因素是如何以及为什么影响着我们的经济和财务决策的。

　　这一章展示了性格和情绪对我们的工作生活、教育成就和财务决策的重要影响。我们中的一些人是喜欢寻求刺激的人,在极限运动、赌博或金融交易中寻找冒险的机会。其他人可能是厌恶风险和谨慎的人,总是喜欢安全的选择。一个具有较高自制力性格特征的人,能够更迅速地抵制住花钱的诱惑,也能够在教育和就业方面做出更好的人生决定。

　　性格和情绪有着复杂的影响,因为经济环境也可能反馈到人们的情绪状态中。心境和情绪也会起作用。我们经常倾向于感受到特定的心境和情绪,部分是由我们的性格特征所驱动的。

如果我们有一个更抑郁的人格,当我们在经济交易中被欺骗时,我们可能会更倾向于感到沮丧和怨恨。如果我们是冲动型人格,我们可能会更容易感到愤怒,使我们更容易与同事、朋友和家人发生冲突,这可能会影响我们可获得的机会。

对性格进行测量

经济研究人员在将性格纳入分析方面一直进展缓慢,部分原因可能是性格不容易测量。心理学家使用着各种各样的性格测试,但至少到目前为止,经济学家使用的性格测试只处于一个相对狭窄的范围。OCEAN测试是行为经济学中最常用的测试之一。OCEAN是由保罗·科斯塔和罗伯特·麦克雷设计的,它基于五大模型而构建,横跨五个维度来体现特征:**对经验的开放性**、**尽责性**、**外向性**、**宜人性**和**神经质**。

行为经济学家也经常使用认知功能测试。至于性格,有很多认知功能测试。一个古老而广为人知的认知功能测试是艾森克的(不一定特别准确的)智商测试(IQ)。行为经济学家还急于使用弗雷德里克的认知反身性测试(CRT),其中包括如下问题:"一个球棒和一个球总共花了1.10美元。球棒比球贵1美元。这个球多少钱?"(慢慢想!详见"参考文献与扩展阅读书目"。)CRT的设计目的是为了体现人们的认知功能,但也与人们的时间和风险偏好有很好的相关性。有些人,包括高智商的人,会急于回答,因为他们没有耐心,所以不给自己时间去仔细思考正确答案。

捕捉性格特征并不容易,因为它们通常是通过自我报告问卷来测量的。这些对于许多偏差来源都是很敏感的。实验参与者通常想给出让自己看起来不错的答案，或者给实验人员留下深刻印象。一个人的性格和表现之间的反馈可能会使结果复杂化。一个更容易感到焦虑的神经质的人可能在认知测试中表现不佳，不过不是因为能力受损，而是因为测试的环境让他们感到不安。智商测试需要付出努力，研究人员无法轻易知道，被试表现不佳是由于缺乏能力、缺少动力，还是两者兼而有之。实验参与者得到多少报酬（或没有得到报酬）也会影响他们的性格测试结果。当给孩子们提供食物时，他们在智商测试中的表现会提高——这些食物不会让孩子们更聪明，但确实会激励他们更加努力。成年人也会受到动机的影响。情绪稳定、认真负责的参与者可能较少受到额外的外部激励（如金钱支付）的影响，因此测量他们的认知功能可能更容易。

性格与偏好

假如我们测量了一个人的性格，那么它的经济含义是什么呢？经济学家通常认为，人们的选择是由他们的偏好所驱动的，性格也起着一定的作用。一个有同理心的人会更有可能做出无私的选择。例如，冲动的人或许会更没有耐心，他们可能不善于为退休储蓄。爱冒险的人更有可能承担风险，这或许会导致他们做出特定的选择——他们更有可能去赌博和/或从事有风险的工作。

基因也起着作用。戴维·塞萨里尼和他的同事们研究了两种类型的双胞胎——同卵双胞胎（基因相同）和异卵双胞胎（基因不同）。他们比较了这两组人，以找出遗传和环境因素对风险偏好的影响。不同组的双胞胎在慷慨程度和冒险行为方面的差异能归到基因因素的只有20%。在一项研究中,塞萨里尼和他的同事们发现,双胞胎过度自信的16%到34%的变异与基因组成有关。在另一项关于养老金计划的研究中,他们发现,双胞胎选择的金融投资组合的风险差异中,有25%可以归因于基因因素。

性格与认知

我们的性格对我们的许多经济和财务的决策与选择都有影响。做决定通常需要一些思考,我们的性格特征可以决定我们的认知能力,并通过我们的认知来驱动我们的选择。这些后果通常会影响我们的一生,因为它们决定了我们的学业成就、工作表现和社交技能。如果一个有责任心的人倾向于更有耐心,那么他们可能也更愿意为他们的退休进行储蓄和/或投资于自己,例如通过获得更良好的教育来做到这一点。

在第六章中,我们考察了沃尔特·米歇尔的棉花糖实验,以及儿童的自我控制和抵制诱惑的能力与其后来的成功相关的证据。米歇尔和他的同事们发现,能够抵制诱惑的孩子在以后的生活中表现得更为成功。其他研究表明,那些抵制诱惑的能力较差的孩子在以后的生活中更有可能从事犯罪活动。

莱克斯·伯格汉斯和他的同事们还对性格与生活机会进行了一些非常深入的研究。他们发现,责任心与学业成绩、工作表现、领导力和寿命有关。但并没有一套独特的性格特征能保证我们在经济和社会生活中取得成功。不同的性格特征在不同的地方有不同的价值。在工作中,我们通常更喜欢值得信赖的同事。在聚会上,我们可能更感兴趣某人是否有幽默感。不同的性格适合于不同的工作岗位。当我们生病时,我们希望我们的医生是有同理心的、可靠的、有良好认知技能的,这样他们就能很容易地在我们的症状和他们的诊断之间找到准确的联系。另一方面,当我们去餐馆时,我们希望我们的厨师是有创造力和富有灵感的——我们甚至可能认为,如果他们喜怒无常、富于想象力或反复无常,将会做出更多美味的食物。但我们可能不希望我们的医生喜怒无常、富于想象力或反复无常。

童年时的性格

性格在我们很小的时候就开始影响我们的生活,而性格和认知在很小的孩子身上是可塑的。环境有重要的影响。莱克斯·伯格汉斯和他的同事们发现,被社会经济地位高的父母收养的孩子,在智商上比被社会经济地位低的父母收养的孩子有更大的提高。来自弱势背景的儿童也可以通过进入良好的托儿中心和家访得到帮助。这些干预措施旨在帮助儿童发展良好的认知技能,但它们也成功地有效提高了社交和个性技能。精心设计的教育干预可以帮助儿童发展需要努力和实践的复杂技能。一旦他们掌握了这些技能,那么在以后的生活中他们的经济成就也有望得到提高。

性格和动机与认知能力和智商对早期成功的影响一样重要。诺贝尔经济学奖得主吉姆·赫克曼和他的同事们研究了这些影响,他们所利用的就是高瞻佩里学前教育研究计划提供的证据。该计划是为来自弱势的非裔美国人家庭的儿童设计的。课程侧重于通过积极、开放的学习和问题解决来发展儿童的认知和社会情感技能。赫克曼和他的团队监测了孩子们之后的成就,并把这些结果与控制组儿童(即那些没有机会参加高瞻佩里学前教育研究计划的儿童)的结果进行了比较。

这种干预的积极影响随着儿童年龄的增长而下降,对弱势儿童的好处远远高于其他群体。赫克曼和他的同事们估计,这些干预措施的益处是巨大的。参与该计划的孩子在成年后的表现要好得多。他们不太可能有犯罪记录,也不太可能在以后的生活中依赖救济金。他们在教育成就、就业能力和收入方面都取得了更高的成就。赫克曼和他的团队估计,高瞻佩里学前教育干预计划的投资总体回报率在7%至10%左右。如今,大多数发达经济体的政府可以以1%左右或更低的利率借款;如果赫克曼的数据具有指示意义,那么政府就愿意借钱用于类似的教育干预措施,特别是那些专门针对弱势群体的教育干预措施,这将是在明智地使用公共资金。

情绪、心境和内心因素

经济学家乔恩·埃尔斯特是研究心境和情绪如何影响经济决策的先驱之一。心境和情绪的区别是什么呢?埃尔斯特将情绪描述为有一个目标,而心境则更加分散,方向性更差。心境也可能是集体经历的,从这个意义上说,心境受性格特征的影响比情绪小。我们将在第八章中更多地讨论宏观经济中的心境,因为心境与信心和情感有关,这两者都是宏观经济波动和金融市场不稳定的主要驱动因素。

情绪,尤其是我们的社会情绪,比我们的基本本能进化程度更高。即便如此,经济学家也经常把情绪视为我们决策过程中的非理性因素。埃尔斯特和其他人挑战了这一假设,解释了情绪和理性是如何相互补充的。当我们感到犹豫不决时,情绪是重要的"决定因素"。情绪通常帮助我们更有效地做决定,因为它们可以快速地运作。但在其他情况下,它们就没那么有用了——例如,当我们面对危险、不确定的情况时,我们经常会感到恐惧,这可能会让我们在需要采取行动时不能正常工作。

情感启发式

情绪对我们的经济和金融选择有复杂的影响,但我们可以通过将情绪和启发式联系起来更好地理解这些复杂性。正如在第四章中所解释的,启发式是快速决策规则,它们通常会很好地指导我们,但有时也会导致我们犯错误。当人们使用可得性启发式时,就会出现偏差——专注于容易记住的信息,而忽略不太容易记住的但可能更重要的客观信息。情绪也在其中发挥了作用。情绪比客观事实和数据更容易接近和获取。情绪往往是生动的,我们可以更容易地记住它们。它们还与更快、更无意识的反应有关。情绪影响记忆,因此决定了什么是要记住的,什么是要忘记的。所以我们用情绪来指导我们的行为——它们是一类启发式,被称为**情感启发式**。

情绪和情感启发式也会干扰我们的认知过程。这是广告商和哗众取宠的新闻会利用的东西。生动的形象很容易被记住。当我们看到生动、可怕的描述时,例如飞机遭劫持和坠毁,这可能会导致我们决定避免乘坐飞机,而实际上乘坐火车更危险。目睹过可怕车祸的人可能对驾驶的风险有扭曲的认识,这反映了他们之前在目睹事故时的情绪反应。这可能使他们决定不去开车,然而作为行人发生事故的概率更大。

基本本能和内心因素

埃尔斯特将情绪与**内心因素**区分开来。内心因素与我们的基本本能有关，比如饥饿和口渴。它们是天生的，经常超出我们的意识控制。内心因素就像情绪一样，帮助我们快速做出决定。它们对人类的生存和基本日常功能至关重要，但它们也很强大，可能会排挤掉我们的其他目标，因为它们更原始、更根深蒂固，比我们的情绪进化得更慢。

其中，心理学家约瑟夫·勒杜和行为经济学家乔治·洛温斯坦做了大量工作，解释情绪和内心因素如何导致自我毁灭行为。洛温斯坦认为，当我们的内心因素驱动我们时，我们会更加短视和自私；并且当我们的内心因素很强烈时，我们就不那么无私了。它们也限制了我们的共情能力：当我们为他人做决定时，我们会忽视/低估他们的内心因素。我们想象着他人对我们内心因素的感受和我们自己的感受方式是一样的，但我们也低估了他人的内心因素对他们行为的影响。内心因素可以帮助解释为什么我们沉迷于冒险和像上瘾这类自我毁灭的行为。部分问题在于，我们的内心因素在现代人为环境中被放大了。今天的科技使我们能够比我们遥远的祖先更快地做出许多决定，因为我们有了电脑和互联网。对于发达经济体的大多数人来说，食物是充裕的，很容易购买和食用，许多成瘾物质也是如此。在现代世界，我们可能不再希望或需要被快速的、本能的冲动所驱动。当我们低估或忽略这些内心因素时，当我们缺乏对它们在我们的决定中所起作用的洞察力时，问题就会变得更加复杂。

所有这些都意味着内心因素会对我们的决定和选择产生令

人困惑的和复杂的影响。它们可能与我们更高层次的认知功能相冲突，它们可能破坏我们与他人的互动和关系。神经科学家乔纳森·科恩对此持相对乐观的态度。他认为，从进化的角度来说，我们的适应性很强。理性和控制是在我们的社会和物理环境迅速变化的同时发展起来的，随着技术的发展，我们旧有的情绪过程会变得不适应。当我们还是狩猎者和采集者的时候，冲动的情绪反应可能在我们的生存中扮演了重要的角色——基本资源稀缺且易腐，所以快速的本能行动是避免饥饿所必不可少的。在现代环境下，这些本能可能不会再提供什么有用的目的，实际上还可能会产生一些有害的行为，比如上瘾。科恩认为，尽管有着所有这些不适应，但进化已经"硫化"并强化了大脑，所以理性和控制可以平衡原始的情绪反应。因此，它使人类开发出了第六章中所提到的一些预先承诺程序——例如储蓄计划、吸烟者的尼古丁口香糖和电子烟。通过这种方式，我们的大脑已经进化到能够缓和冲动、自我毁灭和情绪化决策所带来的影响。

躯体标记假说

神经科学家安东尼奥·达马西奥也对情绪在推动我们的选择方面所起的作用持更积极的看法。情绪与我们身体反应中表现出来的重要生理线索相关——达马西奥称之为**躯体标记**。来自躯体标记的知识通过我们的情绪进行传达，有时这有助于我们更快地做出更好的决定——正如前面所提到的，情绪驱动着情感启发式。

躯体标记可能是有意识思维的结果。然而，更多时候，它们是在无意识地运作的。例如,如果我们在火灾中被烧伤过,当我们再看到火灾时,就会变得很害怕,因此我们会远远地躲开。这是躯体标记如何转化为触发行动的情绪的一个例子。其他的躯体标记则更加明显——例如,企业家的直觉,他们只是凭直觉"知道"一项投资会很好——在某种意义上,直觉代表了对选择和计划的有意识感觉。当专家有预感时——例如,当医生怀疑他们的病人患有某种特定的疾病,却无法清楚地说明其推理时——他们只是有一种感觉或直觉,这代表了他们所有知识和经验的总和。

达马西奥和他的同事们将研究重点放在脑损伤患者身上,其中包括历史上最著名的脑损伤患者之一菲尼亚斯·盖奇,他曾在美国的铁路公司工作。一天,一根铁棒插进了他的大脑。在某种程度上,菲尼亚斯·盖奇是非常幸运的——他康复了,没有明显的外部物理损伤。然而,事故损坏了他的额叶(通常与较高的认知功能相关)。这种脑损伤不仅使他的性格发生了重大变化,还损害了菲尼亚斯·盖奇的工作能力。他最终失去了工作,并遭受了其他各种经济和情绪上的困扰。安东尼奥·达马西奥在自己的病人身上也发现了类似的模式,其中就包括埃利奥特——在切除脑瘤的手术后,他的额叶受损。和菲尼亚斯·盖奇一样,埃利奥特的基本认知功能在很多方面都很好,但他变得极度痴迷。他的情绪反应受损,除了社会后果外,这也影响了他的经济生活,因为他发现在面对一系列选项时,很难做出选择。达马西奥认为,这是因为情绪帮助我们在不同的选择之间做出决定:埃利奥特受损的情绪反应与他无法做出选择和决定有关。这种对他情绪反应的限制,严重影响了他的工作效率。

然而，将这些行为归因于情绪的影响是很困难的，因为情绪不容易测量和观察。丹·艾瑞里和他的团队设计了一种新颖的方法，通过给实验参与者提供彩色和黑白的视觉信息来尝试体现情绪的影响。他们的想法是，彩色图片更生动，因此可以引发更强烈的情绪反应。他们还通过一系列"启动性"练习来操纵参与者的认知：他们要求参与者回忆过去的不同事件，在这些事件中，他们的情绪帮助他们做出了正确的决定。参与者还被要求回忆他们过去的一些事件，在这些事件中，他们的认知能力帮助他们做出了正确的选择。然后，参与者被给予一系列不同产品的选择。他们发现，当参与者对自己的认知能力不太有信心时，他们会更多地依赖情绪；当他们相信自己的感觉时，他们也会更多地依赖情绪；当他们看到彩色照片时，他们也更依赖情绪。艾瑞里的团队发现，当参与者在决定哪些产品能引发更强烈的情绪反应时，他们更有可能做出一致的选择。这一证据证实了安东尼奥·达马西奥和其他人关于情绪的一些洞察：情绪可以产生积极的影响，帮助我们做出正确的决定。情绪并不是非理性的。

双系统模型

我们如何调和所有这些关于情绪是否有用的不同观点呢？其中的一些复杂性和明显的矛盾，在双系统模型中得到了调和——双系统模型体现了情绪/情感与认知之间的相互作用。在《思考，快与慢》一书中，丹尼尔·卡尼曼总结了他在这一领域所做的工作，以及与他和阿莫斯·特沃斯基在启发式、偏差和前景理论上的早期工作之间的联系——如第四章和第五章所述。他将我们的思维过程想象成一类地图,将两种主要的不同决策系统分开——无意识的、快速的和直觉的系统1,以及认知的、深思的、受控的系统2。

行为经济学中关于系统思维的研究非常之多,而且还在不断增长,许多实验旨在表明其中的一些影响。根据第二章中对激励和动机的研究,丹·艾瑞里和他的同事们探讨了金钱激励会损害我们的表现的观点,因为它们转移了我们对有效的无意识过程的注意力。例如,当职业运动员不太去想他们是该如何去做的时候,他们往往表现得更好。温布尔登网球公开赛等备受瞩目的国际体育比赛中的大奖,可能会使运动员在**压力下感到窒息**。艾瑞里和他的团队在美国和印度做了一些实验。他们的实验参与者要完成不同的任务,并根据他们的表现获得报酬,但那些报酬最丰厚组的人不一定表现得最好。他们推断,参与者在争取大奖时,会在压力下感到窒息,因为这些奖励引发了有害的情绪反应以及情感与认知之间的冲突,从而损害了参与者的表现。

一些行为经济学家发展了这些想法,以作为洛温斯坦和勒杜所描述的成瘾的内心因素模型的替代选择。这两组理论是包括加里·贝克尔及其同事们在内的主流经济学家的**理性成瘾**模型的替代选择,他们认为,我们所做的大多数事情,包括成瘾,都是理性选择的结果。这与我们的个人成瘾经历很难调和。双系统模型在表明成瘾驱动因素方面更为直观有力。在伯恩海姆和朗格尔的冷热状态模型中,可以看到一组关键的见解。当我们处于"热"状态、感到压力时,而不是当我们处于"冷"状态、感到平静时,我们的情绪和内心因素更有可能压倒我们。在热状态下,我们更容易误判形势,容易受到诱惑。对于正在康复的瘾君子来说，这可能会引起毒瘾复发。戴维·莱布森举了一个可卡因成瘾者的例子，他在监狱里能够从毒瘾中恢复过来，但只要他被放出来，毒瘾很快就会复发——他回到了那些与他过去的成瘾习惯有千丝万缕关联的地方和环境。

我们的情绪也有更广泛的影响——影响我们的政治和经济生活。在2016年英国就是否应该"脱欧"（即离开欧盟）举行公投之前，丹尼尔·卡尼曼在英国报纸《每日电讯报》上撰文，他洞察到了非理性和愤怒会如何增加脱欧的可能性。在投票的准备阶段，情绪主导了分析。在英国脱欧公投后，情绪再次高涨，许多"留欧派"报告说，他们对这一事件感到沮丧和失落，但这一事件并没有影响到自己或家人，至少没有立即影响到他们。也许其他行为的影响因素，如损失厌恶，也驱动了情绪反应。

神经经济学中的情绪

测量情绪是非常复杂的，甚至比测量性格还要复杂。神经科学家研究情绪的时间比经济学家要长得多，他们的一些工具在研究经济和金融决策时非常有用，而经济学家和神经科学家正在共同研究行为经济学的一个创新分支——**神经经济学**。神经经济学家结合了经济学和神经科学的理论和工具。神经科学为经济学家提供了很多东西，特别是以新的和创新性数据来源的形式。一些实验人员将经济和金融决策与生理反应的测量联系起来，包括心率、皮肤电导和出汗率，以及眼球跟踪。例如，史密斯和迪克奥在拍卖实验中就使用心率数据来推断情绪状态。

测量一般的生理反应不能给出我们关于情绪反应非常详细的信息。脑成像提供了更丰富的信息，但也涉及昂贵的和复杂的技术。大脑成像实验的样本通常非常小,特别是与经济学其他领域使用的非常大的样本量相比。最常用的脑成像技术之一是功能性磁共振成像。这种方法已经在一些神经金融学实验中得到了应用,特别是在表明风险决策和情绪之间的联系时这一方法被使用得更为广泛。其他的实验使用了大脑成像技术来研究参与者在社会环境中的情绪和认知反应,这是一种对前面描述的双系统模型进行测试的方法。这些实验是基于对不同神经区域及其在情绪和认知处理中所起作用的松散分类给出的。

一个经典的例子是桑菲和他的同事们所做的实验。他们使用神经科学技术来表现人们在玩最后通牒博弈时的情绪和认知互动,该博弈在第三章中有过解释。我们来概括一下最后通牒博弈的结构:提议者向回应者发出要约,如果对方拒绝了这个提议,那么双方都得不到任何东西。在桑菲和同事们的实验中,在该博弈的有些轮中,实验参与者是和他们之前见过的人一起玩的。在其他几轮博弈中,他们与计算机对弈。也许毫不奇怪,来自人类的不公平提议被拒绝的频率比来自计算机的不公平提议更高。参与者报告了一些相对极端的情绪反应。当他们收到不公平报价时,他们报告称他们会感到愤怒,并准备牺牲经济利益来惩罚他们的同伴。

桑菲的实验参与者被功能性磁共振成像进行扫描,以测量含氧血在大脑不同区域的流动。简单地说,这种大脑成像方法利用了这样一种观点,即不同的大脑区域与不同的思维类型有关。前额叶皮层是大脑中进化程度更高的区域,通常与更高的认知功能有关。与卡尼曼的不同思维系统的地图类似,前额叶皮层与系统2的认知和控制思维有关。图5展示了额叶皮层和

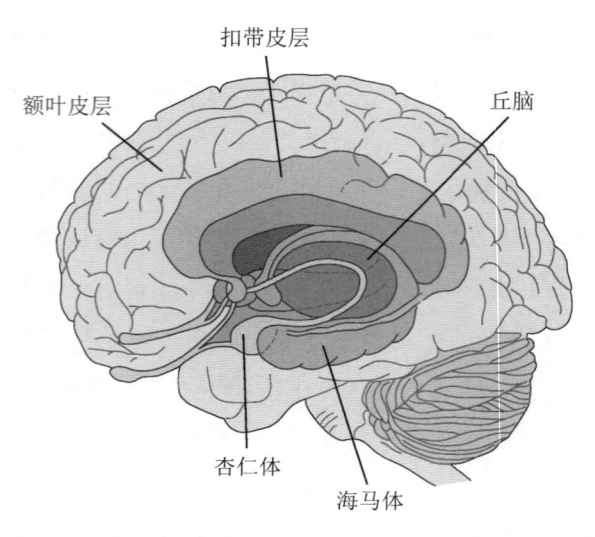

图5 一些大脑区域。杏仁体是边缘系统的一部分,边缘系统是一个相互联系的大脑结构网络,传统上与情绪处理有关

其他一些与情绪处理相关的大脑区域——有时被称为**情绪边缘系统**。

桑菲和他的同事们关注的是大脑中一个被称为脑岛的区域,这个区域通常与痛苦、饥饿、口渴、愤怒和厌恶等负面情绪状态的情绪处理有关。它是边缘系统的一部分,但位于大脑深处,所以在这里不容易说明。脑岛涉及与系统1思维相关的冲动、无意识风格的决策。桑菲和他的同事们对最后通牒博弈的回应者进行了研究,他们发现,与来自计算机的不公平提议相比,来自人类的不公平提议更强烈地激活了脑岛,而且提议越不公平,脑岛的反应就越大。参与者的脑岛激活也具有预测能力:脑岛激活较强的参与者会持续拒绝更大比例的不公平提议。桑菲和他的同事们认为,也许参与者对不公平提议的反应和他们对难闻气味的反应是一样的——不公平提议会产生一种"道德"上的厌恶和愤怒。

当不公平提议被接受时，参与者的前额叶皮层会被更强烈地激活——也许是因为不公平提议更难被接受，需要认知力量来克服拒绝它们的情感冲动。桑菲研究中另一个有趣的发现是，在这种冲突中似乎有一个裁判——一个被称为前扣带皮层的区域，通常与解决冲突有关。扣带皮层如图5所示。也许它被激活，是因为它在解决认知和情感反应之间的冲突中发挥了作用。我们的认知系统想要那些钱；如果提议者很刻薄，情感系统就会惩罚他们。前扣带皮层解决了这种脑内冲突。

其他的神经经济学研究探讨了我们的共情反应。同样是使用脑成像技术，坦尼亚·辛格和他的同事们进行了一些实验，表明当实验参与者观察到他们的伴侣受到痛苦的电击时，他们的共情反应与包括脑岛在内的无意识情绪处理回路有关。共情反应似乎是通过对他人疼痛的反应表现出我们自己的内在感受状态而产生的。

金融决策的神经经济学实验

一些神经经济学研究探讨了情绪对金融市场的影响。研究人员研究了脑损伤患者的经济决策。巴贝·希夫和他的同事们研究了一组病变患者的行为，并将其与健康的控制组的决策进行了比较。两组人都被要求玩一个金融投资游戏。健康的参与者很快学会了选择风险较低的策略。病变患者承担的风险要大得多，但收益明显更高。其他研究发现，经历强烈情绪反应的人在金融交易游戏中的表现则有所不同——罗闻全和同事们发现,作为金融交易员,经历更极端情绪反应的实验参与者的效率更低。

脑成像研究也显示了情绪状态和交易者行为之间的关系。布莱恩·克努森和他的同事们运用功能性磁共振成像技术,对在安全的和有风险的股票之间进行选择的交易者进行了一些脑部扫描研究。克努森和他的同事们发现,情绪处理在金融决策中扮演着重要的角色:有风险的选择与被称为纹状体的大脑区域的激活有关——纹状体与我们处理奖励有关,包括冒险和上瘾的奖励。他们还发现,脑岛激活的显著差异取决于交易员是选择安全的还是风险的选项。这可能反映了脑岛在负面情绪状态中的作用,包括对损失的恐惧——如果对损失的恐惧与风险规避错误有关的话。

我们的激素也可能发挥作用。神经科学家乔·赫伯特和经济学家约翰·科茨开展了一项自然实验,观察一群伦敦即日交易员的行为,这些交易员希望从一天内资产价格的波动中获利。

科茨和赫伯特用唾液样本测量交易员的睾丸激素和皮质醇水平。睾丸激素被认为与更多的冒险和反社会行为有关;而当我们感到压力更大时,皮质醇水平会更高。科茨和赫伯特发现,交易员早上的睾丸激素水平与他们当天晚些时候的表现相关——早上睾丸激素水平较高的交易员似乎在一天的交易中获得了更多的收益。这也许表明,冒险和无情至少在一定程度上是由我们的生理因素驱动的,而不是由标准经济分析中所描述的理性计算过程决定。

其他的研究使用了精神分析的见解。戴维·塔克特是一位精神分析学家,他利用自己的一些专业知识来研究交易员的情绪。塔克特认为，交易员们所专注的金融资产不仅在货币方面有价值。它们就是精神分析学家所说的"幻物"——它们的主人认为它们具有最高级的、特殊的品质。当赚钱带来的兴奋与引起恐慌的亏损恐惧及时分离时，情感冲突就产生了。交易员会在一个阶段获利，在另一个阶段亏损。这或许可以部分解释投机泡沫是如何形成的：交易员很快就会忘记过去的损失。他们编造故事和叙事来把自己的冲动合理化。塔克特表示，欢欣鼓舞的繁荣之后是情绪波动，随着泡沫破裂——最初是由交易员的情绪冲突引发的——最终会以信心的大崩溃告终。

情绪在交易行为中的作用，或许可以解释一些损害宏观经济表现的金融不稳定性。在第八章中，我们将在行为经济学家一个相对较新的未知领域——行为宏观经济学——的背景下探讨其中的一些主题。

第八章
宏观经济中的行为

在第七章中，我们探讨了情绪在经济和金融决策中的作用。当我们把这些情感和心理因素综合起来看时，它会对一些新的宏观经济模型的发展产生影响，这些模型旨在分析这些社会心理影响因素如何驱动我们的集体行为。虽然个人在宏观经济中是微不足道的，但我们所有人的经济行为对政策制定者来说却是一个至关重要的问题，这也是最容易被误解的经济学领域。自2007—2008年金融危机以来，传统宏观经济模型的可信度受到了考验。本章将探讨行为经济学家如何促进创新宏观经济理论的发展，以及新类型行为宏观经济数据的搜集。

行为宏观经济学是一个相对不发达的领域，因为它受到一些重大的限制，这在一定程度上反映了将许多不同类型的人的选择汇集在一起的难度。这些人具有不同的性格，感受不同的心境和情绪，并以复杂的方式使用各种各样的产生更大范围偏差的启发式。因此，行为经济学家倾向于关注消费者、工人、商界人士或政策制定者的微观经济行为。这样做当然是困难的，因为正如第八章所解释的那样，要测量性格、心境和情绪并不容易。因此，对行为宏观经济学家来说，这一分析任务无比艰巨，因为行为测量的问题混合了个体在宏观经济中相互作用的许多复杂方式。

当我们把所有的选择放在一起时，这就会对重要变量产生影响。这些变量通常是日常宏观经济新闻报道的焦点，包括就业、失业、产出和增长、通货膨胀和利率等。心境和情绪会影响我们所有人的幸福，政策制定者也越来越意识到这一点。他们正在设计新的宏观经济政策目标，以体现其中的一些洞见。宏观经济不再是经济学家的专属领域。来自心理学、精神病学、社会学、医学和公共卫生的洞识向我们表明，一个国家的福利不仅仅与公民的经济状况有关。在本章，我们将探讨其中的一些主题。

宏观经济心理学

行为宏观经济学关注社会和心理因素——包括乐观和悲观的情绪——如何帮助我们理解宏观经济波动。企业家往往受到经济整体情绪和商业信心波动的驱动，这会影响到商业增长的速度，以及商界人士是否准备投资于新的商业项目——这对宏观经济产出和增长都有影响。当商界感到乐观时，这可能是一个自我实现的预言，从而推动国民总产出上升。

对待时间的态度也很重要，因为宏观经济波动是由人们今天的消费或为未来储蓄的决定所驱动的。消费者通常是有耐心还是无耐心，决定了他们是否倾向于在今天消费或储蓄。如果他们更有耐心并储蓄更多，就可以为企业家的新投资项目创造资金。如果消费者更没有耐心并消费更多，这可能在短期内提振经济活动，因为企业会扩大生产以满足消费者的需求。企业家必须决定是否投资他们在未来可能会获得发展的业务。把所有这些决定放在一起，就会对整个宏观经济产生重大影响。

我们的心理也会与我们对未来的态度相互作用。心境和情绪决定了我们是否倾向于做出前瞻性决定。希望和乐观以及信心之所以会推动经济前进，其部分原因是，在建设经济体的生产能力方面发挥关键作用的企业家很容易受到信心和情绪变化的影响。2016年英国就是否应该脱离欧盟（"脱欧"或"不脱欧"）举行的公投就是一个鲜明的例子——当支持脱欧的选民（"脱欧派"）获胜时，许多投票支持留在欧盟的人，其中包括大多数英国商业领袖和经济学家，被一种深刻的悲观情绪所震撼。直接的宏观经济后果是深远的。由于公投后经济、政治和金融的不确定性，英镑暴跌，许多投资者撤出了英国。对英国经济的负面影响很快就显现了出来。

我们是有耐心还是无耐心，是乐观还是悲观，将决定我们对未来是否感到积极，这反过来也会影响我们有耐心还是无耐心。实验心理学家塔里·沙洛特已经证明，我们似乎天生就倾向于乐观——我们似乎已经进化出一种过度乐观的倾向，而大多数健康的人都倾向于乐观偏差。脱欧公投也说明了这一趋势——许多支持留欧的选民对公投结果表示了惊讶和震惊，尽管数周以来许多民调一直预测脱欧派将赢得投票，即使优势很微弱。

乐观偏差也影响了建筑和基础设施领域的公共投资，这一点得到了监督政府项目支出的英国审计署的承认。2013年，审计署对建筑行业的过度乐观现象进行了研究。它发现，这与政府项目的成本膨胀有关，因为规划者对项目的未来前景并不总是现实的,因此他们低估了成本,对潜在的延误也是不够现实的。

经济学家约翰·伊弗彻和霍马·扎格哈米使用两种实证工具来体现乐观和耐心之间的一些联系。他们分析了来自美国综合社会调查的自我报告的幸福水平。那些心态更积极的受访者也更有耐心,他们不太可能"活在当下"。伊弗彻和扎格哈米还进行了一项实验,以表明情绪对人们关于未来之态度的影响。其中一组被展示了快乐的电影片段,例如,他们被要求观看一个喜剧演员的日常表演。第二组观看的是中性的影片,例如野生动物和风景的影片。然后,所有的参与者都被要求说明,他们有多看重通过今天的支付来投资未来。看了喜剧节目的那组人表现出了更多的耐心——他们比另一组人更重视对未来的投资,这可能表明快乐的情绪使我们对未来更感兴趣。

早期行为宏观经济学家:卡托纳、凯恩斯和明斯基

将情绪作为宏观经济的驱动因素来关注并不新鲜。乔治·卡托纳是经济心理学的先驱之一,他的许多见解与行为宏观经济学的现代版本遥相呼应。他观察到,情绪因素(如紧张或兴奋)可以诱导消费者情绪、投资者信心和总需求的变化,而这些变化是标准宏观经济学模型所无法体现的。

约翰·梅纳德·凯恩斯也有深远的影响。凯恩斯在其1936年出版的《就业、利息和货币通论》一书的第12章,描述了推动宏观经济的两组主要参与者:投机者和企业家。每个群体都有独特的个性,受情绪的影响也不同。金融投机者追逐金融回报——他们希望通过买卖金融资产实现利润最大化。

凯恩斯的分析集中在股票和股票市场投机者的行为上。金

融技术的快速发展，特别是自20世纪80年代以来的飞速发展，使得股票和股份不再是当今唯一的风险金融资产，但凯恩斯的基本逻辑在现代金融市场也适用。股票市场提供流动性，这是好的一面，因为它为企业家提供资金以提高他们的生产能力，但这种流动性意味着股票买卖非常迅速和容易。金融投机者追逐短期利润，因此他们只关注非常短期的股价波动。他们还会受到其他投机者行为的强烈推动。

凯恩斯推断，投机者通常会认为其他人可能更了解某股票的潜在利润，因此他们在买卖时会模仿他人，尤其是在他们对市场趋势不太确定的情况下。投机者总是关注别人的想法，因为这决定了他们应该为股票支付的价格。投机者不太关心股票的基本价值，也不太关心它在整个生命周期内能赚到多少钱。他们更关心的是，在不久的将来，他们能得到什么样的股票价格。对于这一点，其他投机者的意见是最重要的，因为他们可能明天就会买入这些股票。

凯恩斯用报纸选美比赛的比喻来描绘这种对他人观点的关注。他描述了一项比赛，要求参赛者查看许多漂亮女人的照片，但他们的任务不是选出他们认为最漂亮的，而是选出他们认为别人会认为最漂亮的。从本质上说，他们必须事后猜测其他参与者的判断——因此创造出了这样一种情况，即参与者都在判断别人对别人的决定的看法。就宏观经济而言，凯恩斯认为，当投机者遵循这些惯例并玩选美游戏时，他们对股票的估值将不会有什么坚实的真实信念基础。这导致了不稳定和波动性，并对宏观经济产生影响，因为不稳定和不确定的气氛阻碍了企业家投资建立自己的企业。

企业家是凯恩斯宏观经济理论中的另一类人群。对凯恩斯来说，商业和创业不仅仅是赚钱——如果你想赚钱，投机可以提供相对较大的、可预测的回报，因为投机者的活动都是非常短期的。通常，投机者最关心的是股价在一天、一周或一个月内的波动，而不会关注股价在数年或数十年里的变化（尽管金融投资大师沃伦·巴菲特是个明显的例外）。

企业家面临的任务比投机者复杂得多。他们必须更仔细地考虑长期，这是很困难的，因为未来是如此不确定。如果一个完全理性的企业家必须依靠纯粹的数学计算来支持他们的投资决策，那么他们就不会在自己的业务上投资太多。未来的不确定性，尤其是对于创新型企业来说，意味着很难预测你的企业在一年、五年或十年后会做得有多好。对于企业家来说，还有其他东西可以克服未来的不确定性和恐惧，那就是**动物精神**。动物精神可以部分地从前面讨论的乐观偏差的角度来理解，正如塔里·沙洛特和其他人所分析的那样。佩加蒙的盖伦是古罗马角斗士们的一位希腊医生，他首先提出了**动物精神**的概念。他对动物精神的描述将我们的内部神经生理学与我们的行动联系起来，他的观点是以希波克拉底描述的四体液说——黑胆汁、黄胆汁、血液和黏液——为基础，每一种体液都与一种特定的气质相关：分别是抑郁质、胆汁质、多血质和黏液质。

凯恩斯的动物精神是与多血质的气质联系在一起的，它们是关于行动和去做一些积极事情的渴望。从古代跨越到现代，盖伦的动物精神可能也体现了与企业家的动物精神有关的自发的乐观主义，这种乐观主义推动他们对未来充满信心，并投资建立自己的企业。这与宏观经济有什么关系呢？凯恩斯解释说，企业家活动与投机者活动之间的平衡，将决定股票市场对包括产出、就业、失业和增长在内的宏观经济变量的影响。然而，不确定性和不稳定性很容易削弱动物精神。因此，当金融市场波动时，企业家会感到不安，他们将不太愿意为未来投资建立自己的企业。

金融体系将企业家和投机者联系在一起。企业家需要从金融市场获得资金来建立长期的企业，而金融市场可以提供他们所需的资金。凯恩斯认为，当这些趋势处于平衡状态时，当投机只是稳定的企业流上的泡沫时，一切都会很顺利。但是，如果投机成为一个不稳定的旋涡，那么它将使宏观经济不稳定，放大波动性和不确定性。

现代行为宏观经济学：动物精神模型

如前所述，对行为宏观经济学家来说，从个人决策中搜集数据来体现宏观经济现象特别棘手。行为宏观经济学家可能会发现，很难将所有驱动个体的复杂影响和性格整合到一个连贯的总体宏观经济模型中。传统的宏观经济学通过假设所有的工人和所有的企业都是一样的，各自以同样的方式做出决定，从而避开了这些复杂性。此外，每个人都是完全理性的，所以描述不同的人在宏观经济中如何相互作用相对容易。标准的宏观经济理论描述的是一个人——**一个代表性行为人**，他以相对简单的方式做出决策。在许多标准的宏观经济理论中，代表性行为人反映了所有企业或所有工人的行为。将代表性行为人的行为相乘，就得到了宏观经济模型。在这一分析中，宏观经济学就强有力地建立在微观经济原理的基础之上。

行为宏观经济学家无法令人信服地使用理性的代表性行为人的假设而以同样的方式进行聚合,因为行为经济学的本质是体现性格和情绪的差异,以及行为人之间互动的差异。行为经济学中没有单一的代表性行为人。相反,行为宏观经济学家倾向于关注总体现象——例如,商业信心和消费者信心。

现代行为宏观经济学家建立模型的另一种方式是关注行为的特定心理动机,通常采用动物精神的概念,但定义方式不同于凯恩斯和盖伦的定义。阿克洛夫和席勒在他们的《动物精神》一书中,描述了一系列影响宏观经济和金融体系的动物精神。但他们对动物精神的定义远没有凯恩斯精确。本质上,他们把动物精神等同于一系列心理现象,而凯恩斯的概念更多体现在企业家投资建设自己的生产能力时的直觉上。在阿克洛夫和席勒看来,他们的动物精神超越了企业家的动物精神,包括五种动物精神,每一种都会产生其对经济不稳定的影响——包括信心、公平偏好、腐败、货币幻觉和讲故事。

其他现代行为宏观经济学家围绕动物精神开发了复杂的数学模型,其定义与凯恩斯最初对盖伦概念的宏观经济应用又有所不同。包括罗杰·法默、保罗·德·格劳威和迈克尔·伍德福德在内的宏观经济学家,使用复杂的数学技术对动物精神周期进行建模,从本质上把动物精神作为随机波动(随机噪声)来体现,推动宏观经济从活跃状态转向衰退状态。

金融和宏观经济

行为宏观经济学家还关注金融和金融不稳定性的影响。许多主流宏观经济理论忽视了金融部门,但自2007—2008年的金融危机和随后的全球衰退以来,经济学家和政策制定者们受到提醒,金融部门对宏观经济表现有多么重要。我们可以从投机泡沫的心理学入手。投机泡沫的历史记载很难与标准经济学观点相一致,即冷静理性的行为人在评估购买资产的相对收益和成本时,会进行仔细的数学计算。郁金香狂热,是金融史上最多姿多彩的插曲之一,说明了投机泡沫看上去是多么不稳定和非理性。从1636年11月开始的短短三到四个月里,荷兰对郁金香球茎的需求飙升。对于更稀有的球茎,价格上涨高达六十倍。其中一个球茎特别珍贵——来自变异(多亏一种病毒才有了这种变异的发生)的"永远的奥古斯都"郁金香球茎,它的色彩富有异国情调,非常漂亮。在狂热的高峰期,一个"永远的奥古斯都"郁金香球茎的价格可能相当于阿姆斯特丹市中心一幢三层楼的房子。繁荣之后是萧条,一切都那么具有戏剧性。到了1637年2月,大多数郁金香球茎都卖不出去了,即使价格很低也卖不出去,许多郁金香投机者失去了他们的财富。然而,郁金香狂热并不是只发生过一次:历史上还有很多其他投机泡沫的例子,比如18世纪的南海泡沫,1929年大崩盘中结束的美国猖獗的投机,20世纪90年代末的互联网泡沫,以及导致2007—2008年全球金融危机的次贷危机,这些还只是其中的几个而已。

在解释这种金融不稳定性时,凯恩斯的思想启发了一批经济学家,他们开发了更丰富的金融市场模型,其中包括著名的海曼·明斯基。明斯基发展了信贷周期理论,以体现前面描述的那些金融不稳定性。海曼·明斯基的一些工作在预测2007—2008年的金融危机及其引发全球衰退的实际影响方面,具有特别的先见之明。与凯恩斯一样,情绪因素在明斯基对脆弱的金融体系,以及这种金融脆弱性更广泛的宏观经济影响的分析中发挥了重要作用。明斯基解释了商业周期是如何由恐惧和恐慌的周期所驱动的,金融体系的脆弱性在推动极端的波动中扮演着关键角色。明斯基认为,商业周期首先是由投机热潮和企业家的过度乐观所驱动的。银行放贷太多了。企业借贷也太多了。最终,有人意识到繁荣没有稳定的基础,利率开始上升,这就促发了一场与之前的繁荣一样壮观的萧条。

金融投机更普遍地导致金融不稳定,而这些金融因素可能会对宏观经济产生有害影响。这些信息在好莱坞广为流传,最近的一部电影《大空头》说的就是这样的故事。它讲述了一些金融交易员的故事,他们意识到,随着复杂的新金融产品被开发出来,巨大的金融脆弱性正在积聚,这些产品旨在通过让那些信用评级较差的人获得多项抵押贷款来赚钱。这就是**次级抵押贷款危机**的开始。即使他们为自己赚了数百万美元,但交易员们也意识到,他们是从许多人的背运中获利的,这些人将失去他们的房子和/或工作,因为金融不稳定不仅会对美国经济,而且会对全球宏观经济表现产生毁灭性的影响。正如图6所示,其可能的结果是,由于人们无法再负担得起抵押贷款,他们将积累起信用卡债务,这将影响到银行和其他金融机构,范围所及不仅限于美国,而且会扩大到全世界。

次级抵押贷款危机

这些观点是由一些经济学家提出的。罗伯特·席勒写了很多关于金融市场的"非理性繁荣"(这个词是前美联储主席

图6 次级抵押贷款危机

艾伦·格林斯潘创造的)及其对就业、投资、产出和经济增长可能产生影响的文章。赫什·谢夫林认为,看涨的金融市场中的非理性繁荣反映了恐惧、希望和贪婪之间的相互作用。很多导致金融不稳定的因素都与过度冒险有关,情绪在其中发挥了作用——这与在第七章中探讨的乔治·洛温斯坦和其他人关于内心因素的洞见相关。洛温斯坦认为,对风险的感知与我们的情绪状态有关,而不是像经济学家通常认为的那样,只与简单、稳定的偏好有关。

心境与商业周期

行为宏观经济学家的另一个视角是分析信心和社会情绪对宏观经济结果的影响。共同的因素可能会影响每个人的心境，例如，当阳光明媚的时候，我们大多数人的心情会更愉快。经济学家利用这一洞见，去体现在商业周期的不同阶段心境与宏观经济和金融波动之间的联系。

马克·坎斯特拉及其同事们利用季节性抑郁的数据来检验他们的假设，即金融市场在冬季和夏季的走势不同。季节性抑郁可以用季节性情感障碍（SAD）的发病率来衡量。患SAD的人更可能谨慎和厌恶风险。如果这也转化到金融市场交易员身上，那么他们在冬天会更加厌恶风险——倘若他们生活在日照时间较短的国家也会如此。坎斯特拉和他的团队发现，黑夜、云层覆盖和温度都对股市表现有强烈的影响。他们得出的结论是，季节性萧条增加了交易员的风险厌恶情绪。坎斯特拉的证据在戴维·赫什莱弗和泰勒·沙姆韦（2003）进行的一项类似研究中得到了证实。他们还发现，股市表现与日照时间呈正相关关系。

一些分析人士认为，集体感受的情绪是关键的宏观经济驱动因素，是最终的解释变量。社会经济学研究所的罗伯特·普莱克特和他的团队，将这一洞见应用到金融市场波动的分析中。普莱克特认为，**社会心境**是最终的因果性因素，也是宏观经济趋势最强大的驱动因素。与凯恩斯及其对金融市场波动和实际经济表现之间联系的分析遥相呼应，普莱克特断言，股票市场体现了我们无意识的社会心境。普莱克特认为，这种社会心境驱动了宏观经济周期的活跃阶段。当人们心情更愉快、更乐观时，积极的社会情绪会产生广泛的影响——音乐更"流行"，裙摆也会上升，当职的政客们也会做得很好。股市上涨也是现任总统竞选连任的最佳时机。但当社会心境消极悲观，金融市场不稳定时，时尚是保守的，音乐是压抑的。宏观经济会对社会心境做出响应，因为社会情绪驱动消费者的决定和公司的商业计划。负面的社会心境也影响了政府的决策：政府更为褊狭，倾向于保护主义之类的政策。负面社会心境的所有这些不同方面，都会导致宏观经济的衰退。

幸福和福祉

行为经济学的另一个主题采用了完全不同的视角。行为经济学家也在开发定义和衡量宏观经济表现的新方法。传统上，政府部门的统计人员收集信息以衡量整体宏观经济表现，通常使用以货币衡量的产出/收入（例如物价和平均工资），以及其他衡量经济表现的客观指标，包括就业和失业人数。

行为经济学家并不关注衡量宏观经济表现的货币指标的波动，即以国内生产总值（GDP）衡量的产出和生产的货币价值，他们关注幸福和福祉的心理方面。

衡量幸福和福祉的一个问题是，我们对自己幸福的感知依赖于环境，这与第四章和第五章探讨的参照依赖的思想有关。大多数对幸福和福祉的测量都是基于调查——而且，自我报告的幸福水平就像在一个不太靠得住的时刻拍摄的快照。在我们判定自己有多幸福（或不幸福）之前提出的问题可以作为**启动性**问题。例如，可以通过让学生思考最近发生的事情来操纵学生自我报告的幸福感。在一组实验中,学生被问了一些启动性问题,比如"你昨晚约会了吗?""进展顺利吗?"——这些问题是为了让学生感受到特定的情绪,这取决于他们前一天晚上的表现。学生们自我报告的快乐程度根据问题的顺序而变化。在被问及昨晚的事情如何**之后**,学生被要求表述他们的快乐程度,他们报告了不同的幸福水平。如果之前他们度过了一个悲惨的夜晚,然后他们记录的幸福水平要低得多。如果他们度过了一个美好的夜晚,那么他们的幸福感就会相对较高。另一方面,如果学生在被问及前一天晚上过得如何**之前**先被问及他们的快乐程度,那么他们所宣称的快乐水平就不会受到昨晚事件的影响。让学生回忆最近发生的事情改变了他们对自己快乐的看法。因此,虽然政策制定者应该更多地担心幸福的更广泛定义,但使用幸福调查是有问题的,因为我们自我报告的幸福水平可能会被暂时的因素扭曲。

总部位于伦敦的政治/经济智库列格坦研究所在2014年发布了一份报告,详细阐述了各种文献,探讨了我们的福祉、幸福和生活满意度是如何由广泛的社会心理、经济和金融因素驱动的。该报告还分析了测量幸福和福祉的新数据来源,并提供了一些关于如何使用稳健的计量经济学方法分析这些数据的洞识。

行为经济学家对幸福和福祉的兴趣,已经转到了在世界各地开发这些新的宏观经济数据来源上。公共卫生数据也可以成为集体心境的有用指标,例如,自杀率、精神疾病和压力相关疾病的数据。各类国家和国际统计机构正在搜集关于幸福、福祉和生活满意度的数据,例如,通过包含关于主观幸福感的问题以及关于就业和失业的标准劳动力调查问题的家庭调查,来得到这些数据。

英国国家统计局现在已将对家庭生活满意度问题的回答纳入家庭调查中了。从中国到法国，其他国家也在搜集类似的数据，而经合组织则正在整理国际数据集。这些新数据有可能被用于宏观经济分析，描绘出宏观经济表现更细微和更广泛的图景。也许最具影响力的是，世界银行目前正在发布一份年度《世界幸福报告》，这将有可能为行为宏观经济学家提供一些有用的数据，以表明幸福的宏观经济趋势如何随时间和空间而变化，以及如何将这些新的幸福和福祉指标与更传统的宏观经济表现指标联系起来。

技术创新也有助于搜集更好的行为宏观经济数据。行为研究人员现在可以实施大规模的在线调查，他们也可以使用短信和社交媒体来搜集数据（例如，从谷歌搜索、推特消息和脸书"点赞"中搜集数据）。随着这些类型"大数据"的增长，行为宏观经济学家数据集中的一些空白可能会被填补起来。

使用主观数据是有问题的，但在经济学家、统计学家和政府的合作下，这一领域数据的可信度越来越高。获取幸福数据也会存在问题，需要进行更多的研究来评估这些新统计数据的利弊，以及探索行为宏观经济学家可以更好地理解和衡量幸福与福祉的其他一些方法。

第九章

经济行为与公共政策

最理想的情况下,经济学可以帮助决策者设计政策,以解决广泛的经济和金融问题,既为个人,也为整个经济。传统的经济政策专注于解决市场失灵:如果市场运转不良,价格不能有效地传递相关的供求信息,那么政府政策工具可以帮助解决由此产生的问题。在本章中,我们将探讨行为公共政策的一些关键洞察和证据,重点关注微观经济政策。发展一套连贯的行为宏观经济政策工具是一项复杂得多的挑战,至少到目前为止,还没有人进行过恰当的尝试。

微观经济政策

传统上,税收和补贴一直是政府和政策制定者用来帮助市场更好运转的主要政策工具。一个广为人知的例子是吸烟。如果吸烟给纳税人增加了公共卫生系统的负担,那么对香烟征税就是有用的——这样不仅可以降低人们吸烟的动机,还为政府提供了可以支付给卫生系统的收入。或者,如果某个国家的一个特定地区正在遭受工业衰退的痛苦,那么补贴可以用来刺激该地区的经济活动。

税收和补贴会受到一系列实践、技术和逻辑上的限制,因此现代经济政策也涵盖了一系列更广泛的经济工具,其中就包括那些受到诺贝尔奖得主罗纳德·科斯的市场交易分析启发的工具。科斯的洞见奠定了交易体系人为设计的基础,当价格提供不完善的供求信号时,可以创建交易的人为体系来解决所出现的问题。这些人为的市场取代了"缺失的市场",即由于市场价格将它们排除在外而缺失的市场。污染就是一个简单的例子。当一个企业污染了空气或水,如果不对它采取任何措施,那么该企业就是在免费地造成污染——他们不必为污染的负面后果赔偿任何人。因此,关于污染的市场就缺失了。

基于科斯的洞识,其中一个解决方案就是发展一个人为的市场——在污染的例子里,可能就是采取污染排放交易计划的形式。个人和企业可以买卖污染权(或被污染权)。创建这些人为的市场并不简单,但总体而言,就像税收和补贴一样,它们是为解决市场和制度失灵而设计,而非为个人行为而设计。

什么是行为公共政策?助推行为的改变

行为公共政策从不同的角度看待这些问题。它关注的不是市场失灵,而是**行为的改变**——也就是说,通过助推人们做出更有效率、更富生产性的决策,改变人们做出日常决策和选择的方式。

这一领域的开创性著作是塞勒和桑斯坦的《助推》——英国的政策制定者经常引用《思维导图》,其洞识与《助推》中的观点相似。塞勒和桑斯坦更广泛地借鉴了行为经济学和心理学的大量文献，特别是关于选择过载、信息负载、启发式和行为偏差的思想，这些在第四章和第五章中都有介绍。他们认为，在设计有效的政策工具时，政策制定者需要理解驱动人们决策的启发式和偏差。这样，人们的决策结构就可以重新设计。这一见解构成了塞勒和桑斯坦所说的我们的**选择架构**的基础。我们的选择是如何构成的？在决定我们想做什么和买什么之前，我们是如何处理信息的？我们的决策过程可以重新设计吗？

塞勒和桑斯坦认为，如果政策制定者能更好地理解人们的选择架构，那么他们就能设计出帮助人们更有效决策的政策。给人们简单的选择，设计提示和助推，引导人们的决策向更有建设性和积极的方向发展，不断地提供反馈，以加强"好的"决定，遏制"坏的"决定——所有这些策略都是行为公共决策者工具箱的一部分。

塞勒和桑斯坦认为，从政治和道德上讲，使用"助推"是一种**自由意志的家长主义**。人们保留着自己选择的权力，所以它是自由意志的；但它也包含了来自政府的**助推**，从这个意义上说，它是家长式的。换句话说，它是自由意志主义的，因为人们仍然有选择；它也是一种家长式的政府干预。塞勒和桑斯坦认为，"助推"结合了两个方面的优点（尽管批评者认为它结合了两个方面的缺点）。税收和补贴将成本和收益强加给不同的人群。一般来说，一个普通人无法选择是否纳税（尽管有钱请会计师的个人和企业可能对纳税有更多的控制权）。我们无法轻易选择是否接受补贴，但塞勒和桑斯坦认为，"助推"可以被设计成允许人们做出一些选择的形式，例如通过巧妙地设计默认选项来做到这一点。

实践中的助推：默认选项

"助推"在实践中涉及什么呢？许多助推都是基于对**默认选项**的操作。这些利用了一种特定类型的行为偏差——现状偏差——在第四章和第五章中进行了探讨。如果政策制定者（或企业）设置了默认选项（一个人如果什么都不做就会得到的选项），那么令人惊讶的是，很大一部分人会坚持这个默认选项。这有很多原因。人们倾向于维持现状。他们并不总是能很快放弃默认选项，因为改变选择可能是有风险的，或者还是需要付出努力的。人们可能会把默认选项理解为一种信号，认为它表明了什么是对他们来说最好的选择。如果默认选项被设置为匹配最具建设性的决策，那么更多人可能（尽管是被动地）就会做出该决定。

举个例子，在大多数国家，如何鼓励人们捐献他们的器官是一个大问题。器官的需求远远大于供给。在这一领域也存在政策困境——例如，围绕着付钱给捐献器官的人的道德问题——但在这里我们将集中讨论行为公共政策制定者会如何应对。决策者可以设置默认选项，这样默认选项就是捐献器官。如果一个人不想这样做，那么他们可以选择退出。这样，个人就保留了选择的自由。

默认选项还可以帮助我们为养老金存更多的钱。在第四章中，我们介绍了贝纳茨和塞勒的"多为明天储蓄"养老金计划，该计划也利用了默认选项。为了鼓励员工为他们的退休储蓄更多，这个方案的默认选项是把固定比例的工资纳入员工的养老金，随着工资的上涨，养老金的数额也会增加。但员工并不是被迫这么做的——他们有自己的选择。他们可以选择退出。默认选项是政策制定者的工具——这是助推的家长式的那部分。选择退出是决策者的选择——这是助推的自由意志的那部分。

这些类型"助推"的一个问题是，它们也经常被商业企业利用，从而损害我们的利益。一个营销企业想要通过收集和出售我们的联系方式给其他企业，以图多赚一些钱，它可以设置人们的联系方式表格，从而使我们不会注意到我们已经允许他们传播我们的联系方式。他们太了解我们的选择架构了。

切　换

与默认选项相关的是不频繁切换的问题，这在第四章中也提到过。我们与能源供应商、移动电话公司或银行合作多年，即使它们提供给我们的交易项目价值很低，我们仍然与它们继续合作。我们更换供应商太不勤快了。2016年，天然气与电力市场办公室（英国能源市场监管机构）报告称，超过60%的消费者不记得更换了能源供应商，尽管这样做可以在每年的能源账单上节省200英镑。我们的切换水平低所产生的问题是，它减轻了企业的竞争压力：如果它们提供一个低价值的交易项目时还没有失去客户，它们怎么还能有提供更好交易项目的动机？切换水平低也反映了一种现状偏差，政府政策制定者在越来越多地鼓励我们，当从供应商那里得不到好交易项目时更频繁地切换供应商。他们正在设计的鼓励更多切换的工具，也专注于更好地理解选择架构——例如，通过使我们更容易切换，或通过减少使得切换供应商成为一个认知挑战的选择过载和/或信息负载问题。政策制定者越来越强调鼓励我们进行切换，这在英国取得了一些成功。有证据表明，这些政策在提高切换率方面发挥了作用。天然气与电力市场办公室报告称，2015年按家庭计算的能源供应商切换率比2014年高出了15%。

社会助推

政策制定者设计的另一个强有力的助推机制是，利用我们对社会影响因素的敏感性，这是基于第三章中概述的想法给出的。在能源部门，根据大量学术研究的结果，有一些与家庭能源消费有关的重要发现。例如，韦斯利·舒尔茨和他的同事们分析了加利福尼亚州的家庭。研究人员向家庭提供了两类信息。第一组信息与某一社区其他家庭的能源消费有关。这为家庭提供了一个社会参照点，供他们比较自己的能源消费。我们可以把塞勒和桑斯坦关于设计一种简化选择的选择架构的思想联系起来，如果一个家庭的消费低于当地社会平均水平，那么对其消费相对于社区平均水平的社会赞赏/反对可以通过一个笑脸来传达；如果消费高于当地社会平均水平，则可以通过一个皱眉的脸来传达。第二组信息是一组关于如何减少能源消费的说明。

这些不同类型的信息有什么影响呢？为了测试不同类型信息的差异效果，一组实验参与者（对照组）只得到了节能提示，另一组（处理组）还得到了关于社会平均水平的信息。研究人员发现，社会助推是十分强有力的——与对照组的家庭相比，当被告知他们的能源消费水平高于社区的平均水平时，有了社会信息的处理组的家庭更有可能将他们的能源消费调整到平均水平，即降低他们的能源消费。研究人员推断，这是因为家庭正在根据社会规范或参照点调整他们的选择。大量类似的研究也得到了相同的发现,这些洞见被纳入到了新的能源账单设计中——例如图7所示的OPower账单。

然而,对于政策制定者来说,一个关键的教训是要当心意想

图7　节约能源的社会助推

不到的后果。研究人员发现了**回旋效应**：能源消费低于社区平均水平的家庭，往往会被社区高消费的社会信息所鼓励，从而消费**更多**而不是更少。如果各个家庭的能源消费分布是对称的，那么可能有同样多的人会按照社会平均水平向上调整他们的能源消费，也有同样多的人会向下调整他们的能源消费。如果是这样的话，那么平均消费就不会改变，政策也就没有意义了。

其他的政策举措

行为公共政策原则越来越多地延伸到公共政策的其他领域。例如，有关能源部门社会助推的研究结果已扩展到税收领域。在第三章中，我们注意到税务官员可以如何利用社会影响因素。在英国，税务和海关总署（HMRC）会尝试向逾期缴纳税款的人寄信，告知他们其他部分人已经按时缴纳了税款。这里的想法是利用社会压力作为一种有说服力的工具。据报道，这种社会助推在英国和其他国家都取得了成功。其他政策制定者也在利用默认选项和其他洞识，对竞争政策和金融服务等领域更为传统的政策进行补充。

然而，重要的是，决策者不要忽视传统的经济政策——一些最有效的政策举措都是将标准的经济政策工具与行为修饰相结合。其他的政策将行为洞见与经典方法结合起来，设计出了有效的激励措施。一个例子是对塑料袋收费的政策，这是爱尔兰多年前实施的政策，旨在解决乱扔塑料袋的问题，如图8所示。

乱扔塑料袋是一个严重的环境问题，对野生动物、生活环境和人类健康都有毁灭性的影响。有证据表明，我们的水源正被我们随意丢弃的塑料袋的微小残留物所污染。制造塑料袋还会

图8 到处乱扔的塑料袋

污染和过度使用稀缺的不可再生资源。2015年，英国政府对塑料袋收取5便士的费用，有传言称，在一些家庭，塑料袋的价值超过了他们所住的房子——因为他们囤积了太多现在每个值5便士的塑料袋。

更严重的是，5便士的收费说明了行为经济学的洞识如何能够指导传统经济政策的设计，同时也促进了行为的改变。5便士的收费是一种税收，但它旨在纠正行为偏差，而不是一种市场失灵（假设囤积大量实际上几乎毫无价值的塑料袋不是特别理性）。也许囤积塑料袋是禀赋效应的一种表现——我们高估了已经拥有的东西。无论囤积塑料袋的潜在心理原因是什么，传统的税收都可以让我们避免囤积大量对我们毫无用处的塑料袋，也可以避免使用后扔掉太多。但是，这也带来了意想不到的后果，有证据表明，塑料袋的总体使用量并没有减少。许多人不再重复使用普通的超市塑料袋作为垃圾袋。相反，他们增加了其他更大的塑料袋的购买，包括"生活袋"和耐用的垃圾袋，由此抵消了一些（可能是全部）5便士塑料袋收费所预期的积极环境影响。

政策的未来

行为公共政策的未来是充满希望的。政府政策部门的推广做得很好，最著名的或许是前英国首相戴维·卡梅伦内阁办公室的行为洞察团队——绰号"助推小组"。助推设计在商业上也做得非常好，成为国内和国际很多公众关注的焦点，这种关注既有积极的一面，也有消极的一面。

不过，风险还是存在的。行为公共政策已经变得非常时髦，但与所有时尚一样，它确实会引发过度炒作，而且很容易产生反作用。此外，基于"助推"的行为洞察和政策，也引发了许多兴奋情绪。我们需要更多的证据来证明这些政策干预到底多有效，多么具有"黏性"。我们能否通过稳健的统计分析来确定，这些"助推"是真正有效的，而且起效的范围很大呢？到目前为止所确定的积极影响能否在更广泛的研究中得到复制？助推只是具有短期影响的噱头政策吗？对于那些尝试过"助推"的人来说，他们最终会回到过去的习惯和选择吗？还是说，行为政策的助推会产生更强、更持久的影响？

为了确保最深刻的行为政策经验得以延续，重要的是要建立一个强有力的、科学严谨的证据体系，不仅要证明政策在何时何地起作用，还要证明政策在何时何地不起作用。许多学术研究的问题是，那些负面的结果不容易得到发表。一项关于政策干预**不起作用**的发现，远不如一项关于政策干预产生了惊人积极效益的发现那么令人兴奋和引起兴趣。行为经济学告诉我们，我们往往会过度重视那些最令人难忘的信息，行为公共政策证据也是如此。

  对于政策制定者来说，如果他们不关注传统经济政策，就会出现另一个陷阱。传统经济政策已被证明在解决市场和制度失灵方面很有效。"助推"在政策圈很流行，但它是否导致了对传统政策工具的忽视，而传统政策工具本是可以有效解决市场和其他制度失灵的呢？"助推"可以解决人们的偏差和错误，但帮助人们更有效地做出决定，并不能消除市场和制度失灵。未来，政策制定者需要仔细研究如何利用基于行为洞察的政策来补充，而不是取代传统的经济政策工具。在这种情况下，一个关键的政策问题将会是，如何更有效地协调传统政策和行为政策，而不过分偏向一方。如果我们能正确把握这种政策平衡，那么行为经济学将为我们提供一些强大的工具，解决更广泛的市场失灵和行为偏差，为个人、经济和社会带来更为积极的价值。

索 引

（条目后的数字为原书页码，见本书边码）

A

addiction 成瘾 93—94
 cue-triggers 提示触发 93—94
 and rationality 和理性 93
Aesop's fables 伊索寓言 72
affect heuristic 情感启发式 88—89
aggregation problems in macroeconomics 宏观经济中的加总问题 107
Ainslie, George 乔治·安斯利 69
Akerlof, George 乔治·阿克洛夫 16, 26, 44, 107
alarm clocks, and pre-commitment strategies 闹钟与预先承诺策略 76
Allais, Maurice 莫里斯·阿莱 52
Allais paradox 阿莱悖论 52—53, 参见 certainty effect
altruistic punishment 利他惩罚 25
ambiguity aversion 模糊性厌恶 57
amygdala 杏仁体 95
anatomy of the brain 脑解剖 95—96
anchoring and adjustment 锚定与调整 44—46, 62
Angeletos, George-Marios 乔治-马里奥斯·安杰雷托斯 77—78
animal 动物 77—78
 herding 羊群行为 30, 31
 models, and time inconsistency 动物模型和时间不一致性 69—70

spirit models of the macroeconomy 宏观经济学中的动物模型 107—108
spirits 动物精神 105—108
Animal Spirits, book by Akerlof and Shiller 阿克洛夫和席勒的《动物精神》107—108
Annuities 年金 68, 参见 pensions
ant-grasshopper fable 蚂蚁和蚱蜢的寓言 72
anterior cingulate cortex, and conflict resolution 前扣带皮层与冲突解决 97
Ariely, Dan 丹·艾瑞里 13—14, 92
arithmetic reasoning 算术推理 44—45
artificial markets 人为的市场 117
Asch, Solomon 所罗门·阿希 27
Assange, Julian 朱利安·阿桑奇 55
auctions, housing 房屋拍卖 45
Audit Office, UK 英国审计署 103
automatic responses 无意识反应 88
 in dual-systems models 二元系统中的无意识反应 92—93
availability heuristic 可得性启发式 39—40, 88

B

bank lending 银行贷款 109—110
bat and ball test 球棒和球的测试 83
beauty contests 选美比赛 105
Becker, Gary 加里·贝克尔 93
behaviour change, and public policy 行为变化与公共政策 117—126
behavioural bias 行为偏差 39—48
 cognitive dissonance 认知失调

43—44
   confirmation bias 确认偏差 43
   endowment effect 禀赋效应 62—63
   familiarity bias 熟悉偏差 45
   and mental accounting 与心理账户 78—79
   status quo bias 现状偏差 45—46
   loss aversion 损失厌恶 62
behavioural 行为
   development economics 行为发展经济学 80—81
   life-cycle models 行为生命周期模型 77—78
   paradoxes 行为悖论 52—57
   public policy 行为公共政策 116—126
Behavioural Insights Team 行为洞察团队 125
Benartzi, Shlomo 什洛莫·贝纳茨 46—47, 119
Bernheim, Douglas 道格拉斯·伯恩海姆 93
Big Data 大数据 115
The Big Short《大空头》110
binding choices 约束性选择，参见 pre-commitment strategies
blood donation 献血 11—12
bonobos, and time consistency 倭黑猩猩和时间一致性 70
Borghans, Lex 莱克斯·伯格汉斯 85—86
bracketing 托架，见 choice bracketing
brain anatomy 大脑解剖学 95—96
brain imaging 大脑成像 6, 22—23, 72, 94—97, 98

Brexit 英国脱欧，见 EU Referendum
British Home Stores (BHS), pension fund 英国居家商店的养老基金 32
business confidence 商业信心 101—102
business cycles, impact of season influences 季节性影响对商业周期的作用 111

C

cab driver experiment 出租车司机实验 79—80
Camerer, Colin 科林·凯莫勒 79—80
Cameron, David 戴维·卡梅伦 125
certainty effect 确定性效应 52—55
Cesarini, David 戴维·塞萨里尼 84—85
charitable donations 慈善捐赠 10—15
   experimental studies 慈善捐赠实验研究 13—14
   in Thailand 泰国的慈善捐赠 12—13
Chernev, Alexander 亚历山大·切尔内夫 37
child development 儿童发展 85—87
choice architecture 选择架构 118—121
choice bracketing 选择托架 78—80
choice overload 选择过载 36—37, 120—121
choking under pressure 压力下感到窒息 93
cigarettes tax 香烟税 116
cingulate cortex 扣带皮层 95，参见 anterior cingulate cortex
class action suits 集体诉讼 31
Click-for-Charity experiment "点击慈善"实验 13—14

Clocky "落跑闹钟" 76
Coase, Ronald 罗纳德·科斯 117
Coates, John 约翰·科茨 98
cognition in lesion patients 脑损伤患者的认知 91
cognition in dual-systems models 双系统模型的认知 92—93
cognitive bias 认知偏差, 见 behavioural bias
cognitive constraints 认知约束 3
cognitive dissonance 认知失调 43—44
Cognitive Reflexivity test 认知反身性测试 83, 参见 personality tests
Cohen, Jonathan 乔纳森·科恩 90
Coleridge 柯勒律治 74
collaboration 合作 20
commitment contracts 承诺合同 76—77, 参见 pre-commitment strategies
confidence 信心 101—102
    in the macroeconomy 在宏观经济中 111
confirmation bias 确认偏差 43
conflict resolution, emotional 情绪的冲突解决方案 97
conformity 从众 23
conjunction fallacy 联合谬误 41—42
construction, and optimism bias 建筑业与乐观偏差 103
contingent insurance 或有保险 58
conventions, in the macroeconomy 宏观经济中的惯例 105
cooperation 合作 25, 参见 collaboration
copying 复制, 见 herding
Corbyn, Jeremy 杰里米·科尔宾 43

cortisol 皮质醇 98
Costa, Paul 保罗·科斯塔 83
crowding-out, of motivation 动机的挤出效应 10—12
cue-triggers, and addiction 线索触发与成瘾 93—94
cults 邪教 23
cyber security 网络安全 40

D

Damasio, Antonio 安东尼奥·达马西奥 90—91
data 数据
    in behavioural economics 行为经济学中的数据 4—7
    constraints 数据约束 4—5
    experimental 实验数据 4—5
    ethical considerations 道德权衡 5
    neuroscientific 神经科学 5—6
data constraints 数据约束
    and aggregation in macroeconomics 与宏观经济学中的加总 107
    in measuring macroeconomic performance 在衡量宏观经济表现方面 113—115
    in measuring personality 在性格测量方面 83—84
    self-report measures 自我报告措施 115
de Grauwe, Paul 保罗·德·格劳威 108
default options 默认选项 46—47, 119—120
DellaVigna, Stefano 斯特凡诺·德拉维尼亚 74

Demonizing the President: The Foreignization of Barack Obama《妖魔化总统：巴拉克·奥巴马的异化》43
development economics 发展经济学 80—81
Dickens, William 威廉·狄更斯 43
Dickhaut, John 约翰·迪克奥 94
discounting 折扣，见 time preference
disgust 厌恶 97
dual-systems models 双系统模型
　　and professional sports 职业体育 93 参见 emotions
Duflo, Esther 埃斯特·迪弗洛 80—81

E

economic policy 经济政策 116—125
efficiency wage theory 效率工资理论 15—17
Elliot, in lesion patient studies 脑损伤患者研究的埃利奥特 91
Ellsberg, Daniel 丹尼尔·埃尔斯伯格 55—56
Ellsberg paradox 埃尔斯伯格悖论 55—56
Elster, Jon 乔恩·埃尔斯特 87—89
emissions trading schemes 排放交易计划 117
emotional conflicts, of traders 交易员的情绪冲突 99
emotional limbic system 情绪边缘系统 96
emotions 情绪 87—89
　　and the cingulate cortex 与扣带皮层 97
　　disgust 厌恶 97
　　in dual-systems models 双系统模型中的情绪 92—94
　　during the UK's EU Referendum 2016 在2016年英国脱欧公投期间 94
　　empathy 同理心 84, 97
　　envy 嫉妒 22
　　fear 恐惧 109—110
　　and financial instability 与金融不稳定性 99
　　greed 贪婪 110
　　hope 希望 110
　　impulsivity 冲动 99
　　jealousy 嫉妒 22
　　in lesion patients 脑损伤患者 91
　　and the limbic system 与边缘系统 96—97
　　in the macroeconomy 在宏观经济中 101, 109—110
　　and neuroeconomic analysis 与神经经济学分析 94—99
　　panic 恐慌 109
　　priming of 启动 92
　　primitive 原始的 28
　　rationality of 理性 87—88
　　social emotions 社会情绪 22—23, 95—97
　　and the somatic marker hypothesis 与躯体标记 90—91
　　in trading 在交易中 98—99
　　in the Ultimatum Game 在最后通牒游戏中 22—23, 95—97

venturesomeness 冒险 84
empathy 共情 84, 97
endowment effects 禀赋效应 62—63, 125
energy consumption 能源消费 25, 121—123
energy switching, and nudging policy 能源切换和助推政策 120—121
entrepreneurs, in the macroeconomy 宏观经济中的企业家 101—102, 106—107
entrepreneurs, interactions with speculators 企业家与投机者的互动 104—105
envy 嫉妒 22
ethics, of social manipulation 社会操纵的伦理 32
EU referendum, UK 2016 英国2016年的脱欧公投
    and business confidence 与商业信心 102—103
    and emotions 与情绪 94
    and identity 与身份 26—27
evolution 进化 30
    and cognition versus emotion 与认知与情绪 90
    and visceral factors 与内心因素 89—90
    and vulcanization of the brain 与大脑的硫化 90
evolutionary influences 演化影响 25
executive pay 高管薪酬 15
expected utility theory 期望效用理论 51—52, 65
    Kahneman and Tversky's critique 卡尼曼和特沃斯基的批判 61

expected value 预期值 60
experimental design 实验设计 5
experiments 实验 5
    Allais paradox 阿莱悖论 52—54
    arithmetic reasoning 算数推理 44—45
    auctions and physiological responses 拍卖与生理反应 94
    brain imaging 大脑成像 6, 22—23, 72, 94—98
    cab drivers in New York City 纽约市的出租车司机 79—80
    certainty effect 确定性效应 52—55
    chemical poisoning 化学中毒 63
    on cognitive dissonance 认知失调 44
    Ellsberg paradox 埃尔斯伯格悖论 56—57
    emotional priming 情绪启动 92
    essay choices 文章选择 36
    fear 恐惧 109—110
    fMRI 功能性磁共振成像 6, 22—23, 72, 94—98
    gym membership 健身房会员资格 6—7, 74—76
    holiday prize games 假期奖励博弈 55
    on hormones and trading 激素与交易 98—99
    isolation effect 孤立效应 59—61
    jam shopping 果酱购物实验 36
    Kenyan farmers and fertilizer 肯尼亚的农民和化肥 80—81
    Linda problem 琳达问题 41—42
    line experiment 排队实验 27
    marshmallow 棉花糖实验 70—71, 85

military pensions natural experiment 军人年金自然实验 68
movies and time inconsistency 电影和时间不一致性 73—74
mugs 马克杯 62—63
natural 自然实验 6—7, 68
nursery school experiment 托儿所实验 10—11
optimism and patience 乐观和耐心 103
pigeons and time inconsistency 鸽子和时间不一致性 69—70
public good games 公共品博弈 23—25
randomized controlled trials（RCTs）随机对照试验 6—7
single neuron 单神经元 27—28
on student happiness 学生幸福水平实验 113—114
Ultimatum Game 最后通牒博弈 21—23
external validity 外部有效性 4—5
externalities, herding 羊群效应外部性 29
extrinsic motivation 外在动机 9—11, 13, 参见 motivation
Eysenck, Hans 汉斯·艾森克 83
Eysenck's IQ test 艾森克的智商测试 83—84

F

Facebook 脸书（社交平台）115
fairness, preference for 公平偏好 20—23

familiarity bias 熟悉偏差 45
Farmer, Roger 罗杰·法默 108
fear 恐惧 109—110
Fen-Phen diet pills action 芬芬减肥药的法律行动 31
fertilizer experiment 化肥实验 80—81
financial 金融的
  crisis 金融危机 31—32, 100
  decision-making, neuroeconomic analysis 金融决策，神经经济学分析 94, 97—99
  fragility, Minsky's analysis 脆弱性，明斯基的分析 109—110
  instability 不稳定性 108—111
  instability, seasonal influences 不稳定性，季节性影响 111—112
  speculation 投机 104—105，参见 speculation
  system, and the macroeconomy 金融体系与宏观经济 106—111
  trading, seasonal influences 金融交易的季节性影响 112
Five Year Engagement《五年婚约》71
Flash Crash, Wall Street 2010 2010 年华尔街闪电崩盘 31—32
framing 框架 78—79
Frederick, Shane 谢恩·弗雷德里克 83
frontal cortex 额叶皮层 95，参见 prefrontal cortex
functional magnetic resonance imaging（fMRI）功能性磁共振成像 6, 22—23, 72, 94—98
fungibility 可替代性 78

131

G

Galen of Pergamon 佩加蒙的盖伦 106

The General Theory of Employment, Interest and Money《就业、利息和货币通论》104

Gift Aid 礼物援助（英国慈善捐赠的一种方式）15

gift exchange, at work 工作中的礼物交换 16—17

Gigerenzer, Gerd 格尔德·吉仁泽 3

Glimcher, Paul 保罗·格莱姆彻 72

Gneezy, Uri 乌里·格尼兹 11

golden eggs 金蛋 77

Google 谷歌（搜索工具）115

grasshopper-ant fable 蚂蚁和蚱蜢的寓言 72

greed 贪婪 110

Greenspan, Alan 艾伦·格林斯潘 110

group effects 群体效应 26

group think 群体思维 32，参见 herding；normative social influences

gut feel 直觉 91

gym membership 健身房会员资格 6—7, 74—76

H

happiness 幸福 66, 113—115

happiness surveys 幸福感调查 113—114

Heckman, Jim 吉姆·赫克曼 86—87

Herbert, Joe 乔·赫伯特 98

herding 羊群效应 27—33

　externalities 外部性 29

　in the macroeconomy 在宏观经济中 104—105

heuristics 启发式 33—48

　affect heuristic 情感启发式 88—89

　anchoring and adjustment 锚定与调整 44—46, 62

　availability heuristic 可得性启发式 39—40, 88

　representativeness heuristic 代表性启发式 41—43

targeting 目标定位 79—80

Hirshleifer, David 戴维·赫什莱弗 112

HighScope Perry Preschool Study 高瞻佩里学前教育研究 86—87

hippocampus 海马体 95

Hippocrates 希波克拉底 106

HMRC (Her Majesty's Revenue and Customs, UK) 英国的税务和海关总署 25, 123

homeostasis 内稳态 62

Homer 荷马 74, 75

hope 希望 110

hormones 激素

　testosterone in trader experiments 交易员实验中的睾丸激素水平 98—99

　cortisol in trader experiments 交易员实验中的皮质醇 98

hot-cold models 冷热模型 93—94

housing markets 房地产市场 45, 50

humours, Hippocrates' description 体液说，希波克拉底的描述 106

hyperbolic discounting 双曲线贴现，见 time inconsistency

I

identity 身份 26—27
Ifcher, John 约翰·伊弗彻 103
illiquid wealth 非流动性财富 77
image motivation 形象动机 12—15, 参见 motivation
imagery 形象 88—89
imitation 模仿
    in the macroeconomy 在宏观经济中 104—105, 参见 herding
impatience 无耐心, 见 time preference
impulse 冲动 69, 97, 参见 visceral factors
impulsivity 冲动 99
in-group effects 内群体效应 26
incentives 激励 8—9
    monetary 金钱激励 14—15
    and personality testing 与性格测试 84
    at work 工作中 15—17
income targeting 收入目标 80
inequity aversion 不平等厌恶 20—23
    advantageous 有利地位的 20—21
    disadvantageous 不利地位的 22
inert areas 惰性区域 3
inertia 惰性 40, 62
information 信息
    overload 过载 36, 120—121
    private 私人的 29
    social 社会的 27—33
informational social influences 信息的社会影响 27—29
infrastructure, and optimism bias 基础设施与乐观偏差 103

instinct 本能 89, 参见 visceral factors
insula 脑岛 96—97
insurance 保险
    contingent 或有保险 58
    probabilistic 概率保险 58
intelligence 智力 83—87, 参见 cognition
intelligence tests 智力测试 83—84
intertemporal tussles 跨期斗争 71—73
intrinsic motivation 内在动机 9—12, 参见 motivation
intuition 直觉 91
    in dual-systems models 在双系统模型中 92—93
investment 投资 102
IQ tests 智商测试 83—84, 参见 personality tets
irrational exuberance 非理性繁荣 110
isolation effect 孤立效应 59—61
Iyengar, Sheena 希娜·艾扬格 36

J

jealousy 嫉妒 22

K

Kahneman, Daniel 丹尼尔·卡尼曼 38, 41—42, 44, 51—64, 92, 94
Kamstra, Mark 马克·坎斯特拉 111
Katona, George 乔治·卡托纳 103—104
Kenyan farmers experiment 肯尼亚的农民实验 80—81
Keynes, John Maynard 约翰·梅纳德·凯恩斯 104—106

Knetsch, Jack 杰克·克内奇 62
Kranton, Rachel 雷切尔·克兰顿 26

L

labour costs 劳动力成本 16
Laibson, David 戴维·莱布森 93
le Doux, Joseph 约瑟夫·勒杜 89
Legatum Institute, wellbeing report 列格坦研究所的福祉报告 114
Leibenstein, Harvey 哈维·莱本斯坦 3
Lepper, Mark 马克·莱珀 36
lesion patient studies 脑损伤患者研究 91, 97—98
libertarian paternalism 自由意志的家长主义 118—120
life-cycle models 行为生命周期模型 77—78
life satisfaction 生活满意度 113—115
limbic system 边缘系统 95—96
Linda problem 琳达问题 41—42
line experiment 排队实验 27
living wage 维生工资 17, 参见 wages
Lo, Andrew 罗闻全 98
Loewenstein, George 乔治·洛温斯坦 89, 110
loss aversion 损失厌恶 16, 50, 62, 64, 78, 94
loyalty, at work 工作中的忠诚 16

M

McClure, Sam 山姆·麦克卢尔 72

McCrae, Robert 罗伯特·麦克雷 83
macroeconomic indicators 宏观经济指标 113—115
macroeconomy 宏观经济
　　and business confidence 与商业信心 101—102
　　and emotions 与情绪 101
　　and entrepreneurship 与创业 101—102
　　and the financial system 与金融体系 106—111
　　and moods 与情绪 101
　　and optimism 与乐观主义 101—102
　　and pessimism 与悲观主义 101—102
　　role of psychology 心理学的作用 101—103
　　and time preference 与时间偏好 101—102
Malmendier, Ulrike 乌尔丽克·马尔门迪尔 74
marshmallow experiment 棉花糖实验 70—71, 85
mathematical reasoning 数学推理 35, 42, 44—45, 52
Maxwell, Robert 罗伯特·麦克斯韦 32
measurement, of macroeconomic performance 宏观经济表现的衡量 113—115
measurement problems, subjective data 主观数据的测量问题 115
mental accounting 心理账户 65, 78—79
mental illness 精神疾病 114
microeconomic policy 微观经济政策 116—117

military personel, pension choice study 军人年金选择研究 68
Mindspace《思维导图》117—118
Minsky, Hyman 海曼·明斯基 109
mirror neurons 镜像神经元 27—28
Mischel, Walter 沃尔特·米舍尔 70, 85
missing markets 缺失的市场 117
monetary incentives 金钱激励 87, 见 incentives
moods 情绪
    in the macroeconomy 在宏观经济中 101
    seasonal influences 季节性影响 111—112
motivation 动机 8—18
    crowding-out 挤出效应 10—12
    extrinsic 外在动机 9—11, 13
    image 形象动机 12—15
    intrinsic 内在动机 9, 10—12
    at work 工作中的动机 15—17

N

narratives 叙事 42, 99
natural experiments 自然实验 6—7
    gym membership 健身房会员资格 74—76
    military pensions 军人年金 68, 参见 experiments
neuroeconomics 神经经济学 5—6, 22—23, 27—28, 71—72, 94—99
    and reward processing 与奖励处理 72
neuroscience 神经科学, 见 neuroeconomics

normative social influences 规范性社会影响 27—28
nuclear power plants, regret theory on siting of 关于核电站选址的后悔理论 66
Nudge, book by Thaler and Sunstein 塞勒和桑斯坦的《助推》117
Nudge unit, nickname for Behavioural Insights Team 助推小组,行为洞察团队的昵称 125
nudges 助推
    energy consumption 能源消费 25, 121—123
    organ donation 器官捐赠 119
    pensions 养老金 119—120
    tax bills 税单 25, 123
nudging, and public policy 助推与公共政策 117—126
nursery school experiment 托儿所实验 10—11

O

Obama, Barack 巴拉克·奥巴马 43
OCEAN (Openess, Conscientiousness, Extraversion, Agreeableness, and Neuroticism) personality tests OCEAN (开放性、尽责性、外向性、宜人性和神经质) 性格测试 83
Odysseus 奥德修斯 (又称尤利西斯) 74—75
Odyssey《奥德赛》74—75
Office for Economic Cooperation and Development (OECD) 经济

合作与发展组织（经合组织）115

Office of National Statistics UK（ONS）, life satisfaction surveys 英国国家统计局的生活满意度调查 114—115

Ofgem（UK's energy regulator）天然气与电力市场办公室（英国能源市场监管机构）121

OPower study, of Californian energy consumption 加利福尼亚州能源消费的 OPower 研究 121—123

opt-outs, and nudging policy 选择退出与助推政策 119—120

optimism 乐观主义 106
 in the macroeconomy 在宏观经济中 101—102
 and patience 与耐心 103

optimism bias 乐观偏差 102—103
 in construction 在建筑业中 103

orangutans, and time consistency 猩猩与时间一致性 70

organ donation 器官捐赠 119

Osama bin Laden, killing of 击毙奥萨马·本·拉登 43

out-group effects 外群体效应 26

P

panic 恐慌 109

Partlett, Martin 马丁·帕利特 43

passwords 密码 40

patience 耐心 67
 and optimism 与乐观主义 103, 参见 time preference

penguins, and social learning 企鹅与社会学习 30—31

pension funds 养老基金 32

pensions 养老金 46—47
 for military personel 军人养老金 68
 individual differences in pension choice 养老金选择的个人差异 68

Pentagon papers 五角大楼文件 55—56

personality 性格
 in childhood 儿童时期的 85—87
 and cognition 与认知 85—86
 of entrepreneurs 企业家的 104—105
 and genes 与基因 84—85
 and preferences 与偏好 84—85
 of speculators 投机者的 104—105

personality tests 性格测试 83—84
 Cognitive Reflexivity test 认知反身性测试 83
 Eysenck's IQ test 艾森克的智商测试 83—84
 intelligence tests 智力测试 83—84
 IQ test 智商测试 83—84
 OCEAN（Openess, Conscientiousness, Extraversion, Agreeableness, and Neuroticism）开放性、尽责性、外向性、宜人性和神经质 83
 self-report 自我报告 83

personality traits 性格特征 83

pessimism, in the macroeconomy 宏观经济中的悲观主义 101—102

phantastic objects 幻物 99

philanthropy 慈善事业, 见 charitable donations

Phineas Gage, in lesion patient studies

脑损伤患者研究中的菲尼亚斯·盖奇 91
physiological responses 生理反应 94—95
pigeons, and time inconsistency experiments 鸽子与时间不一致性实验 69—70
plastic bag charging 塑料袋收费 123—125
Pleeter, Saul 索尔·普利特 68
policy tools, from government 政府提供的政策工具 116—118
politics 政治 26, 43
pollution 污染 117, 124
pre-commitment, and income targeting by cab drivers 预先承诺策略与出租车司机的收入目标 80
pre-commitment strategies 预先承诺策略 73—77, 90
　　alarm clocks 闹钟 76
　　commitment contracts 承诺合同 76—77
　　of naïfs versus sophisticates 天真汉和老油条 73—74
　　quitting aids 戒烟的辅助手段 76, 90
pre-frontal cortex 前额叶皮层 96—97，参见 frontal cortex
Prechter, Robert 罗伯特·普莱克特 112
present bias 当前偏差 68
　　Kenyan farmers and fertilizer 肯尼亚的农民和化肥 80—81
　　参见 time inconsistency
price comparison sites 比价网站 40

primacy effects 首因效应 39
priming, in experiments 实验中的启动性 92, 113
privacy, online 网络隐私 40
pro-social behaviour 亲社会行为 12—15, 23
probabilistic insurance 概率保险 58
probability weighting 概率权重 55
probability theory 概率论 42
procrastination 拖延 62
prospect theory 前景理论 48, 61—65
　　value function 价值函数 63—64
　　versus expected utility theory 与期望效用理论 51—52
psychoanalysis, of traders 交易员的心理分析 99
psychology, in the macroeconomy 宏观经济中的心理学 101—103
public good games 公共品博弈 23—25
public goods 公共品 23—24
public health indicators, of macroeconomic performance 宏观经济表现的公共健康指标 114
public policy 公共政策
　　and behaviour change 与行为改变 117—125
　　behavioural 行为的 116—126
　　economic instruments of 公共政策的经济工具 116—117
　　nudging 助推 117—126
　　traditional instruments, taxes, and subsidies 传统工具、税收和补贴 116—117
public spending, and optimism bias

索引

137

公共支出与乐观偏差 103
punishment, third party or altruistic 第三方或利他惩罚 25

Q

quitting aids 戒烟的辅助手段 76, 90

R

randomized controlled trials（RCTs）随机对照试验 6—7
　Kenyan farmers and fertilizer study 肯尼亚的农民和化肥研究 80—81
　Rangel, Antonio 安东尼奥·朗格尔 93
rational addiction models 理性成瘾模型 93
rationality 理性 2—4
　in addiction 成瘾 93
　bounded 有限理性 2—3
　ecological 生态理性 3
　and emotion 与情绪 87—88
　selective 选择性理性 3
recency effects 近因效应 39
reciprocity 互惠 20
reference points 参照点 23, 61—63
　and energy consumption 与能源消费 121
reflection effect 反射效应 57—58
regional subsidies 地区补贴 116—117
regret theory 后悔理论 64—66
　and siting of nuclear power plants 与核电站选址 66

representative agents 代表性行为人 107
representativeness heuristic 代表性启发式 41—43
reputation 声誉 29—30
resentment 怨恨 22
reward processing 奖励处理 72
risk aversion 风险厌恶 54, 58
risk preference 风险偏好
　and financial instability 与金融不稳定性 110
　seasonal influences 季节性影响 112
risk-taking 承担风险 54, 57—58
　and testosterone 与睾丸激素 98—99
Rustichini, Aldo 奥尔多·鲁斯蒂奇尼 12

S

Save More Tomorrow（SMarT）pension scheme "多为明天储蓄" 养老金方案 46—47
saving 储蓄 77—79
　by scrub jays 丛林松鸦 70
　and time inconsistency 与时间不一致性 69
school performance 学校表现 85—87
Schultz, Wesley 韦斯利·舒尔茨 123
scrub jays, and time consistency 丛林松鸦与时间一致性 70
Seasonal Affective Disorder（SAD）, impacts on financial trading 季节性情感障碍对金融交易的影响 111—112
seasonal influences, in the macroeconomy

宏观经济中的季节性影响 111—112
security, online 网络安全 40
self-control 自我控制 73—77
self-harm 自残 26
Sharot, Tali 塔里·沙洛特 102, 106
Shefrin, Hersh 赫什·谢夫林 110
Shiller, Robert 罗伯特·席勒 108, 110
Shiv, Baba 巴贝·希夫 97
Shumway, Tyler 泰勒·沙姆韦 112
Simon, Herbert 赫伯特·西蒙 2
Singer, Tania 坦尼亚·辛格 97
single neuron experiments 单神经元实验 27—28
Sirens 塞壬 74
Smith, Vernon L. 弗农·L.史密斯 3, 94
social emotions 社会情绪，见 emotions
social emotions, in the Ultimatum Game 最后通牒博弈中的社会情绪 95—97
social influences 社会影响 19—33
　informational 信息的社会影响 27—33
　in the macroeconomy 宏观经济中的社会影响 104—105
　normative 规范的 27
　and public policy 与公共政策 121—123
　reputation 声誉 29—30
social learning 社会学习 27—33
social media 社交媒体 25
　in measuring well-being 在幸福感测量中 115
social mood 社会心境 111—112, 114, 参见 moods
social nudges 社会助推 121—123
　and tax payment 与纳税 123

social reference points, and energy consumption 社会参照点和能源消费 121
social signalling 社交信号 26, 参见 image motivation
socionomics 社会经济学 112
somatic marker hypothesis 躯体标记 90—91
speculation 投机 31—32, 108—110
speculative bubbles 投机泡沫 108—110
　dot. com bubble 互联网泡沫 109
　South Sea Bubble 南海泡沫 109
　sub-prime crisis 2007—2008 2007—2008 年次贷危机 110—111
　Tulipmania 郁金香狂热 108—109
　Wall Street Crash 1929 1929 年华尔街的崩盘 109
　Wall Street 2010 Flash Crash 2010 年华尔街的"闪电崩盘" 31—32
speculators 投机者
　interactions with entrepreneurs 投机者与企业家的互动 104—105
　in the macroeconomy 宏观经济中的投机者 106—107
SplashData 飞溅数据（一家安全公司），见 passwords
status quo bias 现状偏差 45—46
　and behaviour change 与行为改变 119—120
stories 故事 42, 99
stress 压力 114
Strotz, Robert 罗伯特·斯特罗茨 71
sub-prime mortgage crisis 2007—2008 2007—2008 年次贷危机 110—111

subsidies 补贴 116—118

suicide 自杀 114

sunshine, impacts on financial markets 晴天对金融市场的影响 111—112

Sunstein, Cass 卡斯·桑斯坦 117, 121

surveys, of happiness and life statisfaction 幸福和生活满意度调查 113—115

switching 切换 40

 and social nudging 与社会助推 120—121

System 1 thinking 系统1思维 92—93, 96, 参见 dual-systems models

System 2 thinking 系统2思维 92—93, 96, 参见 dual-systems models

T

Tajfel, Henri 亨利·泰弗尔 26

tangibility 有形性 70

targeting 目标 79—80

tax breaks, on charitable donations 慈善捐赠的税收减免 14—15

taxation 征税 116—118, 123

 social influences on payment 对纳税的社会影响 25, 123

taxes, as a policy instrument 作为一种政策工具的税收 25, 116—117, 123—125

temperaments, and Hippocrates' humours 性格与希波克拉底的体液说 106

temptation 诱惑 70—71, 73, 85

testosterone in trader experiments 交易员实验中的睾丸激素水平 98—99

thalamus 丘脑 95

Thaler, Richard 理查德·塞勒 46—47, 62, 65, 79, 117, 119, 121

Thinking, Fast and Slow《思考，快与慢》38, 92

third party punishment 第三方惩罚 25

time consistency 时间一致性 68—69

time inconsistency 时间不一致性

 and Aesop's ant-grasshopper fable 与伊索寓言中蚂蚁和蚱蜢的寓言 72

 in animal models 在动物模型中 69—70

 and pre-commitment strategies 与预先承诺策略 73—77

 and saving 与储蓄 69

time preference 时间偏好

 economic approach 经济方法 67—68

 individual differences 个体差异 67—68

 in the macroeconomy 在宏观经济中 101—102

 and optimism 与乐观主义 103

tobacco tax 烟草税 116

trading, seasonal influences 交易的季节性影响 112

transaction costs 交易成本 77—78

transcranial magnetic stimulation (TMS) 经颅磁刺激 6

trust, at work 工作中的信任 16, 20

Tuckett, David 戴维·塔克特 99

Tulipmania 郁金香狂热 108—109

Tversky, Amos 阿莫斯·特沃斯基 38, 41—42, 44, 51—64, 92

twin studies, and personality 性格与双胞胎研究 84—85
Twitter 推特(社交平台) 115

U

Ultimatum Game 最后通牒博弈 21—23
　neuroeconomic analysis of emotions in 情绪的神经经济学分析 95—97
Ulysses 尤利西斯，见 Odysseus
uncertainty 不确定性 105—106
unit labour costs 单位劳动力成本 16

V

value function 价值函数，见 prospect theory
visceral factors 内心因素 87, 89—90
Viscusi, Kip 基普·维斯库西 63

W

wages 工资 15—17
　fair wage 公平工资 46
　living wage 维生工资 17
　and status quo bias 与现状偏差 46
Wall Street Crash 1929 1929年华尔街的崩盘 109
Wall Street 2010 Flash Crash 2010年华尔街的"闪电崩盘" 31—32
Warren, John 约翰·沃伦 68
Washington Times《华盛顿时报》43
Waterhouse, J.W. 沃特豪斯 74—75
wealth 财富 77, 79
weather, impacts on financial markets 天气对金融市场的影响 111—112
weighting, of probability 概率的加权 55
well-being 幸福 113—115
well-being report, by the Legatum Institute 列格坦研究所的福祉报告 114
willingness to accept 接受意愿 62—63
willingness to pay 支付意愿 62—63
Woodford, Michael 迈克尔·伍德福德 108
work 工作
　incentives at 工作中的激励 15—17
　and personality 与性格 85—86
　参见 wages; efficiency wage theory
World Bank 世界银行 115
World Happiness Report《世界幸福报告》115

Z

Zarghamee, Homa 霍马·扎格哈米 103

Michelle Baddeley

BEHAVIOURAL ECONOMICS

A Very Short Introduction

*To my grandmother Irene Baddeley, née Bates,
1916–2009, on the centenary of her birth.
In memory of her practical wisdom and
unstinting support for her granddaughters.*

If all the year were playing holidays,
To sport would be as tedious as to work;
But when they seldom come, they wish'd-for come,
And nothing pleaseth but rare accidents.

William Shakespeare, King Henry the 4th,
Part I (Act 1, Scene 2, 173–95)

Contents

Acknowledgements i

List of illustrations iii

1 Economics and behaviour 1

2 Motivation and incentives 8

3 Social lives 19

4 Quick thinking 34

5 Risky choices 49

6 Taking time 67

7 Personalities, moods, and emotions 82

8 Behaviour in the macroeconomy 100

9 Economic behaviour and public policy 116

References and further reading 127

Acknowledgements

My thanks go to Joy Mellor, my copy editor, for her enthusiasm, meticulous work on the manuscript, and lots of good suggestions; and also to Dorothy McCarthy—for her thorough proof-reading and for her vote of confidence in the content. Thanks also to all at the Oxford University Press for their help—including Andrea Keegan, for her wise advice and for guiding the proposal through the early stages; Jenny Nugee, for efficiently guiding the manuscript through to publication; Deborah Protheroe, for her help and advice with illustrations; and Ruby Constable, Chloe Mussen, and Martha Cunneen, for their editorial assistance. Thanks also to Saraswathi Ethiraju, for overseeing the production process. The anonymous reviewers of the proposal and first draft also contributed some excellent thoughts and advice, so my thanks to them too, though, as always, errors and omissions remain my own.

My gratitude also goes to all those who took a look at the script—including my family, friends, students, and colleagues. I am particularly grateful to Pete Lunn, for reading the manuscript so thoroughly and making some excellent suggestions; and to Nissy Sombatruang, for her enthusiastic feedback on the first draft, and also for suggesting the Thai examples included in Chapter 2. A special mention goes to my former UCL student,

Josephine Pletts, for suggesting that a *Very Short Introduction* might be a nice writing project to consider in the first place.

A final thank you to my husband Chris—for his generosity, warmth, and patient support for all that I do.

List of illustrations

1. The Linda problem—a conjunction fallacy **42**

2. Confusing default options **47**
   © Jon and Mick / Modern Toss. This cartoon first appeared in *Private Eye*.

3. The prospect theory value function **64**

4. Ulysses pre-committing himself to resist the Sirens' calls **75**
   © National Gallery of Victoria, Melbourne, Australia / Bridgeman Images.

5. Some brain regions **95**

6. Sub-prime mortgages mess **111**
   © Feggo / CartoonStock.com.

7. Social nudges for saving energy **122**
   Courtesy of Opower.

8. Plastic bag littering **124**
   © Neil Juggins / Alamy Stock Photo.

Chapter 1
Economics and behaviour

Behavioural economics is a hot topic. Behavioural economics research is regularly featured in the top academic journals in economics and science. It has a high profile on social media, and journalists regularly write about the new books and research emerging in the field. Governments and other policy-makers, from all over the world, are embedding insights from behavioural economics into their policy designs, as, increasingly, are more mainstream economists when designing their models.

What is behavioural economics and why so much interest? Behavioural economics extends economic principles by allowing that our decisions are affected by social and psychological influences, as well as a rational calculation of benefits and costs. It also broadens economics, making it more accessible to a wider audience. Undeniably, economics is a critically important subject because it is all about our welfare—at an individual level, nationally and internationally, and for our children and future generations. But it is also perceived by many to be an esoteric, technocratic subject. People without economics qualifications struggle to understand the key concepts. Behavioural economics has the potential to change this because it strikes many as being much more interesting. It provides a more intuitive and less mathematical account of our decision-making.

Behavioural economics is also interesting because of the pluralism and diversity in its underlying principles. Behavioural economists bring economics together with insights from a wide range of other disciplines, for example psychology (especially social psychology), sociology, neuroscience, and evolutionary biology. Using this multidisciplinary blend of ideas, behavioural economists enrich our understanding of economic and financial behaviour, without necessarily abandoning the analytical power often associated with conventional economics.

Why is behavioural economics different?

Most economists describe people as mathematical calculators—able easily and accurately to add up the money costs and benefits of their choices in pounds and pence, dollars and cents—and without worrying about what others around them are doing. Most economists start with the presumption that economic problems emerge, not because people as individuals are fallible, but because of failures in markets and their supporting institutions. Barriers stop small firms from entering markets and allow large, rich monopolies to dominate markets, elevate prices, and constrain production. Information may be distorted. There may be missing markets—for example there are no natural markets for cigarette smoke and pollution, so prices do not fully capture the balance of benefits and costs of smoking or pollution.

Rationality in behavioural economics

While conventional economists direct their attention away from limits to rationality, behavioural economists do not assume that people are super-rational beings. Instead they focus on some limits to rational decision-making. Many behavioural economists draw on some ideas from Herbert Simon who was a psychologist and computer scientist as well as Nobel Laureate in Economics. He is famous for his concept of *bounded rationality*, capturing the idea that we are limited and bounded by various constraints when we are deciding. Cognitive constraints may limit our ability to choose the best strategies. Limits on memory or numerical processing ability mean that sometimes we are forced towards a particular option because we do not have the information or cognitive processing time or power to consider other options.

Behavioural economists develop other conceptions of rationality too. Another Nobel Laureate, Vernon L. Smith, develops the concept of *ecological rationality*. He hypothesizes that rationality is malleable because it is determined by the contexts and circumstances in which we find ourselves. Similarly, Gerd Gigerenzer argues that we are driven by a practical rationality—in the real world we have to decide quickly and 'frugally'—we do not have time to collect lots of information, or to apply complex decision-making rules. We decide quickly and simply. Often this works well, but other times it leads us into systematic behavioural biases.

Another economist with interesting insights about what it means to be rational is Harvey Leibenstein, who developed the concept of *selective rationality*—similar to Vernon L. Smith's ecological rationality. We choose when to be super-rational and sometimes we do take full account of all available information. At other times, however, we may decide to stick with the status quo, and remain in what Leibenstein describes as *inert areas*. This makes our choices 'sticky'. We do not always adapt our behaviours effectively to new circumstances. When our behaviour is sticky Leibenstein argues that there are two explanations: either we have decided that the costs of changing choices are too high or, in other cases, we are just too lazy and apathetic to change.

So behavioural economists have a complex range of views about what it means to be rational. Mostly, they allow that our rationality is variable and dependent on the circumstances in which we find ourselves. When we do not have access to good information, when we are in a hurry, when we are facing cognitive constraints or social influences—then we might be led into decisions that, in a perfect world with plenty of time and information, we could improve.

Data constraints

While this form of economics has plenty of potential, a key constraint for behavioural economists lies in finding relevant and reliable data. Behavioural economists often use experiments to collect data—in contrast to the traditional empirical approach in economics of using econometric, statistical methods to analyse published, historical data, collected by governments and international statistical agencies.

Often behavioural economists are trying to infer something about people's thinking and feeling processes, not yet knowing exactly what is driving people's choices. Standard economic data sources are not so helpful in this because traditionally economic data is about observed choices and outcomes (e.g. employment and unemployment statistics in a macroeconomic context). Behavioural economists can rely on survey data—for example, questions about people's perceptions of their own happiness and well-being are being incorporated into household surveys. But survey data has limitations—how does a researcher identify a representative sample? How does a researcher cope with untruthful or ill-informed answers to survey questions?

Experimental data

Laboratory experiments are probably the most common data source for behavioural economists. The problem with many lab experiments is that they are conducted in universities, often with university students as experimental participants. Students' choices in experiments may not correlate well with real-world choices, in which case this experimental data will lack *external validity*—the experimental findings will not translate well to the real world. So, for example, if a student participates in a trading experiment, their observed choices may have little connection with how real traders would behave, because students have limited knowledge and experience, and are likely to be less strongly motivated to succeed.

Another significant obstacle to reliable experimental data is experimental design. Experimenters can find it difficult to construct a 'clean' controlled experiment in economics. Some economists have criticized early findings from behavioural economists on the basis that the experimental participants' responses demonstrated confusion about what they were supposed to be doing, and the behavioural anomalies identified were not genuine systematic biases. There are ethical trade-offs too. What should an experimenter be allowed to put his or her participants through, especially if they are, for example, vulnerable hospital patients? Is it legitimate to deceive experimental participants; and is it possible to design an artificial experiment that involves no deception at all?

Online experiments are enabled by tools such as Survey Monkey, Prolific Academic, and Task Rabbit as well as, increasingly, mobile apps. These methods are cheap and can be a very quick and easy way to get large batches of experimental data. But how does the researcher ensure that they are using a representative sample? How do they deal with the problem of unmotivated participants who may just tap computer keys at random, being most interested in simply earning money from the exercise? Motivating experimental participants to behave realistically in experimental trials is a significant problem for behavioural economists, especially as academic research budgets are often limited.

Neuroscientific data and neuroeconomics

Combined with experimental data, neuroscientific data can help illuminate some key influences. There is a wide range of neuroscientific techniques. Choices made by brain-lesion patients can help to inform us about which brain areas are implicated in economic decisions. Similarly, brain-imaging techniques (e.g. functional magnetic resonance imaging, or fMRI) can capture how our economic decisions correlate with neural responses in specific brain regions. Another technique increasing in popularity is transcranial magnetic stimulation (TMS), which involves zapping specific areas of the brain and seeing how people's choices subsequently change as a consequence of this temporary interference. There are other simpler and cheaper neuroscientific tools too, including monitoring physiological responses (heart rate, pulse rate, etc.); or measuring hormone levels (e.g. oxytocin levels in studies of trust; and testosterone levels in studies of financial risk-taking).

The key advantage for neuroscientific data is that it is relatively objective. With surveys, respondents may be expressing a possibly unreliable subjective opinion; or they may have reasons to lie or manipulate their responses. It is much harder, if not impossible, for an experimental participant to control the physiological responses measured using neuroscientific tools, though this does not remove an experimenter's bias in their experimental designs.

Natural experiments and randomized controlled trials (RCTs)

One problem with standard experiments, as mentioned earlier, is that they can lack external validity. *Natural experiments*, if we can find them, are a solution—natural experimental data that emerges by chance from real-world events and behaviours. One example is a study by economists DellaVigna and Malmendier of gym membership and attendance data, described in Chapter 6, showing that many people pay large sums of money for gym memberships that they rarely use. But good data from natural experiments are rare and we would not get far if we relied only on these data sources. One solution is to use RCTs. These are experimental methods commonly used in clinical trials to identify treatment effects: impacts on experimental participants receiving a trial treatment are compared with impacts on experimental participants in a control group receiving just a placebo.

Behavioural economists borrow these methods to compare a control group's responses to a treatment group's responses. However, as experimenters would find it difficult to design a socio-economic equivalent of a placebo, the control group in these studies receives no treatment at all. This means that with behavioural economics RCTs it is not possible to establish whether or not it is the intervention itself that is changing behaviours, or just some economic equivalent of a placebo effect from people responding positively to any intervention regardless of how genuinely effective it might be. Nonetheless, RCTs are now widely used by behavioural development economists to study impacts of development interventions on socio-economic outcomes.

Key themes

There is an enormous literature in behavioural economics—it could fill a library of its own. In this Very Short Introduction, we will focus on a few key themes, each explored in the following chapters: what motivates us; how we are affected by social influences; how and why we make mistakes; how we judge and misjudge risk; our tendency to short-termism; and how personality, mood, and emotions drive our choices and decisions. Once these key behavioural, microeconomic principles have been explored, we will explore how this can all be brought together in behavioural macroeconomics. Then we will turn to the policy implications and lessons adopted by public policy-makers—illustrated by a number of examples of influential policy studies based around behavioural economic insights.

Chapter 2
Motivation and incentives

If you were to watch some economists talking together—at a conference, for example—it would not take long for someone to mention 'incentives'. Incentives are the fundamental driver in economic analysis. Incentives encourage people to work harder and better. They encourage businesses to provide more and better products. Economists usually assume that money is the main incentive, and there is no doubt that money can provide an objective (though not necessarily accurate or fair) measure of value. Money motivates us in much of our ordinary lives. It determines the prices we pay or do not pay for the goods and services we buy, and the wages we earn or do not earn. Higher prices and wages reward better, more productive decision-making. Monetary incentives underpin the markets that coordinate the choices of many different people and businesses.

As a behavioural economist, I would not argue against the idea that prices and money are powerful incentives motivating us to work harder and better, but rather that a complex range of other socio-economic and psychological factors drive our decision-making too. We are motivated by far more than just money. As an academic, perhaps I am not paid as well as I might be in the private sector. If I look at my lifetime's earnings, perhaps the fact that I have a generous pension and far more job security explains why I am not maximizing my earnings today. But there is something else going on too because there are parts of my job that I genuinely enjoy—they tap into my other non-monetary motivations. Sometimes, I think that if I won the lottery and so did not have to worry about having enough money to live, I would not give up my job. Sometimes my job gives me a pleasure all of its own, quite apart from the money I am paid.

Intrinsic versus extrinsic motivations and incentives

We see this every day in our working lives—at work we are motivated by a number of different monetary and non-monetary rewards. Most people want to be paid for the work they do, but some people do not work just for money. Some people may also be incentivized by social rewards, such as social approval, that come from working hard and having a well-respected job. Some people are driven by moral incentives—for example, those who work for charities. Others just enjoy what they do and so work at it even though it is not well paid—for example, many artists.

Behavioural economists capture these wider influences on our decisions and choices by categorizing two broad groups of incentives and motivations: *intrinsic* and *extrinsic*.

Extrinsic motivation

Extrinsic motivations capture the incentives and rewards external to us as individuals—for example, when the world and the people around us encourage us to do something we would otherwise be reluctant to do. Then our actions must be driven by something outside ourselves: we need extrinsic motivation in the form of an incentive. A common and powerful incentive is money: we work because we are paid a wage or salary. A more powerful external incentive is physical threat. But extrinsic motivations can also come from non-monetary incentives—for example, social rewards such as social approval and social success. Higher wages, good exam results, prizes and awards, and social approval are all external rewards.

Intrinsic motivation

Intrinsic motivations reflect the influence of our internal goals and attitudes. An internal response sometimes encourages us to make an effort—for our own sake, not because we are driven by some external reward. When we are intrinsically motivated by something inside ourselves—whether it be professional pride, a sense of duty, loyalty to a cause, enjoyment from solving a puzzle, or pleasure in being physically active—then we do not need external incentives. When we play a game of chess or cards, or a computer game, we enjoy the challenge—and that enjoyment is internally driven from within us. Many artisans and craftspeople enjoy their job and take pride in it, and, while the money they are paid is not irrelevant because they and their families need money to live, the money is just one of many motivating factors.

Crowding out

Extrinsic and intrinsic motivations are not independent of each other. Extrinsic motivations can *crowd out* our intrinsic motivations. This occurs when our intrinsic motivations are dampened by external rewards. Some experiments have shown how this can happen. One set of studies to capture the crowding out of intrinsic motivation involved experimenters asking university students to solve a series of puzzles. Students were sorted randomly into two groups: one group was paid; the other group was not. Surprisingly, some of the students in the second group did better than students in the first. The unpaid students were enjoying the intellectual challenge; the paid students were perhaps demotivated by relatively low rates of pay. When the students were paid, they were distracted from enjoying the intellectual challenge of the task (the intrinsic motivation), and were focused instead on whether or not they were being paid enough (the extrinsic motivation). Other studies have also shown that small payments can be demotivating, leading to worse performance than when there is no payment at all, because small payments crowd out intrinsic motivation without offering sufficient external incentives to fully develop an extrinsic motivation.

Extrinsic incentives and disincentives affect our ordinary lives too and often in surprising ways, as shown in a study of nursery schools by economists Uri Gneezy and Aldo Rustichini. A nursery in Israel had a problem with parents arriving late to collect their children. Teachers were often forced to wait behind after closing time to care for the children until their parents turned up. This was costly and disruptive for the nursery and its teachers, so the nursery managers decided to introduce a fine as a deterrent.

The impact was surprising: with a fine, *more* parents started arriving late—not fewer. The researchers postulated that this might be because parents were not interpreting the fine as a deterrent. They were interpreting it as a price. The nursery was providing an additional service—looking after children after normal school hours. Some parents were willing to pay for this additional service, and because the parents perceived this as a reciprocal and mutually beneficial arrangement (the nursery was getting more money, after all) they did not feel the guilt that had previously stopped them turning up late too often. Again, this might reflect crowding out of intrinsic motivations. Before the fine, many parents might have been intrinsically motivated to be cooperative and considerate in turning up on time as often as possible. After the fine had been introduced, their perception of the situation changed—they were just paying for the luxury of arriving late. The monetary disincentive of the fine was crowding out the intrinsic motivation to be a cooperative parent.

Blood donations are another important example of when and how extrinsic motivations crowd out intrinsic motivations. Low levels of blood donation are a big problem in many countries and some economists have explored new ways to encourage more people to donate blood. The obvious economic solution is to pay donors. However, when researchers experimented with introducing payments for blood donation to encourage more donations, they found that it had a perverse and unexpected effect: it lowered rather than raised people's willingness to donate. One explanation could be that the extrinsic motivation from monetary payments undermined donors' intrinsic motivation to be good citizens.

Pro-social choices and image motivation

Charitable donations are another example of the complex interplay between extrinsic and intrinsic motivations. Some people give to charity because they feel a moral or religious obligation. Others give to charity because it makes them look good. Many of us probably do it for a mixture of reasons. When Mark Zuckerberg and his wife donated most of their fortune to mark the birth of their first child, was this choice about an intrinsic moral motivation to help the world? Or was their choice about being admired by others as generous philanthropists, and a way to enhance their social reputations?

Behavioural economists have studied these charitable motivations in more depth, exploring when and how extrinsic rewards can 'spoil' the reputational value of pro-social behaviours such as generosity and philanthropy. They find that when people accrue personal benefits from their 'generosity' and information about these benefits is made publicly available then people are less likely to be generous. One of our young researchers has told me that, in Thailand, when there is a festival or a funeral, people put the money they want to donate into an envelope with their names on the envelope. Alternatively, they give money directly to a collector, who notes the donor details and amounts donated. Organizers then announce publicly and loudly, through loud-hailers installed around the village, the names of donors and the amounts donated. Apparently, villagers within a kilometre radius can hear the announcements and children are instructed to pay attention to the names.

These types of behaviour show that our social reputations are important to us, particularly in the context of generosity and charity, and they illustrate a social type of extrinsic motivation: *image motivation*. Some of our choices reflect the fact that we want to boost our reputations and improve our image.

To explore the impact of image motivation, Dan Ariely and colleagues explored how people's pro-social choices are affected when external rewards are visible to others. He and his team started with the premise that donations to charitable causes are driven by image motivation and are a way of signalling to others that you are a good person. However, if additional benefits are available as a reward for philanthropy, and if everyone can see our charitable choices being rewarded in other ways, then the image motivation is weakened. When it is public knowledge that we have given to charity, we signal to others that we are good people. But if others can see that we are earning personal benefits from our generosity, then the social signalling value of our generosity is diluted.

To test these ideas, Dan Ariely and his team designed a 'Click for Charity' experiment. In their experiment, they assigned people randomly to one of two charities: a 'good' charity—the American Red Cross; and a 'bad' charity—the National Rifle Association. Then they asked their experimental participants to perform a task requiring very little effort—pressing 'x' or 'z' on a keyboard, for example. For all the experimental participants, performance in this simple key-pressing task was rewarded by donations to their charity. To test the impact of additional private benefits, the experimental participants were divided into two groups: some of them were able to earn money for themselves if they performed well; others were given no additional payments at all. These two groups were divided again according to whether their performance in the 'Click for Charity' task was made public to the rest of the experimental group or whether it remained private, known only to the individual participants and the experimenters.

Unsurprisingly, Ariely and his team found that the groups making the most effort, measured by the number of key-presses, were those performing for the 'good' charity (the Red Cross). More surprisingly, the participants exhibited some complex interactions of extrinsic motivations in terms of money incentives versus image motivation. The best performing group was not paid money, but its efforts were made public. Image motivation is the most likely explanation for their superior performance—they worked hard to enhance their social reputation because their efforts would be made public. The worst performing group also received no additional money incentive, but their efforts remained private. They had nothing to gain: no extra income and no social value because no-one would know whether or not they had made an effort. In fact, what reason did this latter group have to make any effort at all given that their rewards were neither social nor monetary?

The most interesting finding was seen in those who were earning additional private income for their efforts. They worked less hard than the best performing group (i.e. those who received no private income, but their efforts were made public). From this study, it seems that image motivation is a more powerful incentive than monetary payments, at least in the context of charitable donations. But image motivation does not completely crowd out conventional monetary incentives: for the two groups being paid, those whose efforts were also made public did still perform better than those whose efforts remained private. Both image motivation and monetary payments played a role in incentivizing effort.

Overall, the findings from this and other studies confirm what most economists would probably predict: monetary incentives can encourage anonymous giving. Perhaps this is why tax breaks for charitable giving—GiftAid in the UK, for example—work well in the real world. But in some cases monetary incentives do not work. Many people do not take advantage of tax breaks on their charitable giving, but this could reflect the transaction costs involved in claiming tax rebates and/or procrastination—a theme explored in Chapter 6. These studies suggest another, potentially more powerful, policy lesson: if people's charitable impulses can be made public more easily then the inclination towards philanthropy will increase, and this effect might be more powerful than conventional monetary incentives such as tax breaks. In a world dominated by social media where we have an opportunity to publicize our good character and generosity, then charitable giving is more likely.

These findings also connect to debates about executive pay in the charitable sector. Paying chief executives of charities high commercial salaries might have a counter-productive impact on the charity—both in terms of the people attracted to these jobs and the negative perceptions of potential donors. If a charity's chief executive is apparently strongly motivated by monetary incentives, this runs counter to the expected ethos for charity work, and so the charity's reputation is likely to suffer—potential donors like myself may decide that this is not the sort of charity we would wish to support.

Motivating work

Incentives and motivations, both intrinsic and extrinsic, are also powerful influences in our working lives. Most workers are motivated by interplays of internal and external influences. Extrinsic incentives and motivations include the wages and salaries we earn, and also the social approval we get when we are employed—especially if it is in a job perceived to be worthy (e.g. medicine or education). Working also reflects intrinsic motivations, for example: we enjoy a challenge; it is satisfying to be doing something; or we are motivated by personal ambition.

These insights from behavioural economics about incentives and motivation can link into one of the most powerful and influential approaches to understanding wages and employees' efforts and productivity—*efficiency wage theory*. Efficiency wage theory captures how economic and socio-psychological influences motivate effort at work. Efficiency wage theorists explain what constitutes an efficient wage—defined as the wage that minimizes a firm's labour costs. If raising a worker's wage leads to a more than proportionate increase in the worker's productivity then the firm's profits will rise, not fall. For example, if a worker's wage is increased by 1 per cent but the higher wage encourages them to work much harder so that they produce 2 per cent more output, then labour costs per unit of output have fallen. All things being equal, profits will rise.

A simultaneous rise in wages and profits can be explained partly in terms of standard economic concepts. If an employee is paid well, they will value their job more, will not want to lose it, and so they will work harder. In very poor economies, paying more might help workers to afford better food, shelter, healthcare, and clothing—so, physically, they will be stronger and more able to work longer and harder, and take less time away from work through illness. Paying more might deter strike activity amongst unionized workers.

However, higher wages motivate employees to work hard not just because of the money benefits but also because of social and psychological rewards and incentives, including the impact that being treated well has on an employee's trust and loyalty. When your boss treats you better than you expect, you will want to reciprocate by being a better worker. The employer–employee relationship is not just about monetary exchange. It is also about social and psychological incentives and drivers, including loyalty, trust, and reciprocity. George Akerlof and colleagues describe this as a form of 'gift exchange'. My boss treats me well and pays me well, so I return the favour by working harder.

Many of us may have experienced this in our working lives. The jobs we do over our lifetimes, and the contrast between our best and worst jobs, can illustrate how workers' motivations are complex. Imagine that you are working in a shop, filled with things you might usually like to buy—sports equipment, good food, or nice shoes. To start with, you are more likely to enjoy your job and work hard. If, in addition, your boss treats you well and your job is intrinsically satisfying, then you are likely to work without close monitoring, which saves your boss supervision costs—you and your boss trust each other and so you show initiative in working hard. You might also spread the word amongst your friends and other networks, which will help your boss to attract good new workers without having to advertise very widely. This will save your boss labour search costs, and also reduces their risk of hiring a shirker.

So incorporating non-monetary incentives into the analysis of labour markets is not just about our charitable impulses. It also has important implications for businesses and policy-makers. Lowering wages does not necessarily increase business profits; paying a *higher* wage, however, might increase profits. Efficiency wage theory also brings insights into policy debates about minimum wages and the *living wage* (i.e. a wage that allows workers to meet the local cost of basic living). Higher, fairer wages can benefit everyone—employers and employees. If paying a higher wage motivates workers to work harder for a business both inside and outside work, then the case for better pay is easier to defend.

This chapter has shown how behavioural economists take basic economic insights—for example, that people respond to incentives—and define the concepts (incentives and motivations, in this case) more broadly, allowing that socio-psychological influences play a role too. Once we allow that our choices and behaviours are affected by a wider set of social, economic, and psychological motivations, this significantly changes the standard economic prescriptions for better performance. How we think about our own and others' image and social reputations affects our donations to charity and our responses to fines. Our social interactions with others drive our performance at work as well as our firm's profits. Markets capture the interactions of people, and while it is clear that people respond to monetary incentives, there is a range of other powerful influences too. As individuals, employees, employers, policy-makers, and citizens, insights from behavioural economics can help us to develop a much richer understanding of the complex motivations driving our choices and efforts, and their consequences.

This chapter has explored some of the influences on our choices and decisions, including social influences that reflect some of the extrinsic motivations that drive us. In Chapter 3, we will see how people are affected by a wider range of social influences—including aversion to unequal outcomes, trust and reciprocity, social learning, and peer pressure.

Chapter 3
Social lives

In Chapter 2, we explored the ways in which our economic and financial decisions are determined by a range of factors, apart from money. Most economic theories start by assuming that we are independent and self-interested creatures, who do not look to others when deciding what to do. All things being equal, anonymous markets are the best way to coordinate economic activity and ensure that consumers and producers get the best, most mutually beneficial, deal possible.

The standard assumption in economics is that we all behave as if others do not actually exist as individuals. We are affected by other people only indirectly, because their decisions about supply and demand drive market prices. This leaves out an important dimension of people's economic lives. Prices are impersonal and by only focusing on prices in economic analysis, economists can easily forget the importance of human relationships and social interactions in economic decision-making. There are many ways in which economic choices are affected by the others around us. Literatures from social psychology and sociology are illuminating in showing how and why this happens. In this chapter we will explore some of the main ways in which social influences drive behaviour.

Trust, reciprocity, and inequity aversion

We care about others around us, or not; they care about us, or not. We worry about fairness and tend to prefer fair outcomes over unfair outcomes. We are also inclined to trust others in some situations, and they sometimes trust us in return. When other people are trustworthy and treat us well, we are more likely to reciprocate by trusting and being trustworthy in return. For example, if my colleagues help me out with my lecturing and administrative tasks, then I will feel more willing to help them with their lecturing and administrative tasks. This interplay between trust and reciprocity is a key element in many of the cooperative and collaborative activities that we undertake every day—everything from collaborative teamwork when we are working or studying, through to the altruism we show when donating to charity, and the cooperation that is necessary for family life, community projects, and political movements to succeed.

The analysis of trust and reciprocity in behavioural economics starts from the insight that people do not generally like to see unequal outcomes. People do not like to be treated unfairly, and they do not like to see others being treated unfairly either. If we feel that we are being treated unfairly then we are less likely to trust and reciprocate. This key element in our social interactions links our preference for fairness with how we feel we are doing relative to others. We do not like situations when others seem to be doing much better or worse than we are because we do not like inequitable outcomes. Behavioural economists call this preference *inequity aversion*.

There are two main types of inequity aversion both of which can be captured by thinking about a banker meeting a homeless person on the streets of London. The banker may be distressed to see someone suffering from poverty—he would prefer that living standards were more equal—if so, he is feeling *advantageous inequity aversion*. The banker is coming from a position of advantage, but perhaps he does not want to see others suffering from a much lower standard of living, and would like to see a fairer outcome for the homeless person. The homeless person also does not want to suffer from inequity. She would prefer to have enough money to afford a safe and comfortable place to live—her predicament is unfair and she will experience a preference known as *disadvantageous inequity aversion*; from her position of disadvantage, she does not want to be relatively worse off than others around her.

While both are experiencing a similar aversion to unequal outcomes, it is likely that the beggar is far more concerned about her unequal position than the banker: people are much more affected by disadvantageous inequity aversion than by advantageous inequity aversion. The banker is likely to feel mild discomfort at seeing a homeless person on the street; the homeless person, however, will be feeling much more unhappy about the inequity.

Our preference for fairness can also explain altruism—for example, when we volunteer or give to charity. We may do this because we enjoy being generous and sometimes get a warm feeling from our generosity. Some experiments show that it is not always about pure altruism, sometimes it is about signalling to others that we are good and generous people. As noted in Chapter 2, people are more likely to give more when their generosity is made public.

Many experimental studies have confirmed that inequity aversion is a strong tendency, not only among humans across most countries and cultures, but also among our primate cousins. The basic experimental game used to test inequity aversion is the *Ultimatum Game*. In its simplest form, this game is played by two players. Player A, the proposer, has a sum—say £100—and can offer whatever amount she likes to Player B—the responder.

If the responder rejects the proposer's offer then neither player gets anything, and the proposer has to return the £100 to the experimenter. Non-behavioural economists would probably predict that people will play this game perfectly selfishly and aim to get as much as they can, given what they believe about the other player's strategies. Player A will assume that Player B would prefer £1 to £0 because something is better than nothing. So Player A will make a £1 offer because she thinks that Player B will probably accept it. If Player B does not care what Player A thinks or does, he will prefer £1 to £0 and so will accept Player A's offer. Player A has deduced that Player B will react in this way and therefore offers £1 and keeps £99 for herself.

The Ultimatum Game is one of the most used experiments in behavioural economics—and it has been adapted to test responses to different sums of money, and to explore differences across a wide range of countries and cultures. The experiment has even been used in animal experiments. Chimps playing the game for juice and fruit treats exhibit similar behaviour to humans. Across all these different studies, the robust finding is that real-world behaviour is very different from what most economists might expect: the proposer is often very generous—offering much more than £1 or its equivalent, while the responder is often seen rejecting offers even when offered 40 per cent or more of the total sum available.

Some behavioural economists explain inequity aversion as a type of emotion—a social emotion. Our social situations can lead us to feel particular emotions such as envy, jealousy, and resentment, and there is probably an emotional element when people are treated unfairly in the Ultimatum Game. For example, if the responder (Player B) resents the proposer (Player A) for making a mean offer, then he may be prepared to pay £40+ to punish the proposer. Neuroscientists have used brain-imaging studies to unravel what might be going on with our brains. One study involved imaging the brains of experimental participants in the responder role. Their brain responses suggested that the same neural areas that were activated, for example, when people were disgusted by a bad smell were also activated when people were treated unfairly in the Ultimatum Game. Some neuroscientists and neuroeconomists interpret these findings as evidence that we experience a form of social disgust when others treat us unfairly.

Cooperation, punishment, and social norms

Social norms are another set of social influences that drive our behaviour, and these are often reinforced through peer pressure. Given our social natures, we generally reward (and are rewarded for) pro-social behaviour—if teenagers copy their peers in their choices and habits, then they are probably more likely to be invited to the coolest parties. Conformity has a strong influence and it drives our customs, traditions, and religious life. When driven by blind conformity, social influences are not always benign—for example, when cults form. Cults are an extreme example of destructive social behaviour but conformity has power in more ordinary contexts too. We often compare our own behaviour with what others are doing, and others' behaviour provides us with what behavioural economists call our *social reference points*: we make our own decisions with reference to what we believe to be the average decision of the group. Many organizations, from government policy-makers to those in marketing, use information about our social reference points to leverage more constructive behaviour, for example, or more profits.

Social norms help to explain how and why we have evolved as a cooperative species, but how do we ensure that no-one free rides on the generosity of others? This question is explored by behavioural economists who study a group of games known as *public good games*—an experimental vehicle for studying not only our tendencies to cooperate but also the role of social sanctions and punishments in sustaining cooperative behaviour. Public good games are developed from the economic concept of a public good.

In its purest form, a public good is something to which everyone has free and easy access—no-one is stopped from consuming the good and so it cannot easily be brought into private ownership. The classic example of a public good is a lighthouse—everyone sailing past a lighthouse can get the benefit of the light, but it is difficult to *charge* any single individual for the benefit of the light. So anyone wanting to make money out of a private business is unlikely to invest in a lighthouse because it would be difficult to make any money out of it. Some other motivation is needed to ensure that public goods such as lighthouses are provided. And economists have found that local communities are surprisingly good at ensuring that public goods are provided and maintained.

Behavioural economists have unravelled some of the factors that affect our behaviour towards public goods by using public goods games. In one such game, a group of experimental participants is gathered together and asked to make a contribution to a communal pot of money that will later be shared equally between the members of the group. This is a little like what a community would have to do if it wanted a pot of money to build a community park, for example. Many economists would predict that most people would make a contribution of nothing because they would reason that, regardless of whether or not they decided to contribute, the pot of money will be shared equally. So the best way for an individual to maximize her net gain is to have a share of the pot without also having to make a contribution herself. The problem with this reasoning is that if everyone thinks this way, and everyone plans to free-ride on the others' contributions, then there will be no money at all in the pot to share, and there will be no public goods. In this case, selfish individuals will create an outcome that is bad for the group as a whole.

Behavioural and experimental economists have found that, luckily, in public goods game experiments, people are surprisingly generous—in much the same way that people are generous in ultimatum games. Most participants will give quite a bit more than nothing. Variants of the public goods game experiments show that, when a third party observes others being mean in public goods experiments, then he is willing to pay to punish the uncooperative players—this phenomenon is known as *altruistic punishment*. People are prepared to forgo something themselves in order to punish others for violating social norms of generosity and cooperation. This is a form of cooperation in itself because altruistic punishment reinforces the cooperative behaviour of those who do give generously, and discourages the selfish behaviour of those who do not. Altruistic punishment in public goods games has been studied by neuroeconomists and neuroscientists. They find that experimental participants engaging in altruistic punishment experience neural activations in the brain's reward centres—this suggests that we feel pleasure when we punish others for violating social norms.

Altruistic punishment is an important phenomenon in the evolution of cooperation. In the modern world, altruistic punishment can help to explain why we are quick publicly to condemn socially unacceptable behaviour. Social media has made this much easier, with negative consequences too—for example, Twitter trolls. More generally these tendencies to cooperate and reinforce social norms can also explain why social information is such a powerful tool in manipulating behaviour. One example is the evidence on energy consumption—when energy consumers are told about the consumption of their neighbours, they are likely to adjust their own consumption towards the social reference point of friends' and neighbours' energy consumption. Similarly, when the UK's tax agency—Her Majesty's Revenue and Customs (HMRC)—wrote letters to late payers of tax bills containing some social information about others' behaviour and informing the recalcitrant that her behaviour was socially anomalous because most of her peers had paid their bills on time, this led to many (not all!) of the remaining late-payers paying up more quickly than a group of late payers who had received letters containing no reference to the social information about others' payment decisions.

Identity

Identity is another manifestation of our social natures and, in many ways, is like a very specific form of social signalling, similar in that sense to the role that image motivation plays in charitable giving, as discussed in Chapter 2. We identify with some groups more than others and this links back to social psychologist Henri Tajfel's early analysis of prejudice and discrimination. Tajfel wanted to understand why so many ordinary people were so in thrall to Hitler and the Nazi party. He focused on intergroup relations where we identify with a particular *in-group* and we are prepared to challenge and clash with *out-groups*, whom we see in some sense as our opposites. Tajfel also noted that it takes very little for a group of people to identify with each other and decide they want an ongoing relationship of mutual favourism. Simple preferences for particular types of art, even a simple coin toss, can separate one group from another. We are prepared to incur costs to identify ourselves with a particular group—for example, fans of pop stars such as Katy Perry will spend thousands of pounds or dollars in a year because they identify with other Katy Perry fans. Tajfel's insights about groups link into behavioural economists' analyses of identity. George Akerlof and Rachel Kranton have developed the analysis of identity—observing that what seem like perverse behaviours, including incurring self-harm in the form of tattoos and piercings, are an attempt to signal to our in-groups that we are with them.

Identity plays a particularly powerful role in politics. Most of us have a strong need to identify with others socially, politically, and culturally. In the aftermath of the UK's vote to leave the EU in June 2016, commentators observed that many who had voted 'Leave' were motivated by the sense that their identities had been lost or diluted by the growth of immigration from the EU. The irony is that, with a couple of notable exceptions (for example, Boston in Lincolnshire), the most ardent 'Leavers' among the general public, the ones who felt they had most to fear from immigrants, were living in areas with low immigration rates. Perhaps they were deciding that immigrants were an out-group on the basis of little direct experience at all, a phenomenon that would not have surprised Tajfel.

Herding and social learning

An important facet of our social natures is our tendency to imitate, herd, and follow the crowd. Sociologists explain herding as a reflection of two types of influence: *normative* and *informational*. Normative influences are the social norms that drive our decisions—many of us often want to fit in and do what others do. They may reflect evolved, instinctive responses. Many of our decisions, including economic and financial decisions, involve following other people, perhaps because we believe we can learn from them or perhaps because there is some more primitive instinctive process going on.

Social psychologist Solomon Asch found that, even in very simple decision-making tasks—for example, judging the relative length of lines—others can easily manipulate us. Asch found that when single, genuine experimental participants were included in groups of, say, nineteen experimental confederates all giving obviously wrong answers to very simple questions, the genuine experimental participants would often change their minds and switch from obviously correct answers to wrong ones, because that is what the group had decided. And this is not necessarily irrational behaviour, if the person is judging that it is not very likely that he is right and the nineteen others are wrong.

Fascinating new research into how and why we copy others is emerging, and one promising area for investigation for economists is the neuroeconomic analysis of *mirror neurons*. Mirror neurons are found in human and primate brains, and in some other animals too. Scientists believe that they may play a role when we imitate others. Neuroscientists have conducted experiments on monkeys using single neuron experiments, which involve monitoring firing rates from a single neuron. When a monkey moves in a certain way, the mirror neurons fire not only when the monkey under observation moves, but also when that monkey sees another monkey move. The fact that similar responses are seen in our primate ancestors may indicate that herding behaviour is automatic and 'hard-wired', and perhaps reflects our more primitive emotions including impulsiveness. It is possible that similar neural processes are generating our herding behaviour in economic and financial contexts too.

An important element in the economic analysis of herding builds on sociologists' insights about informational influence. Informational influence is about learning from others' actions. Where these actions are easily observable they can be a useful guide when alternative information is hard to find. Other people may know something we do not and so it might make sense to copy them—following the crowd may be a rational social learning device. However, sometimes following the crowd is just impulsive and we do it without thinking, perhaps reflecting evolved herding instincts.

There are very many examples in ordinary life. When I need some cash in a hurry and I see a long queue behind one ATM and no queue behind the next ATM, I save myself time by assuming that people are not using the second ATM for a reason—it is broken or the bank is charging an excessive fee. I learn from the group's decisions. This is neither wrong nor right—sometimes the herd has chosen the correct strategy, other times the herd has chosen the wrong strategy. Whether or not it is clever for me to follow the herd will depend on the circumstances. Other people's choices are also informative when we are choosing a restaurant. I would not usually go into an empty restaurant when the restaurant next door is crowded. I prefer the crowded restaurant even if I have to queue because the herd might know something I do not about the dodgy wine and food in the first restaurant, or the tasty food in the second. Is herding good or bad? It depends on whether those group judgements and decisions are right or wrong.

Herding also generates negative spillovers. If I am choosing between an empty restaurant and a crowded restaurant—why pick the crowded one? If I follow others into a crowded restaurant then I am using social information about group decisions—but what if I have other, private information that is valuable but not directly observable by others? Imagine I have two pieces of information: one is a recommendation from a personal friend who has been visiting from Sydney and told me that the empty restaurant is the best undiscovered restaurant in London; the second is the information I can infer from observing other people's preferred choice of restaurant.

I may decide to follow the herd into the popular restaurant—and in ignoring my private information (my friend's recommendation) that information is now lost to anyone observing my behaviour. They would infer from my selection of restaurant that the empty restaurant does not have much to recommend it at all—they cannot see or know that I have private information suggesting the empty restaurant could, in fact, be very good. So they are likely to queue for the less good but crowded restaurant too, as are others following along behind them. In this way, social information about others' choices cascades through the herd. When herding leads to valuable private information being ignored because people are misled by the behaviour of the herd, it generates negative effects on others—a negative *herding externality*. The herd provides safety; and collective decision-making can, under certain assumptions, lead to better decisions. Collective information can be more accurate. But herding can also mean that valuable private information is ignored and lost.

Another reason to herd is because what others think of us matters to us. Our reputation is valuable and we try to guard it carefully, and this also links to the image motivation factors discussed in

Chapter 2. Our reputations often survive better if we are only wrong when others are wrong—to paraphrase economist John Maynard Keynes: reputations fare better if we are conventionally wrong than if we are unconventionally right. Rogue traders are an example of the vulnerability of a reputation built on contrarian choices. Spectacular gains can be made when a trader bids against financial market conventions. But when the crowd is right and the contrarian is wrong, her reputation cannot so easily be rescued if she cannot defend herself by saying: 'it was a common mistake'.

Evolution may well play a significant role because many other species share our social learning behaviour. The Adelie penguins of the Antarctic exhibit strong herding tendencies. They are in the middle of a food chain—they eat krill and are eaten by leopard seals. When finding food they face a dilemma—if they dive into the sea, they may find some krill to enjoy, or they may be attacked and eaten by a seal. Their best strategy is to employ some social learning and observe their fellow penguins before deciding what to do. The bravest and/or hungriest penguin will take a risk, and if the rest of the colony can see that no seal attacks him, then the others will follow—herding behind him into the sea. There are modern human parallels—we use consumer feedback and reviews to guide our purchases—made much easier with the growth of the Internet and online shopping. We are responsive to information about celebrities using particular products. All these ways in which we look to others when choosing what to buy reflect our susceptibility to social information.

Similarly, human herding is often about the security of being in a group. There is safety in numbers. Imagine crossing a busy road in Jakarta jammed with cars and motorbikes. The only way to get across that road is to move with a group of locals—learning from them the local pedestrians' habits, but also enjoying the safety and shelter of the crowds. A car is far more likely to run over a lone pedestrian than a crowd. There are corollaries in our civil lives:

class action suits rely on the fact that the crowd has more power and influence than single individuals, and it can protect us from injustice too—for example, if we group together to take legal action. An example is the Fen-Phen diet pills class action suit. The US Food and Drug Administration found that using Fen-Phen was associated with heart disease. More than 125,000 users of the diet pills filed a class action suit against the manufacturers, Wyeth, who eventually settled out of court at a cost of almost $16.6 million. Individuals who were powerless alone gathered together as a group to get justice for their collective.

Many of these are modern examples, but our herding instincts are old, deep-seated, and antediluvian. Our herding instincts are shared by many other species—for example, the penguins mentioned earlier. Herding is very much associated with animal behaviour. Cows' herding behaviour is an instinct that has evolved as a protection against predators. In humans as with many other animals, following others is an evolved survival strategy that enabled our ancestors to find food, shelter, and fertile mates. How do these deep-seated instincts play out in modern artificial environments in which internet and mobile technologies mediate our social relationships and interactions—when we buy and sell on eBay; and book our holidays and taxi cab rides using TripAdvisor, Airbnb, and Uber? Both the virtues and the vices of herding and social influence are magnified in our fast-moving computerized world. Financial crises today are driven by speculators chasing other speculators in search of profit, as they have done for centuries, from the time of Tulipmania (the 17th-century Dutch speculative euphoria around buying and selling tulip bulbs) and before.

Financial herding is a type of herding that has affected us all profoundly—either directly or indirectly. We live in a globalized, computerized, interdependent, financial system. The speed and magnitude of financial flows can be overwhelming— exemplified in the case of Navinder Singh Sarao, who was accused of contributing to Wall Street's 2010 trillion-dollar 'Flash Crash' by spoof trading from a computer in his parents' suburban London home. Herding has the power to destabilize markets and financial systems. It also has the power to disrupt our buying patterns, voting habits, religious views and practices, and cultural preferences. It can distort our social relationships and interactions.

Herding has wider implications too—in terms of welfare and well-being. Ethically, it could be problematic if business and government are using social information to manipulate decision-making, taking us towards a *1984*-style world of group-think and Big Brother. If there is commercial value in manipulating social decision-making then there are powerful incentives for business and government to invade individuals' privacy and mine personal information, leading to exploitation by modern hi-tech businesses. It can also affect our financial futures—for example, if group-think dominates pension fund trustees' decision-making processes, enabling mendacious individuals and groups to siphon off money, then large numbers of people will face a financially vulnerable old age. Unfortunately, pension fund fraud is not rare—and from Robert Maxwell onwards there have been many such stories—most recently in the UK are concerns about pension fund management for former employees of British Home Stores. The good news is that regulators are aware of these influences and are working on developing policies to limit the risks and ensure that pension funds are properly managed.

This chapter has explored the many ways in which social influences affect a wide range of our economic and financial decisions. We respond to social influences reflecting our perceptions of how we are doing relative to others, and how they are doing relative to us. Many people prefer to see more equal outcomes and do not like inequity, especially if it affects them personally. We trust and reciprocate, and many economic relationships depend on this social behaviour. We learn from others and we copy others. Many types of herding and social learning affect our economic and financial decisions. In all of this, behavioural economics brings together insights from social psychology, sociology, neuroscience, and evolutionary biology to explain how and why social influences have such a powerful pull on our economic and financial behaviour.

One interpretation of herding is that it is a quick decision-making tool—what behavioural economists call a *heuristic*—enabling us to economize on the time and cognitive effort of making all our decisions from scratch. For example, imagine you need to buy a new fridge, and you know that your neighbour has just spent a lot of time investigating the best brand of fridge to buy. Why would you repeat all that effort when you could just ask him for a recommendation? Your heuristic is to ask your neighbour—which will save you a lot of time and energy. But the problem with heuristics is that, while they are quick and convenient and often work well enough, they are associated with systematic behavioural biases. When we follow our neighbours and friends, we may be leveraging valuable social information, or we might just be repeating their mistakes. Furthermore, herding is only one type of heuristic—the behavioural economics literature on heuristics is vast, and in Chapter 4 we will cover some of the key insights.

Chapter 4
Quick thinking

Chapter 3 covered some of the ways in which our decisions are affected by social influences and the behaviour and attitudes of other people. Herding is a key example—we follow others because copying them is a quick way to decide what to do next. In many of our everyday choices we use these quick rules and this chapter explores some of the main heuristics and the consequences of using them, especially in terms of behavioural bias.

Traditionally, economists focus on the role of markets in coordinating the decisions and choices of many consumers and firms. In markets, prices play the pivotal role by signalling information about costs of production, and the balance of demand and supply. While markets serve a very important purpose, the price mechanism is fallible and all sorts of failures in markets mean that prices do not effectively capture all aspects of supply and demand. Economists know this better than anyone and many economists spend their lives analysing how and why markets fail—mostly focusing on market and institutional failures.

Behavioural economists bring in an additional dimension, not by looking at markets and their supporting institutions such as governments and legal systems, but by examining the behaviour of the individual decision-makers that constitute a market. In this, behavioural economists move away from the standard economic assumptions—that people use relatively complex and mathematical decision-making rules when deciding what to do, what to buy, what to sell, and how hard to work.

Traditionally, economists assume that, while markets fail, the people using markets are super-rational beings. Sometimes these super-rational beings make decisions that, with the benefit of hindsight and better information, they could improve. But, on the basis of the information available at the time, they do their best and they do not repeat their mistakes. These rational agents' choices are a stable reflection of their underlying preferences—for example, if a rational being prefers books to chocolate, and prefers chocolate to shoes, then they will also prefer books to shoes. Their preferences are stable and consistent. They process all the most up-to-date information they have and use mathematical reasoning to figure out from that the best, most optimal solution. There is plenty of economic analysis addressing what happens when this information is unreliable or imperfect in some way, but most economists do not focus on other, less mathematical ways of choosing and deciding. This is where behavioural economics comes in—with a softer view of rationality.

For behavioural economists, the problem with traditional economics is that these assumptions about people's decision-making tools are incomplete and/or unrealistic. In reality, we make many of our everyday decisions quickly, without too much thought at all. This is not stupid or irrational—quite the opposite. We would be more stupid and irrational to spend hours collecting information and carefully calculating a strategy for some of the everyday decisions that have just a fleeting impact on our lives. Sometimes we want or need to decide quickly. That does not mean that thinking quickly is a good thing either. When we decide too quickly, we make mistakes. When we reflect back over the day we might decide that, if we had taken more time deciding, we might have made better choices. This chapter explores some of these themes, focusing on the quick thinking rules and associated mistakes that we make in our everyday decision-making.

Quick decisions using heuristics

Deciding quickly is difficult when we are overwhelmed by information: when we face *information overload*. It is also difficult to decide quickly and accurately when we are overwhelmed by choices: when we are facing *choice overload*. Traditionally economists have assumed that choice is a good thing and that having more choices is better than having fewer choices. Many choices mean that each of us can more easily find products and services that neatly match our needs and desires, thus boosting our welfare. In the real world however, having a very wide range of choices available does not seem to improve outcomes.

Choice experts Sheena Iyengar and Mark Lepper explored how and why choice can demotivate shoppers and students. In one set of experiments, they asked shoppers in a grocery store to browse stalls selling jams: one stall had twenty-four varieties of jam on offer; the other displayed just five. While shoppers spent more time browsing the stall with lots of jams on offer, they bought more from the stall with the smaller range. Perhaps the shoppers were so overwhelmed and demotivated by the range of choices available, their ability to make any choice at all was impaired.
In another choice experiment, two groups of students were set different assessment tasks. Students in one group were instructed to choose one essay topic from a list of thirty. Students in the other group were instructed to choose one essay from a list of six. Like the shopping scenario, performance and motivation was better for the students facing more limited choices. The students offered the more limited set of choices wrote longer and better essays.

In the modern world, the problem of choice overload is particularly profound and is exacerbated by information overload too. When facing choice overload, consumers decide quickly; for example, they may choose one of the first items on a list rather than fully considering all the options offered to them. If choices are too complex, and especially if they relate to 'boring' decisions that have no tangible and immediate benefits (e.g. choosing a pension plan), we might just abandon our attempt to choose anything at all. Subsequent evidence about choice overload has been mixed but a recent study from Alexander Chernev and colleagues has shown that context is important: the complexity of choices offered, the difficulty of tasks, participants' uncertainty about their preferences, and their desires to minimize effort—all are associated with increased susceptibility to choice overload.

Paralleling the wide range of choices we face in buying everything from jam and bread through to complex financial products, there is a large volume of complex information, both online and offline, which is not necessarily quick and easy to navigate. In contrast to the standard view from economics, behavioural economists are discovering that more information is not necessarily better. In many everyday situations, we do not want to waste time and energy with complex calculations and instead we use simple rules of thumb to help us to decide quickly. Behavioural economists call these simple decision rules *heuristics*. Sometimes heuristics work well, but not always. Other times they lead us into errors and mistakes.

It is often sensible to use heuristics. Only a foolish person would spend days exploring all the different online and offline sales outlets before deciding to buy a particular type of car, TV, fridge, or phone, just in the hope of saving a few pounds. For smaller, everyday choices this is particularly true. I do not conduct a comprehensive research exercise each time I buy a loaf of bread. I do not waste time comparing prices of bread across all London supermarkets because, while I might save 50 pence on the bread, I would have to spend £5 travelling to the cheapest supermarket, as well as having to factor in the value of the time I had wasted.

This insight is consistent with standard economic analyses of the costs of transacting. Most economists would agree that we economize not only when deciding what to buy but also in the process of trading, bargaining, and collecting information.

Behavioural economists take the insight further, however, in arguing that we are not making calculations about these transaction costs either. We use heuristics and these stop us wasting time thinking about *any* of the direct and indirect costs of our different options too deeply at all. Going back to my choice of bread—I might use a range of heuristics. I might buy the same brand I bought last time because I remember it was tasty. If I am trying to be healthy, I might pick a brand with packaging that represents healthiness—more paper, less plastic perhaps, illustrated with imagery of green plants and seeds. If I am at home and feeling lazy, I will just go around the corner to my local convenience store, even though I know that their prices are significantly higher than those of the big supermarkets. But these processes will operate almost unconsciously. I will not consider the information offered by the bread bakers and suppliers with any sort of analytical depth, and I will not think too deeply about the relative transaction costs of the different options either.

The problem with using heuristics is that, often, they lead us into mistakes and bias. Psychologists Daniel Kahneman and Amos Tversky were pioneers in analysing heuristics and this work has been popularized in Kahneman's 2011 book—*Thinking, Fast and Slow*. Using a range of experiments and insights, Kahneman and Tversky showed how a small set of heuristics lead us into making systematic, predictable mistakes. When we decide quickly, sometimes our choices are distorted away from what is best for us.

Kahneman and Tversky explore three main types of heuristics and the behavioural biases associated with them: availability, representativeness, and anchoring/adjustment.

Using available information

When we are making a decision, particularly if we are in a hurry, we do not reflect carefully on all the information we have. Instead, we will use information that is easy to access, retrieve, and recall. Using our knowledge is like rifling through a filing cabinet when we are in a hurry to get to a meeting. We tend to go to the first folder we can find that has any relevance, but we do not have the time and energy to go through every folder carefully looking for the most relevant information. Sometimes this means that we miss important information and make mistakes.

When we rely on easily retrievable information instead of looking fully and carefully at all relevant information—Kahneman and Tversky call this the *availability heuristic*. Availability also links with concepts from psychology: *primacy* and *recency effects*. We remember more easily the first and last bits of information we come across, and information in the middle is much more easily forgotten.

The availability heuristic can explain our habitual behaviours. My husband and I enjoy travelling, and I usually book the flights and hotels. I am aware that there is a large, complex range of travel agencies online and offline, but I tend to use the same one each time because I can easily remember how to use it. I remember how good (or bad) my last experience was—and the online sites help me with that by allowing me to store information about my past experiences. Frequent email reminders from the online providers reinforce these memories. I might be missing out on all sorts of bargains because I do not shop around enough. I do not want to be a sucker so I do occasionally take a look around on other sites, but usually the prices for hotels and flights are not that different—whether this reflects collusive over-charging by the travel agents, competitive price pressure, or a combination of both, I do not know. Either way, when I think about it carefully,

I feel reassured that my speedy use of readily retrievable information is not leading me into big, important mistakes, though I may be wrong.

Sometimes we use the availability heuristic more consciously (e.g. when we are choosing our passwords) and this increases our vulnerability to cyber privacy and security violations by hackers, spammers, and phishers. A good password is hard to remember. We might use the availability heuristic to devise memorable passwords for ourselves—but a password that is easy to remember is also easy to crack. Security firm SplashData compiles an annual list of the worst passwords. The commonest and most enduring password is '123456' (it has made the top of SplashData's list for a few years running). The second most common is 'password'. Both are easily retrievable using the availability heuristic, but it would be well-known to any hacker that these passwords are commonly used.

Policy-makers and competition regulators are interested in how we use heuristics, especially in the context of consumers' 'switching' behaviour—we are slow to switch our energy, mobile phone, and financial services suppliers, even when we could get a better deal elsewhere. Why not switch to better deals more often? Perhaps it is laziness and procrastination—but it might also be the availability heuristic at work. Unless we have had a memorably bad experience, we tend to stick with what we know, because we know what we know. Policy-makers are increasingly concerned that businesses can exploit consumers' inertia. When businesses are not disciplined by competitive pressure from consumers (i.e. consumers deciding to go for a better bargain elsewhere), then businesses have no incentive to improve the deals they offer. What is the solution? Price comparison sites are one way to help us access better information more quickly. Governments are also working on ways to make it easier for us to switch suppliers, as will be explored in more detail in Chapter 9—'Economic behaviour and public policy'.

Using representations

Another of Tversky and Kahneman's heuristics that leads us into bias is the *representativeness heuristic*. We often decide by analogy—we draw, sometimes spurious, comparisons with other superficially similar events. Behavioural economists and psychologists have used a wide range of experiments to show how we jump too quickly to the conclusion that scenarios are similar. We also fit our perceptions of others with our pre-existing stereotypes.

Tversky and Kahneman illustrate the representativeness heuristic with a range of experiments. In one, they ask their experimental participants to judge a person's likely profession. Some people were given a description of Steve. They were told that Steve is shy and withdrawn and has an eye for detail. Given this information, participants were more likely to predict that Steve is a librarian, even when the objective information about the relative likelihood that he is a librarian does not support their judgement.

Tversky and Kahneman capture a similar phenomenon in their experiments exploring 'the Linda problem'. They asked another group of experimental participants to read some information about a woman named Linda. The participants were told that Linda is in her 30s. She is clever, single, and outspoken. She is concerned about social justice and discrimination, and has been an anti-nuclear protestor. Then the experimental participants are asked:

> 'Which is more probable?
> 1. Linda is a bank teller
> 2. Linda is a bank teller and is active in the feminist movement.'

Many people select option 2: that Linda is a bank teller active in the feminist movement, even though this category is a sub-set of

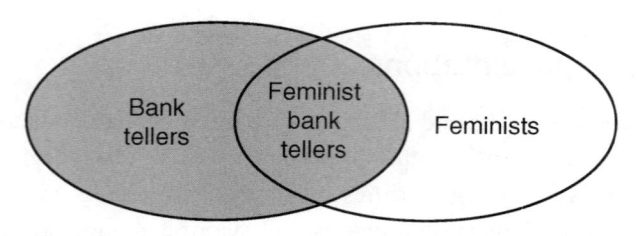

1. The Linda problem—a conjunction fallacy.

option 1—(all) bank tellers. At most, option 2 is as probable as option 1. It cannot be more probable. This mistake is called the *conjunction fallacy*: it is about the probability of what theorists call 'conjoint events'—events occurring together, as illustrated in Figure 1.

The conjunction of the two events—first, that Linda is a bank teller and, second, that she is also a feminist, is judged by many people to be more likely than just a single event—that Linda is a bank teller, even though Linda as a bank teller covers a larger set of possibilities—all bank tellers, feminist or not. Given that there is some chance that Linda is not a feminist given the information presented, then, if people are properly applying the rules of probability, they should decide that option 1 is more likely.

Why do so many people ignore simple rules of probability? The idea is that we do not make our decisions purely on the basis of mathematical, statistical rules. Instead, we form narrative accounts in our mind. Stories have a powerful pull on our imaginations. Employing the representativeness heuristic, we match our judgements with our knowledge of prior scenarios and stereotypes. Linda's story makes us think she is more likely to be a feminist and so we choose the option that explicitly includes the possibility that she is a feminist. Even if we know the rules of statistics and probability, this knowledge of probability rules does not seem relevant to us and we discard it in favour of a coherent narrative—a story that seems to capture who Linda is and what she does.

The representativeness heuristic can also distort our judgement if we are slow to adjust our prior beliefs to new information, and this links to the problems of *confirmation bias* and *cognitive dissonance*.

Confirmation bias occurs when we anchor our judgement rigidly to our prior beliefs. This is a common phenomenon in political debates and in disputes between the Left and Right. In his 2014 book, *Demonizing the President: The Foreignization of Barak Obama*, Martin Parlett explores reactions to Barak Obama's role in the killing of Osama bin Laden in April 2011. On the surface, it might be hard to imagine that Barak Obama's role in bin Laden's killing could be interpreted as a pro-terrorism action, however the conservative newspaper *The Washington Times* suggested that Obama had honoured bin Laden by allowing him full traditional Muslim burial rites. The conservative view was that Obama is a terrorist sympathizer, and so any of Obama's actions, even the killing of a terrorist leader, was interpreted from a conservative perspective as pro-terrorist.

In the UK in 2015, the surprise election of Jeremy Corbyn as the Labour Party's Leader of the Opposition also illustrates confirmation bias. On his first outing at Prime Minister's Questions he included questions from voters when usually the questions are formulated by the UK Members of Parliament, with the Leader of the Opposition taking the lead. His supporters interpreted this as an excellent illustration of his laudable democratic inclinations; his detractors interpreted it as evidence that he did not know what he was doing and could not think of any questions of his own. In either case, Jeremy Corbyn's actions mostly did not change people's opinions of him; his actions just confirmed what they already believed.

While confirmation bias is about interpreting new evidence in the light of our existing beliefs, *cognitive dissonance* is about conflicts between our beliefs and our actions. We may believe ourselves to be good, charitable people and yet regularly walk past homeless people asking for money. Our actions conflict with our belief about ourselves and so we rationalize our actions. We might decide that the homeless person should be selling the *Big Issue*—we would buy a magazine from them if they were selling one. Or we might conclude that the homeless person is a con artist who really just wants to steal our wallet. Or we might decide that giving them money will not help them really because they would just spend it on drugs. In any of these cases, we have manipulated our perception of a situation so that our prior beliefs, in this case about our capacity for generosity, remain unchallenged.

George Akerlof and William Dickens confirmed this tendency with some behavioural experiments. They asked students to insult each other, for example by telling them: 'you are shallow, untrustworthy, and dull'. Akerlof and Dickens found that the students delivering the insults adjusted their attitudes towards their targets by becoming more genuinely critical of the victims of their insults. The students delivering the insults did not want to challenge their own belief in themselves as a 'nice' person, and the only way to reconcile this dissonance was to adjust their beliefs about others. Akerlof and Dickens conclude that the students' responses may parallel the ways in which people justify violent and aggressive behaviour more generally.

Anchoring and adjustment

The third sort of bias occurs when we anchor our decisions around a reference point, and adjust our choices relative to this reference point. Again, Tversky and Kahneman use a range of experimental evidence to illustrate the idea. In one study, they asked school children to make quick guesses about arithmetic tasks. One group of children were asked to estimate 8 x 7 x 6 x 5 x 4 x 3 x 2 x 1. A second group of children was asked to estimate 1 x 2 x 3 x 4 x 5 x 6 x 7 x 8. The guesses should have been similar but the children who were asked to start with 8 x 7 x... came up with higher estimates than the children asked to calculate 1 x 2 x.... One explanation for this is that the first group of children were anchoring their estimates around the first number they saw—'8' and getting a higher answer than the second group, who were anchoring their estimates around the '1'. The children's answers illustrate the more general problem we get when we adjust around an initial anchor—insufficient adjustment. Our decisions and choices are distorted by our starting position.

One everyday example of anchoring and adjustment can be illustrated using the Sydney housing market. In Australia, many houses are sold via auction and this gives academics a rich database to study. Auction clearance rates are an important signal about the buoyancy of the Sydney housing market, and 2015 was a bumper year with house prices growing, on average in Sydney, by around 20 per cent. This bubble burst (temporarily) in late 2015, and auction clearance rates plummeted from rates of up to 90 per cent (i.e. 90 per cent of the houses listed for auction were successfully sold) down to under 50 per cent (see <www.abs.gov.au/ausstats/abs@.nsf/mf/6416.0>). By early 2016 potential home-sellers had responded to this downturn and auction clearance rates were going up again, but only because the number of sellers putting their houses up for auction had fallen so fast—the number of houses listed for auction fell from hundreds in late 2015 to just a handful by early 2016. One possible explanation could be that potential sellers had anchored their expectations to a particular sale price. Once they saw that they were not likely to achieve this price, they decided not to sell rather than just allowing market forces to determine the outcome for them.

In some senses, the anchoring element of anchoring and adjustment heuristics overlaps with the availability heuristic described earlier. Our reference points are often more cognitively accessible than other information. For example, often we use the status quo as the reference point—we tend to avoid change away from the existing situation. Sometimes this leads to *status quo bias* and *familiarity bias*—people are resistant to change, or they judge events according to how different they are to the current situation. In our everyday lives, many of our judgements are based around how much our decisions will move us away from the status quo. When we are looking for a new job, or selling a house, our perception of a fair wage or a fair house price will be based around what we are earning today, or the price we paid for our house when we bought it, or how much our neighbour got when she sold hers. The problem is that these judgements may have very little to do with market forces of supply and demand. These judgements may also stop markets working smoothly.

Businesses and policy-makers can exploit our status quo bias in manipulating our decision-making—for example, by setting the status quo through default options. The default options we are offered represent the status quo, and we have to make a conscious effort to change away from these defaults. Businesses often cynically exploit this tendency by designing complex default options to confuse us—as Figure 2 implies.

However, status quo bias and default options can be used in more constructive ways by policy-makers—to solve the problems that can emerge from our inertia. One key example relates to pensions. Finding the money to pay for people's retirements, given ageing populations and lengthening life expectancies, is a serious and growing policy problem for many advanced economies. Behavioural economists Shlomo Benartzi and Richard Thaler devised a pensions scheme based around the status quo bias and the related idea that people tend to stick with default options, where the default represents the status quo. Their scheme, which they called 'Save More Tomorrow' (SMarT), was designed so that a proportion of future pay rises goes into workers' pension pots. So, unless a worker opts out, when they get a pay rise, part of it will go into their SMarT pension fund. This scheme also means that workers do not feel that they are losing anything relative to their current pay because only salary *increases* are taken into the

DESPERATE BUSINESS

how come I'm still paying for this subscription?

yeah you didn't tick the box that said you don't want to not renew it

2. **Confusing default options.**

SMarT fund. And the workers still have a choice. Automatically contributing a proportion of any salary increases is the default option, but if a worker does not want to lose any of their pay rise into their pension fund, then they can opt out. Benartzi and Thaler found that pension contributions increased significantly just by manipulating default options in this way—an insight that has led to the redesign of pension schemes and policies in a number of countries.

Since Kahneman and Tversky's pioneering studies in the 1970s, the range of heuristics and biases identified by economists and psychologists has grown rapidly. The Wikipedia entry for 'cognitive bias' currently lists well over a hundred different types of bias. Developing an analytical structure to these insights would help us to understand more deeply how and why these biases affect our choices. Many behavioural economists have been working on this—to develop theories to capture the key insights. One of the most influential theoretical developments in this field is *prospect theory*. In constructing this theory, Kahneman and Tversky developed their early ideas about heuristics and bias into a richer and more systematic analysis of decision-making, applied in particular to how we decide in risky situations. We will explore prospect theory, and some other competing theories about risky decisions, in Chapter 5.

Chapter 5
Risky choices

In Chapter 4, we explored a range of ways in which our quick decisions can lead us into making mistakes, and this is particularly true when we are facing risk and uncertainty. When we decide to cross the road, buy a lottery ticket, invest our money, or take out a payday loan, all these decisions involve risk and uncertainty. Economists usually think of risk as quantifiable—if we can just figure out that the chance that we will get hit by a bus when crossing the road is, say, 1 in 8,000, then we can decide whether or not we want to take that risk, depending on how we value the consequences.

Economists also usually assume that we decide between risky options according to how much we like taking risks, or not. Our risk preferences do not change just because one of the options we are facing is presented and framed in a different way. If I buy a lottery ticket, my chance of winning £1 million is 1 in 14 million—so I am not likely to win, but I balance these low odds against the prospect of a very large prize, and decide according to my risk preference. Do I like taking risks? Or do I prefer to avoid risks if I can? Or perhaps I am risk neutral and do not mind too much either way? If I prefer to avoid risk, I will not buy the ticket; if I like taking risks, I will.

Behavioural economists challenge this understanding of risk. They focus on the way our perceptions of risks shift in different situations. One example is the way we judge risks depending on how easily we remember information, and this links to the availability heuristic, explored in Chapter 4. We choose, not on the basis of all the information we can find, but just on the basis of information that is quickly available to us—information we can recall or retrieve quickly and easily. Newspaper headlines about plane crashes are an example: we read about plane crashes regularly and these stories are often accompanied by very memorable, vivid, and emotive images of wreckages and distraught relatives. This leads us into a misperception that airplane crashes are a lot more likely than pedestrian fatalities. We are more likely to be killed crossing the road, but pedestrian fatalities rarely get beyond the local newspapers. We may take a lot more care and worry a lot more when we are deciding to fly, when really we should be taking more care when we are crossing the road.

Another mistake we make when making risky decisions is we inflate the impact of losses relative to gains. Many behavioural experiments have shown that people suffer more from a loss than they gain pleasure from an equivalent gain—for example, we tend to care a lot more about losing £10 than we do about winning £10. This phenomenon is called *loss aversion*—and it has been found to apply to a wide range of people's decisions.

One example affects housing markets: when homeowners see house prices falling, they are reluctant to sell because, by selling, they probably would have to experience a loss from the lower house prices. So homeowners postpone their selling decisions, until, suddenly, many more homeowners are forced to sell simultaneously—perhaps because economic conditions have deteriorated or mortgage interest rates have risen. The housing market gets flooded with properties for sale, and ironically, homeowners' losses are then likely to be magnified, all because loss aversion delayed people's decisions to sell sooner.

Behavioural economists are developing theories that capture some of the human, psychological aspects of risk-taking—to compete with the standard economics assumption that people carefully, consistently, and mathematically balance information about risks.

Prospect theory versus expected utility theory

The key model of risk in behavioural economics was developed by Daniel Kahneman and Amos Tversky, and, to some extent, it formalizes some of the key concepts from their analyses of heuristics and bias explored in Chapter 4. Prospect theory is about future risky prospects: when we buy a house, for example, we may have two prospects available to us. Imagine a first-time buyer who is not sure whether to buy a flat, in a convenient but expensive urban location; or a larger house in a less convenient but cheaper suburban or rural location. Another person might be balancing two employment prospects. Imagine a young graduate who faces two prospects: she can choose an unpaid internship that might lead to a much more interesting and/or more highly paid job in the future; or she can choose a steady, quite well-paid job which will earn her a steady income. Every day we are balancing different risky prospects against each other.

As a starting point in the development of prospect theory, Kahneman and Tversky critique some of the key elements of the standard economic approach to risk: *expected utility theory*. What is expected utility theory? 'Utility' is the word economists use to denote happiness and satisfaction, and expected utility theory explores how we decide about different options depending on what we expect the options to deliver in the future—in terms of our future utility. But we are not perfect forecasters and sometimes these expectations may turn out to be wrong.

Expected utility theory is founded on a range of restrictive assumptions about behaviour. Expected utility theorists assume that people make full use of all relevant, available information.

They also assume that we use relatively complex mathematical tools to ensure that we are maximizing our utility—they assume that we are doing the very best we can possibly do, and so we are choosing the options that give us the highest level of expected happiness and satisfaction that we could hope to achieve, given the information we have when we decide. Once we have identified this best choice, we do not change our minds. Our choices are not inconsistent. If we prefer apples to oranges, and oranges to bananas, then we will also prefer apples to bananas.

Behavioural paradoxes

According to Kahneman and Tversky, the problem with expected utility theory is that it cannot easily explain some common behavioural paradoxes, including (amongst others) the Allais Paradox and the Ellsberg Paradox.

Maurice Allais, the 20th-century French economist, showed how people's choices in risky situations are often inconsistent and one famous behavioural paradox—the *Allais Paradox*—is named in his honour. It shows that people do not have a stable, steady response to different risky outcomes. Specifically, if someone is given the option of a certain outcome alongside a series of risky options, then they will prefer the certain outcome even if, with a different set of prospects, they would be prepared to take risks. Kahneman and Tversky called this effect the *certainty effect*, and confirmed its existence with their own experiments. They wanted to see if people were prepared to take a small additional risk in order to increase their payoffs by—say $1. If people have consistent preferences for risk-taking, then a risk-loving person would take the risk and a risk-averse person would not. Kahneman and Tversky tested for the Allais Paradox by including an option that was guaranteed with certainty so they could see if this distorted people's choices, especially the choices of those who were usually more inclined towards risk-taking.

Table 1 Allais Paradox games

	Choose one option	
	Game 1	Game 2
Option 1	$24 with certainty	34% chance of $24
		66% chance of $0
Option 2	1% chance of $0	33% chance of $25
	33% chance of $25	67% chance of $0
	66% chance of $24	

Kahneman and Tversky's experimental participants were asked to assess different sets of prospects across two games: Game 1 and Game 2. If you were one of their participants you would have been asked to choose one of two options for each game. For Game 1 you have two options. You can either have $24 guaranteed with certainty (i.e. a 100 per cent chance you will get $24) or you can take a gamble giving you a slightly higher, 1 per cent, chance of nothing but the possibility of winning more than $24—including a 33 per cent chance of $25 and a 66 per cent chance of $24, with an overall 99 per cent chance at winning at least $24. These options are summarized in Table 1.

On its own, the set of prospects from Game 1 cannot reveal anything. A risk-averse person might select Option 1 because it offered $24 with certainty. A risk-seeking gambler might decide to take a chance on an additional $1 from winning a $25 payoff by selecting the second option, even though it increases his chances of $0 by a small amount. Either person's choice would be consistent with expected utility theory. But we can see if there are *inconsistencies* by comparing the players' choices with those from Game 2, which includes a second set of options—also summarized in Table 1.

The key difference between Game 1 and Game 2 is that Game 2 does not offer any certain outcome: the first option is a 34 per cent chance of $24 and a 66 per cent chance of $0. As for Game 1, the second option offers a slightly lower chance to win a little more—a 33 per cent chance of $25, but also a slightly higher chance of nothing at all—a 67 per cent chance of $0. So Game 2 is similar in many ways to Game 1 *except* it does not include any certain option.

Expected utility theory predicts that the outcome will be determined by a person's risk preferences, and there will be a trade-off between risk and rewards. If there are two types of people—a risk-averse, cautious person and a risk-loving gambler—the cautious person will always take the safe option, the gambler will always take the risky option. For Game 1 the gambler will take an extra chance in the hope of getting $25—they will trade the slightly higher risk of nothing for the slightly higher reward. For Game 2, they will also take a chance on $25—in both cases they would choose Option 2 because they like taking risks.

The cautious person should be the opposite—in both cases they would choose Option 1 because, for both Game 1 and Game 2, this is the safe option associated with smaller chances of getting nothing at all. For Game 1, choosing Option 1 means no chance of getting zero. For Game 2, the risk of zero is lower with Option 1 at 66 per cent, than for Option 2, when the chance of zero is slightly higher at 67 per cent.

How do real people play this game? Confirming previous experimental studies, Kahneman and Tversky found that people's choices are not consistent: gamblers are not always risk-takers. Many people will select Option 1 (the certain, safe option) from Game 1, but Option 2 (the more risky option) from Game 2. Kahneman and Tversky interpreted this evidence as confirming the existence of the certainty effect. Many people will be happy to take a chance and gamble, but when they are offered a certain outcome this distorts their choices away from taking additional risks for higher rewards.

How does this link into everyday choices? Perhaps it affects how we play for prizes in competitions. Kahneman and Tversky also designed a holiday games version of the certainty effect games. In one game, participants were asked to choose between an option for a 50 per cent chance of a three-week tour of England, France, and Italy versus a certain (100 per cent guaranteed) outcome of a one-week tour of England. Notice that the chances of the lesser English holiday are twice as good as the chances of the better European holiday. Most (78 out of 100 participants) chose the lesser but certain option—the guaranteed one-week tour of England.

In a second game, however, participants were prepared to take more risks when playing for holiday prizes. The relative probabilities were the same as for the first game—the English holiday was twice as likely as the European holiday—but no certain, 100 per cent option was included. The prospects were a 5 per cent chance of a three-week European holiday and a 10 per cent chance at the one-week English holiday. When offered the 5 per cent chance at the European holiday, 67 out of 100 participants took that option in preference to the better chance of the holiday in England. Even though the relative balance of probabilities was the same, participants had swapped their preferences from the more probable (in fact certain) but lesser prize, to the better but more unlikely prize. So the certainty effect appeared to be driving participants' decisions in the holiday games too. Kahneman and Tversky attributed this to *weighting*: we do not weight all probabilities equally, and tend to give certain outcomes more weight than less certain outcomes. Certainty distracts us.

Another famous behavioural paradox described by Kahneman and Tversky is the *Ellsberg Paradox*, named after the economist and military analyst Daniel Ellsberg, once employed by the RAND Corporation. He was also perhaps an early role model for modern day whistle-blowers and journalists including Edward Snowden and Julian Assange: Ellsberg released the 'Pentagon Papers',

Table 2 Ellsberg Paradox games

	Which would you bet on?	
	Game 1	Game 2
Option 1	Red	Red or yellow
Option 2	Black	Black or yellow

documenting the US government's controversial decisions during the Vietnam War for the *New York Times* in 1971.

Ellsberg's PhD research was a study of risky decisions and in one of his experiments, he told his experimental participants that he had filled an urn with ninety balls: thirty of which were red and sixty of which were either black or yellow, but the experimental participants were not given precise information about how many of the sixty balls were black and how many were yellow. Ellsberg then asked his experimental participants to choose which option they would select if they were asked to take a bet on the colour of a ball to be drawn at random from the urn. The options for this set of games are set out in Table 2.

Notice that both sets of options are essentially similar. For Game 1, Option 1 is to choose 'red'; Option 2 is to choose 'black'. For Game 2, the options are the same as for the Game 1 choices, except that 'or yellow' has been added in the same way to both options. Expected utility theorists might predict that if someone chooses Option 1 (red) for Game 1, they would also choose Option 1 (red or yellow) from Game 2 because the chances of drawing a red ball are not going to change from Game 1 to Game 2. Similarly, their choices will be consistent if they choose Option 2 (black) from Game 1 and Option 2 (black or yellow) from Game 2.

One interpretation is that people can calculate exactly the chances of 'red' and 'black or yellow' because they have been given the information they need to calculate this beforehand. But given the prior information, they have no exact information about the separate chances of picking a black or yellow ball (they just know the overall chances of black or yellow). So for Game 1, Option 2 is ambiguous; and for Game 2, Option 1 is ambiguous. Most people avoid the ambiguous option—they experience *ambiguity aversion*. We are not being at all irrational when we avoid ambiguous outcomes, but Kahneman and Tversky argue that ambiguity aversion is not easy to explain using expected utility theory, and they aimed to develop their prospect theory so that it *was* consistent with ambiguity aversion.

Inconsistent choices

In developing prospect theory, Kahneman and Tversky were keen to develop an alternative to expected utility theory which could incorporate the anomalous behaviour identified in the Allais and Ellsberg experiments, and also some additional effects that Kahneman and Tversky had noted in their own experiments.

What are these effects? Kahneman and Tversky also found that people were prepared to take on more risk if they were trying to avoid losses, and less risk when gambling for gains. Kahneman and Tversky argued that preference for taking risks when facing losses is the mirror image of the preference for taking risks in the context of gains—and so they called this effect the *reflection effect*.

Kahneman and Tversky demonstrated the reflection effect with the set of games shown in Table 3.

The payoffs for these two games are similar. In both games, participants choose between a risky option (Option 1) and a certain outcome (Option 2). The only difference is that Game 1 involves a gain and Game 2 involves a loss. Expected utility theorists would predict that a risk-seeking player would choose

Table 3 Reflection effect games

	Which would you choose?	
	Game 1	**Game 2**
Option 1	An 80% chance of winning $4,000, and a 20% chance of winning $0	An 80% chance of losing $4,000, and a 20% chance of losing $0
Option 2	A certain payoff of $3,000	A certain loss of $3,000

Option 1 in both cases, and a risk-averse player would choose Option 2 in both cases, but Kahneman and Tversky found that people's behaviour did not follow the pattern predicted by expected utility theory. Most participants (80 out of 100) chose the certain outcome for Game 1, but most (92 out of 100) chose the risky option for Game 2. They were prepared to take risks to avoid a loss, but preferred the certain outcome when offered prospects of gains. With this evidence Kahneman and Tversky confirmed the existence of a reflection effect—people are willing to take on more risks to avoid losses.

Kahneman and Tversky suggested that this could explain why people prefer *contingent insurance* (i.e. insurance payouts contingent on specific events such as fire, damage, or theft) versus *probabilistic insurance* (i.e. policies in which there is no guaranteed cover and payouts are determined by chance).

A probabilistic insurance deal could incorporate a reduction of regular insurance premiums by half for the insurance policy-holder if, in return, they were prepared to take some chance that they would bear all costs themselves. Then, if there is loss or damage, a toss of a coin will determine what happens next—either a 50 per cent chance that the policy-holder pays the remaining half of the premium and the insurance company covers all the costs of losses, or a 50 per cent chance that the policy-holder covers all the costs of the losses themselves and the insurance company returns their premium payments. Kahneman and Tversky argue that, in essence, the purchase of a burglar alarm is similar—people pay for a reduced risk of loss, not for eliminating the loss entirely, yet when offered probabilistic insurance most people avoid it. If they were consistent in their risk preferences, a risk-seeking person might prefer probabilistic insurance.

Kahneman and Tversky also identified a third effect—the *isolation effect*. This is about when we ignore important elements in the alternatives we face. We isolate specific bits of information, rather than looking at all the relevant information in its entirety. Kahneman and Tversky set out their findings from another set of experimental games to illustrate the isolation effect. One of the games includes options involving a sequence of possibilities, as shown in Table 4.

These games are set up carefully so that the payoffs the players could expect from both games are identical. To show this we need to think about the chances of the different range of options.

Table 4 Isolation effect games

	Game 1: a sequential game	**Game 2: a one-stage game**
	Stage 1: you have a 25% chance of moving to Stage 2 (and a 75% chance of not moving to Stage 2). If you were to move to Stage 2, which option would you choose?	**Choose one option**
Option 1	An 80% chance of winning $4,000, and a 20% chance of winning $0	A 20% of winning $4,000, and a 80% chance of winning $0
Option 2	A certain payoff of $3,000	A 25% chance of winning $3,000, and a 75% chance of winning $0

For Game 1, players have only a 25 per cent chance of moving to Stage 2—so there is a 75 per cent chance they will win nothing at all because this is the likelihood that they will not even get to Stage 2. When calculating their payoffs, participants should allow for this fact—that they only have a 25 per cent of getting to a stage when they will actually win anything at all.

So—for Game 1, Option 1, the *expected value* of the different options will be 25 per cent (the chance of moving to Stage 2) multiplied by an 80 per cent chance at $4,000 and a 20 per cent chance of nothing:

25 per cent x {(80% x $4,000) + (20% x $0)} = $800

For Game 1, Option 2, given the 25 per cent chance of getting to the second stage, when the player is guaranteed $3,000, the expected value will be 25 per cent x 100 per cent x $3,000:

25 per cent x {100% x $3,000} = $750

For Game 2, Kahneman and Tversky constructed the expected value of the options to be identical to those in Game 1 but there is no first stage—the players go straight to two options outlined and it is easier to calculate the payoffs because even the cleverest mathematicians need only to think about a single set of options:

Option 1:
= 20 per cent x $4,000 = $800
Option 2:
= 25 per cent x $3,000 = $750

Notice that, just in terms of the expected value of the options, these games are identical. The expected value from Option 1, in both games, is $800. The expected value from Option 2, in both games, is $750. So we can make some comparisons. If expected utility theory is correct, a person choosing Option 2 from Game 1 should choose Option 2 from Game 2 too. Yet Kahneman and Tversky found that a majority of their participants (78 out of 100) chose Option 2 from Game 1, but a majority (65 out of 100) chose Option 1 from Game 2. Kahneman and Tversky suggest that perhaps people were forgetting about the first stage of the game in Game 1. They were forgetting that, to start with, they had only had a 25 per cent chance of moving to the second stage. Kahneman and Tversky's interpretation is that people do not include this 25 per cent chance of reaching Stage 2 in their calculations of the expected values for Game 1. People are isolating the different options presented to them by focusing their attention, selectively, only on Stage 2 of Game 1.

Building prospect theory

Kahneman and Tversky argued that any decision-making theory should be able to explain the three effects outlined earlier: the *certainty effect*, the *reflection effect*, and the *isolation effect*. Their critique of expected utility theory revolved around the fact that expected utility cannot explain these effects and they decided to develop a theory that could—*prospect theory*. They argued that prospect theory has much more real-world explanatory power than expected utility theory.

Prospect theory is based around the idea that we make judgements about the value of different options in particular ways, which are not consistent with the standard economics approach as captured by expected utility theory. The first insight is about the relative comparisons we make when we are choosing and deciding. We do not decide to buy a new mobile phone based just on all the information we are given about that particular mobile phone and the other new offers—we compare the mobile phone options we are offered with the deal we already have and decide whether or not the new deal is an improvement. We do not start completely afresh when we are making our choices—we compare the options against a starting point—a *reference point*. One implication is that our decisions are driven by *changes* relative to our reference points, and not by all the information we have available to us.

The idea of a reference point develops Kahneman and Tversky's earlier insights about anchoring and adjustment heuristics, discussed in Chapter 4: we anchor our choices around our reference point, and adjust our choices accordingly. As we saw in Chapter 4, often the status quo is our reference point. Kahneman and Tversky link this to the physiological concept of homeostasis which is about how, physiologically, we have a set point and our bodily responses are determined by that set point. The same event will have different impacts on our physiology depending on our starting point: for example, if we are too hot and we feel a blast of cold air, we will find that pleasurable. But if we are too cold and we feel the same blast of cold air, it will be unpleasant. Our choices around our reference points are sticky and less likely to change. We exhibit a lot of inertia in our everyday behaviour. This might be because the effort involved in changing is too much, we procrastinate, we are lazy—there is probably a complex set of socio-economic and psychological reasons to explain our resistance to change.

A second key feature of prospect theory develops from Kahneman and Tversky's insights about the reflection effect covered earlier in this chapter, which links into the concept of loss aversion—we care much more about losses than we do about gains. According to many behavioural economists, one manifestation of loss aversion and the status quo bias is the *endowment effect*. We care much more about the things we have and therefore could lose, than we care about things we do not have and could buy. Daniel Kahneman, Jack Knetsch, and Richard Thaler illustrated the endowment effect in some experiments with students. Students were randomly sorted into different groups including 'buyers' and 'sellers'. The sellers were given mugs—which they could sell. The buyers were given the opportunity to buy mugs. The sellers were asked if they were prepared to sell their mugs at various prices. The buyers were asked if they were prepared to buy at various prices. There was a large difference in sellers' versus buyers' prices: the median price that the sellers were willing to accept was $7.12; the median price that the buyers were willing to pay was $3.12.

Just on the basis of this evidence, we would find it difficult to argue this is definitely the endowment effect at work. You might expect a profit maximizing seller to start with a disproportionately high price, in case they could get away with it. The process of bargaining would see the sellers lowering their willingness to accept and the buyers raising their willingness to pay until an equilibrium is found. Nonetheless, there is evidence that divergences between willingness to pay and willingness to accept are relevant in other choices too.

Demonstrating similar divergences in a wider context, Kip Viscusi and colleagues conducted some experiments on people's attitudes towards chemical poisoning. They showed consumers cans of insecticide and toilet bowl cleaner, and asked people how much they would be willing to pay for a safer product with a lower risk from poisoning. Then people were asked if they would be willing to accept a price reduction on a product with an increased risk of poisoning. Most economists might predict that consumers' responses to these questions should be symmetrical: the amount they are willing to pay for a safer product should be similar in magnitude to the amount of compensation they would expect to get in terms of a price reduction on a relatively unsafe product, but Viscusi and colleagues' experimental findings did not support this conclusion. People's responses to reducing risk exhibited a standard pattern predicted by economic theory: there was a diminishing willingness to pay for higher levels of risk reduction. But people were very unwilling to accept *any* sort of increase in poisoning risk in return for compensation.

Kahneman and Tversky bring their insights together by depicting a *prospect theory value function* to capture our subjective perceptions of value, as illustrated in Figure 3.

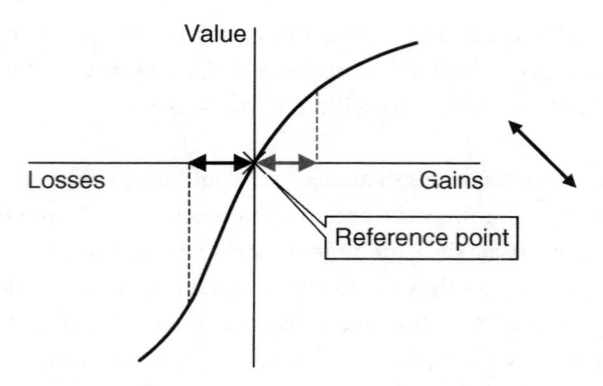

3. The prospect theory value function.

Many of the phenomena identified in this chapter can be seen in the prospect theory value function. It is anchored around a reference point (not necessarily zero). The value function has a sigmoid shape and is not symmetrical around the reference point, reflecting the fact that losses have more impact on value than gains. From looking more closely at Figure 3, we can see the disproportionate impact that losses have in our evaluations of value. The double-headed black arrow illustrates a loss. The double-headed grey arrow illustrates a gain equal in magnitude to the loss. The dashed vertical lines are drawn down to the value function to illustrate the impact of the loss versus the gain on value. The black dashed line is much longer than the grey dashed line: a loss of a given magnitude erodes our perceptions of value much more than an equivalent gain increases our perceptions of value. In this way, loss aversion is captured in the value function, to show how people care much more about losses than equivalent gains. When we lose £100 it upsets us much more than it pleases us to win £100.

Regret theory

Even though it has been very influential in behavioural economics, prospect theory (and its variants) is just one theory that behavioural economists have used. There are others, including

Richard Thaler's mental accounting model and regret theory. Mental accounting builds on some of the ideas about framing and context that emerge from prospect theory, but it also relates to planning about the future—we will explore this model in more detail in Chapter 6.

Graham Loomes and Robert Sugden developed regret theory as an alternative to prospect theory. They argue that regret theory gives us a simpler and more intuitive way than prospect theory to resolve some of the behavioural paradoxes and inconsistencies associated with expected utility theory.

What is the essence of regret theory? Regret theory allows for different states of the world—which we cannot know because we cannot predict what will happen tomorrow. The interaction between our choices today and an unknown future come together to determine how much pleasure (or not) our choices give us, in the end. We regret some decisions; we 'rejoice' in others—but whether or not we regret or rejoice is determined by future states of the world, which might be completely beyond our control. This is a key distinguishing feature of regret theory relative to prospect theory. Prospect theory assumes just one possible state of the world whereas regret theory allows two (or more) states, and our evaluations of our own happiness will depend on which state of the world emerges in the end, and also on our anticipations of future regret.

Imagine that you are deciding whether or not to take an umbrella to work, for example. You have no information about what the weather might be like today (say you live in England). Taking an umbrella involves some hassle—it might not fit easily in your bag; if you are a little absent-minded, umbrellas might be one of the objects you frequently lose. If it rains, however, it will be worth the trouble. So your happiness/satisfaction is determined by something completely beyond your control: the English weather. If it rains you will rejoice at your perspicacity in bringing an umbrella with you. If it is sunny you will regret taking the trouble to pack it, especially if you lose it. Happiness is not dependent just on our perceptions, preferences, and choices. Happiness also depends on how we judge our past choices retrospectively, given the state of the world which unfolds *after* we have made our choices—when it is too late to change our mind. We have no control over these states of the world and yet our happiness is very much dependent upon them.

Economists have studied more serious examples, including the siting of nuclear power plants. If a nuclear power plant is sited in an area where, unexpectedly, there is an earthquake and tsunami (as in Japan in 2011), the planners regret their choice. If there is no earthquake they rejoice at their clever choice of location for the plant. Consequences are determined not only by our own choices but also by events in the world around us.

In this chapter and Chapter 4, we have focused on heuristics, biases, behavioural paradoxes, and the behavioural theories designed to explain them. The focus so far has been mainly on the biases that relate to our decisions and choices in risky situations. Behavioural economists have developed a whole additional literature on the types of biases that emerge when we are deciding over time. Time and risk do interact of course, but for the purpose of this book we will keep it simple and in Chapter 6 we will focus just on the biases that emerge over time.

Chapter 6
Taking time

In Chapters 4 and 5, we focused on risky choices. Another important dimension of our decisions is our attitude towards time. Are we patient? Are we impatient? Or does it depend on the situation? Many of our everyday decisions unfold over time, and what we want today is not always consistent with what we might want tomorrow. How do real people deal with time, and with current decisions that have important future consequences? We are not always good at saving for our pensions in the future. We may struggle to cope with energy bills because we are too fond of turning up the heating or air conditioning, when feeling a little too cold or too hot, without thinking very hard about the consequences in terms of future energy bills. In staying healthy too, we are not always good at planning for the future: with unhealthy habits and lifestyles today we are often storing up health problems for the future.

Standard economic theory does allow that people are different in terms of their *time preference*—or their levels of patience versus impatience. For most economists, people's time preferences can differ *between* individuals but they should be stable *within* individuals. In standard economics, if someone is impatient to get something today and cannot wait until tomorrow, then they will exhibit the same impatience if they are choosing over the same time interval (one day) but rolled forward into the future. This is *time consistency*—our levels of patience versus impatience do not change over time; they are stable. For example, if I am given a choice between chocolate cake today or chocolate cake tomorrow and I choose chocolate cake today then, if I am time consistent, my preference should not change if this same set of choices is rolled forward a year. I should also prefer chocolate cake in a year over chocolate cake in a year and a day. My choices do not change when I am deciding for the near future versus the distant future.

Nor does the standard approach preclude *different* people from making different choices—for example, one person deciding to have their cake sooner rather than later; another later rather than sooner. Again, this is not necessarily inconsistent. Decisions to consume and spend in the very short-term may be strictly rational and consistent, especially if you are facing immediate financial problems and/or your life expectancy is low. For most economists, if people are consistent in favouring smaller rewards sooner over larger rewards later, then they are still strictly rational.

In a study of military personnel and their pension choices, economists Warren and Pleeter found significant individual differences. Military personnel were given two choices: they could take either a large, one-off, lump-sum payment or a small annual payment (an 'annuity') but continuing for the rest of their lives. Warren and Pleeter found that around 51 per cent of the officers chose the lump-sum payment but a much higher proportion of the enlisted personnel—92 per cent—took the lump-sum payment. Warren and Pleeter analysed the data and found that there were significant variations across different groups: white, female, and college-educated groups were more likely to take the annuity. This evidence shows that there are differences across people—which is not a sign of time inconsistency in itself because standard economic theory does not preclude different people having different levels of patience versus impatience. So what can behavioural economics add?

What is time inconsistency?

Behavioural economics draws on evidence from psychology suggesting that the consistency in time preferences, as assumed in standard economic approaches, does not apply for humans (and other animals). We are *disproportionately* impatient in the short-term (we want our chocolate cake today) but when planning for the future, we are more patient (we are prepared to wait a year and a day for our chocolate cake). This is *time inconsistency*—our preferences for delayed outcomes are shifting over time. Our time preferences are not stable. We suffer from *present bias*—we have a disproportionate preference for smaller, immediate rewards over delayed but larger rewards—a reflection of underlying time inconsistency. Our capacity for patience is shifting over time. We are patient in some contexts, but impatient in others. For example—if we have £10 and we are deciding about spending it today, or saving it until next week, we are more likely to spend it today. When we are thinking about more distant decisions, we might be more patient—if we are thinking about spending £10 in a year, or saving it to spend in a year plus one week, then our choices may shift, and we will plan to save for that extra week. Trouble emerges when our impatience today means we have nothing left to spend or save in a year's time, in a decade's time, or when we retire.

Animal models

Some of the early evidence about time inconsistency comes from *animal models*—which draw parallels between our behaviour and other animals' behaviour. Psychiatrist and psychologist George Ainslie observed time inconsistency in a study of pigeons' impulse control. Pigeons were held in a chamber. They could get some food by pecking at keys illuminated with either red or green lights. If they pecked the key when the red light was on, the food rewards were smaller but came sooner. If the green light was on, the rewards were larger but the pigeons had to wait. The pigeons quickly learnt the difference between the rewards they got from pressing green versus red keys, but they were also impulsive—they preferred to peck when the key was red, to get their food more quickly. Other animal behaviourists have identified more constructive, long-term planning behaviour among animals, however. Biologists Mulcahy and Call observed bonobos and orangutans selecting and saving tools to use later, suggesting that they were planning their future actions. Scrub jays and other animals will save and store food too.

Why are we more patient when planning for a distant future? Scott Rick and George Loewenstein explain this in terms of the relative tangibility of benefits versus costs. Today's temptations are hard to resist. Resisting temptation involves tangible short-term costs, and these stop us from achieving future goals. There are numerous examples—dieting, going to the gym, and giving up smoking. We have to forgo an immediate, tangible pleasure—say, of eating chocolate or smoking a cigarette. Or we have to incur some immediate discomfort (e.g. going to the gym and working out). Future goals can seem distant and less tangible, making it harder to exert self-control today. When people fail to control immediate temptations, it can lead to serious problems such as obesity, and drug and gambling addictions, all of which have serious impacts on individuals, families, and public health systems.

The famous *marshmallow experiments*, conducted by psychologist Walter Mischel and his team, illustrate this phenomenon in children's choices. Walter Mischel and his team offered children a range of sweet treats (including marshmallows). If the children were able to resist the temptation to take one treat immediately, they would be rewarded with a second treat later on. The children were able to wait longer if they were distracted, and they also employed their own ways of distracting themselves from temptation. There was also a link with the children's future life chances. The children who were better able to resist temptation demonstrated superior emotional and cognitive function as teenagers, and were more socially and academically competent as adults. The marshmallow experiments inspired Hollywood scriptwriters to create a fictionalized example. In the movie *The Five Year Engagement*, Violet, a psychologist (played by Emily Blunt), decides that her sous chef fiancé Tom (played by Jason Segal) is feckless because he is unable to resist the temptation to eat stale donuts rather than to wait for fresh ones. (Towards the end of the movie, when Tom discovers that Violet had judged him in this way, he defends his behaviour by arguing that there might be all sorts of other reasons to eat stale donuts.)

Intertemporal tussles

Evidence from the marshmallow experiments and other similar studies suggests that our temptations generate internal conflicts. It is as if we are in a struggle with ourselves—as if we have two personalities: a patient self and an impatient self, and these selves are in conflict. Economist Robert Strotz drew on Ainslie's evidence to develop early economic insights about time inconsistency, connecting with this idea of intrapersonal conflict. He postulated that we faced an *intertemporal tussle* between our patient and our impatient selves. While Strotz set out his ideas in great technical detail, it is also an idea that has a lot of intuitive power. Most of us procrastinate about something; many of us probably procrastinate about going to the gym. Our patient self worries about the future—and the impact of a lack of exercise on our future healthiness. Our impatient self likes a comfortable life now, and prefers to sit on the sofa eating chocolate and chips. The net impact will depend on which self dominates.

Neuroeconomic analyses of immediate versus delayed rewards

Neuroscientific tools can be used to capture some of our neural responses when we are facing choices between delayed versus immediate rewards. Sam McClure and colleagues used functional magnetic resonance imaging (fMRI)—a technique for monitoring oxygenated blood flow through the brain and underlying neural areas. They were inspired by Aesop's fable of the ant and the grasshopper to develop a multiple-selves model. The patient ant works hard in the summer, collecting food. The impatient grasshopper enjoys himself by singing away the summer. No prizes for guessing who wins out in the end—when winter comes, the grasshopper begs the ant for food because he is dying of hunger, and the ant tells him to get lost and sing away the winter as he had sung away the summer.

Do we have something like an intertemporal tussle between our ant and our grasshopper selves when we are deciding about immediate versus delayed rewards? To find out, McClure and colleagues asked their experimental participants to value immediate rewards and delayed rewards during a brain scan. They identified different neural activations depending on the timing of rewards. Neural areas associated with high-level cognitive functioning were activated more strongly for delayed rewards. Neural areas associated with more primitive, impulsive instincts were activated more strongly for immediate rewards. They concluded that different neural processes are interacting when we confront choices between immediate, smaller rewards versus delayed, larger rewards, and this could reflect intrapersonal conflicts between multiple selves—a patient planner and an impatient short-termist.

The neuroeconomic evidence is mixed, however. Paul Glimcher and colleagues tested some of the McClure team's assertions. Glimcher's team adjusted the experiment so *all* choices were delayed. The earliest rewards were available only after a sixty-day delay. They found the same patterns as for the McClure study of immediate rewards. Glimcher's team concluded that their evidence demonstrated that time inconsistency is not a reflection of impulsiveness and intertemporal tussles between multiple selves. It is ordinary temptation, and this can be explained in terms of a single self with coherent beliefs and goals.

Pre-commitment strategies and self-control

What is the solution to these self-control problems? Partly it depends on our self-awareness. Ted O'Donoghue and Matthew Rabin argue that some people have more insight into their behaviour than others and they distinguish two broad types: naïve and sophisticated decision-makers—*naïfs* and *sophisticates*. These different types of people will respond to time inconsistency in different ways. Both types will suffer present bias, but the *sophisticates* will be aware that their capacity for self-control is limited, and will implement strategies to force themselves along a more constructive path.

O'Donoghue and Rabin illustrate with an example of students choosing movie trips—the students like to go to the movies on Saturday nights but they have to work on one weekend in the next four because they have an important essay to finish within the month. They have to decide which Saturday they will work instead of going to the movies. O'Donoghue and Rabin set the problem up so that not all the movies in the next four weeks will be the same—the movie in the first week is mediocre, in the next week is good, for the third week it is excellent, and the movie in four weeks will be the best—an outstanding Johnny Depp movie. The optimal choice would be to get the essay done in the first week and go to all the better movies in the subsequent weeks, including the outstanding movie in the fourth week.

The trouble is that students might not have the self-control necessary to ensure this, but the *sophisticates* may do a better job of balancing the trade-offs. The *naïfs* will under-estimate their future self-control problems completely and will procrastinate until the last Saturday and, because they will have an essay to write, they will miss the best, Johnny Depp movie. The *sophisticates* will suffer self-control problems too and will procrastinate a little (they might go to see the mediocre movie in the first week) but they will also have the insight to realize that they might procrastinate too much and miss the best movie. So they prepare themselves by getting the essay done in the second week because they realize that, if they leave it until later, they risk missing out on the Johnny Depp movie. This links to what behavioural economists call a *pre-commitment strategy*: *sophisticates* limit their menu of future choices in order to achieve their long-term goals.

The idea of binding ourselves to ensure we stay on a constructive path is an age-old phenomenon captured in classical literature. In Homer's *Odyssey*, Odysseus (also known as Ulysses) is sailing past the Sirens—mythical creatures who lure sailors to their destruction with their songs. Odysseus ties himself to the mast of his ship while his crew—deafened by wax plugged in their ears—is able to sail by, leaving Odysseus to listen to the Sirens' sweet songs without being seduced into sinking his ship. J. W. Waterhouse illustrated this classical story in his famous painting *Ulysses and the Sirens*—shown in Figure 4. Ulysses' forward-looking self is binding his impatient short-termist self in his attempt to survive.

Coleridge is another example—he realized well the destructive consequences of his opium addiction, so he hired servants to keep him out of opium dens—a far-sighted attempt to bind his immediate desires to indulge his drug habit.

Natural experiments illustrate self-commitment behaviours too. As explained in Chapter 1, natural experiments study real choices and behaviours, not artificial, hypothetical choices as many experimenters are forced to do. DellaVigna and Malmendier studied a set of real data on gym membership. Attendance records showed that people were paying thousands of dollars on annual memberships and then going to the gym only a couple of times—even though they could save a lot of money by using the

4. Ulysses pre-committing himself to resist the Sirens' calls.

cheaper pay-as-you-go option offered by the gym. On the surface, we might think that only a stupid person would pay a lot of money for a gym membership they rarely use—but many of us do exhibit this type of behaviour, and maybe it is not so stupid. Some behavioural economists interpret it as a type of pre-commitment strategy: by spending a lot on a gym membership, we are trying to force our impatient self to be more responsible in the short-term. Our patient self reasons that, if we have spent a lot of money, even our short-termist self will not want to waste it.

Modern businesses now offer services designed around the insight that people's self-control is not perfect. Resisting the temptation of short-term rewards is hard and many of us are prepared to buy our way out of temptation. There are many examples in the dieting world, and also in quitting aids for smokers—most recently e-cigarettes. For anyone who ever has trouble getting up in the morning, they can buy themselves a roaming alarm clock. The original product—Clocky—is an alarm clock that runs around the room so you have to chase it to turn it off, and hopefully by then you will have woken up properly.

The growth of online services has also delivered some pre-commitment services, including Bee-minder and Stikk. The latter offers a service to help people manage their limited self-control problems using financial incentives. Stikk users define their goal online. This forms the basis of a *commitment contract*: if users do not achieve their commitments, then they are charged and the money goes to their chosen beneficiary. Users can make their least favourite charity the beneficiary. If they fail to achieve their goal, a Democrat voter might commit to giving money to the Republicans. Stikk does rely on honest participants, but dishonesty in itself is often a short-termist strategy and how can Stikk devise a watertight contract given that they would find it impossibly difficult and costly to check on their own users' honesty?

BeeMinder is a similar service but with a different underlying business model. BeeMinder offers 'in-your-face' goal tracking for 'flexible self-control'. Like Stikk, their customers set themselves goals to form the basis of their commitment contract with BeeMinder. If they fail to achieve their goal, then BeeMinder charges them. These services can have a powerful impact, especially if they leverage modern technology as a way around the dishonesty problem seen with Stikk. A truly committed BeeMinder client can connect their exercise goals to output from personal fitness monitoring gadgets such as FitBits and iWatches. Technology provides the monitor.

Behavioural life cycle models

If we are not good at saving our money, if our pension pots are not sufficient for us to look after ourselves after retirement, then this will have implications for government budgets and debt. These patterns are explored in behavioural life cycle models, developing David Laibson's insights about how we are disproportionately better at looking after our *golden eggs*—our illiquid stores of wealth which most people hold mainly in the form of pensions and housing wealth—than we are at managing our credit card bills.

Behavioural life cycle models blend behavioural insights about time inconsistency with standard life cycle models assuming time consistency, to study how our patterns of saving, investment, and spending evolve over our lifetimes. George-Marios Angeletos and colleagues used these models in explaining why people might simultaneously hold a lot of credit card debt alongside large stores of illiquid wealth in the form of housing or pensions.

Transaction costs are part of the explanation. Selling a house to settle credit card bills is a complex and expensive process. People have credit cards as a buffer against unexpected bills but, for Angeletos and his colleagues, that is not enough to explain it. They simulate patterns of spending and saving by making some assumptions to match the average experiences of people today, for example that a person will live for a maximum of ninety years, and will work for an average of forty-three years, with household sizes varying over a lifetime as people leave home, marry and have families, and then retire. Then Angeletos and his colleagues use actual data on key variables such as interest rates and employment rates to match their simulations against real-world data about spending and saving patterns. Their findings are consistent with behavioural theories of time inconsistency: the simulated patterns assuming time inconsistency matched real-world macroeconomic trends better than simulated patterns from models incorporating standard economic assumptions about time consistency.

Choice bracketing, framing, and mental accounting

In deciding about consuming today versus tomorrow, the context of our decisions plays a crucial role. For example, as explained in Chapter 5, if a decision is framed as a loss then the final choice may be different from the choice taken when a decision is framed as a gain. How our choices are bracketed together influences our final decision. This forms the basis of another explanation for choices that might seem inconsistent: *choice bracketing*. When we face many complex but related decisions, we may simplify our task by bracketing our choices together.

Richard Thaler developed some of these insights in his model of *mental accounting*. Mental accounting helps to explain why we might not always save as much as we could or should. Framing, reference points, and loss aversion will all determine our perception of our potential spending and saving decisions. Thaler defines mental accounting as the set of cognitive operations we use to organize, assess, and track our financial decisions. Thaler argues that we do not treat all money as equivalent. Money is not *fungible*—we do not perceive it to be exactly the same thing no matter when and where we spend it. How we think about our money and how we spend it will depend on the context in which we win or earn it. We have a set of separate mental accounts and, in our minds, we assign different choices to different accounts. There is a windfall account for money we acquire through lucky events (lottery winnings and other chance events); an income account for the money we earn; and an illiquid wealth account for the money we save.

Our decisions about our money will depend on which mental account we perceive is most relevant. If we win money in a lottery, we might splurge on a treat. If we earned the same money through hard work, then we might be more likely to save it. If we spend large amounts of money online shopping using our credit card, we will perceive that to be cheaper in some sense than paying cash. We treat purchases on credit very differently to cash purchases—possibly partly reflecting poor forward planning too.

Mental accounting means that our evaluation of our economic decisions will depend on the context. We will bracket our choices together and combine choices in our minds. How we perceive a bargain is not determined purely by what we are buying—sometimes the process of shopping, or of finding a bargain, has a value in itself. Thaler illustrates with the example of a woman buying a quilt: all quilts cost the same regardless of size, yet she will buy the biggest quilt even if it is too large for her bed.

Colin Camerer and colleagues explore another manifestation of bracketing: income bracketing and targeting by New York City cab drivers. Camerer and his team were able to get hold of a cab company's daily records of cab drivers' trip sheets and so were able to study working patterns and earnings. Standard economic theory predicts that the cab drivers should maximize their daily earnings, bringing in more on busy days and less on quiet days. They discovered something surprising, however: the cab drivers did not earn more on the busy days. Rather than maximizing their earnings, they were working towards a target and so on busy days they allowed themselves to finish early. Camerer and colleagues offered another explanation too—perhaps cab-drivers were using income targeting as a form of pre-commitment. If a cab driver pre-commits herself to a steady income over time then she will not work extra on busy days because her impatient self might be tempted to splurge her extra income on frivolous spending and trips down the pub. If instead she is working towards a steady target each day, working longer hours on quiet days and shorter hours on busy days, then once in a while, instead of being tempted into excessive spending, she can go home for an early night.

Behavioural development economics

Insights about time inconsistency have been applied in the developing world too. Esther Duflo and her team have used a range of randomized controlled trials (RCTs) to improve agricultural output for poor rural farmers. As explained in Chapter 1, RCTs are a technique borrowed from the medical sciences, where they are used in clinical trials to test the efficacy of drug and other medical interventions. RCTs involve separating participants into two or more groups: a treatment group and a control group. The participants in the control group receive no intervention. The treatment group receives a policy intervention and, to test whether or not the intervention has had an impact, the outcomes for the treatment group are compared to the outcomes for the control group.

In one of their experimental trials, Duflo and her team focused on Kenyan farmers purchasing fertilizer. Fertilizer is relatively expensive in poor rural communities, but if farmers are able to save then they can usually afford the small fixed costs of purchasing fertilizer. The problem in many poor rural regions of the developing world is that the financial infrastructure needed to enable savings (i.e. banks and building societies) does not exist. Without the capacity for saving, farmers may not have the money needed to buy fertilizer because they have to wait for harvest time for their money (a standard economic problem) and cannot use savings from previous harvest income. Another problem might be farmers' present bias: they may procrastinate and postpone their fertilizer purchases. Either way, their agricultural yields will be much lower than they would have been had they bought fertilizer earlier. If, however, the farmers are offered small, time-limited discounts on fertilizer to overcome present bias, and just after the harvest when they have the money to pay for them, then they are more likely to buy the fertilizer they need, leading to significant gains in their agricultural productivity and annual earnings.

Research into time inconsistency and present bias by psychologists, neuroscientists, and evolutionary biologists, as well as behavioural economists and economic psychologists, is some of the most important research in behavioural economics. Most of us know that we struggle to resist temptation, and the standard economic model does not really help us very much because of its unrealistic assumption that we are always cleverly able to make decisions that promote our long-term welfare. Understanding why many people do not behave in a way that is consistent with their own long-term best interests, and what to do about it, is a key challenge for behavioural economists and policy-makers, and the time inconsistency research has a lot to add to these debates.

Chapter 7
Personalities, moods, and emotions

Economists often assume that all people are super-clever and able easily to choose well. As explained in earlier chapters, however, psychological biases lead us to make mistakes more often than standard economics predicts. So far though we have not focused strongly on the underlying psychological reasons, and in this chapter we will explain how and why psychological factors such as personality, mood, and emotions affect our economic and financial decision-making.

This chapter shows the important impacts that personality and emotions have on our working lives, educational attainments, and financial decisions. Some of us are thrill-seekers, looking out for risky opportunities whether in extreme sports, gambling, or financial trading. Others may be risk-averse and cautious—always preferring the safe options. A person who has personality traits associated with higher levels of self-control is able to resist the temptation to spend his money sooner, and is also able to make better life decisions about education and employment.

Personality and emotions have complex impacts because economic circumstances may also feedback into people's emotional states. Moods and emotions will play a role. We are often predisposed to feel particular moods and emotions, driven partly by our personality traits. If we have a more depressed personality, we may be more inclined to feel despondent and resentful when we are cheated in an economic transaction. If we are impulsive, we may be quicker to feel anger, making us more vulnerable to conflicts with our colleagues, friends, and families, and this may affect the opportunities available to us.

Measuring personality

Economic researchers have been slow to incorporate personality into their analyses, perhaps partly because personality is not easy to measure. Psychologists use a wide range of personality tests but economists, so far at least, have used a relatively narrow range. The OCEAN tests are some of the most commonly used tests in behavioural economics. OCEAN was devised by Paul Costa and Robert McCrae and based around the Big Five Model—capturing traits across five dimensions: **O**penness to experience, **C**onscientiousness, **E**xtraversion, **A**greeableness, and **N**euroticism.

Behavioural economists often use cognitive functioning tests too. As for personality, there is a wide range of cognitive functioning tests. One old and widely known cognitive functioning test is Eysenck's (not necessarily particularly accurate) Intelligence Quotient (IQ) test. Behavioural economists in a hurry can use Frederick's cognitive reflexivity test (CRT), which includes questions such as this one: 'A bat and a ball cost $1.10 in total. The bat costs $1.00 more than the ball. How much does the ball cost?' (Think slowly! And see 'References and further reading' for the answer.) The CRT is designed to capture cognitive functioning but also correlates well with people's time and risk preferences. Some people, including highly intelligent people, will jump to an answer, because they are impatient and so do not allow themselves time to think through carefully to the correct answer.

Capturing personality traits is not easy because they are usually measured using self-report questionnaires. These are susceptible to many sources of bias. Experimental participants often want to give answers that make them look good, or impress the experimenter. Feedback between a person's personality and their performance can complicate the results. A neurotic person who is more likely to feel anxious may perform less well in cognitive tests, again not because of impaired ability but because the context of the tests unsettles them. IQ tests require effort and researchers cannot easily discover whether poor performance is a function of a lack of ability, a lack of motivation, or a mixture of both. What experimental participants are paid (or not) will also affect their personality measurements. When children are offered treats, their performance in IQ tests improves—the treats do not make children cleverer, but they do motivate them to try harder. Adults are affected by motivation too. Emotionally stable, conscientious participants may be less affected by additional external incentives such as money payments—and so measuring their cognitive functioning may be easier.

Personality and preferences

Once we have measured a person's personality, what are the economic implications? Economists often assume that people's choices are driven by their preferences, and personality plays a role. An empathetic person is probably more likely to make altruistic choices. Impulsive people are more likely to be impatient and may not be so good at saving up for their retirement, for example. Venturesome people are more likely to take risks, which might lead them into particular choices—they will be more likely to gamble and/or take risky jobs.

Genes also play a role. David Cesarini and colleagues studied twins—identical twins (with the same genes) and non-identical twins (with different genes). They compared the two groups to pick up the impacts of variations in genetic versus environmental factors on risk preferences. Only 20 per cent of the variation in generosity and risk-seeking behaviours across the different twins could be attributed to genetic factors. In one study, Cesarini and colleagues found that about 16 to 34 per cent of the variations in the twins' over-confidence was linked to genetic make-up. In another study of pension plans, they found that 25 per cent of the variations in the riskiness of financial portfolios selected by twins could be attributed to genetic factors.

Personality and cognition

Our personalities have an impact on many of our economic and financial decisions and choices. Often making decisions requires some thought, and our personality traits can determine our cognitive skills and, through our cognition, drive our choices. The consequences often unfold over a lifetime because they determine our academic achievements, job performance, and social skills. If a conscientious person is inclined to be more patient, then they may also be more willing to save for their retirement and/or invest in themselves, for example by getting a good education.

In Chapter 6 we looked at Walter Mischel's marshmallow experiments and the evidence correlating a child's ability to exert self-control and resist temptation with her later success. Mischel and colleagues found that children who were able to resist temptation were more successful later in life. Other studies have shown that the children who were less able to resist temptation were more likely to engage in criminality later in life.

Lex Borghans and colleagues also conducted some very thorough research into personality and life chances. They found that conscientiousness was correlated with academic achievement, job performance, leadership, and longevity. But there is not one unique set of personality traits that guarantees us success in our economic and social lives. Different personality traits are valuable in different places. At work, we generally prefer to have trustworthy colleagues. At a party, we are probably more interested in whether or not someone has a sense of humour. Different personalities suit different jobs. When we are ill, we want our doctors to be empathetic and reliable with good cognitive skills so they are able easily to make an accurate link between our symptoms and their diagnosis. On the other hand, when we go to a restaurant, we want our chefs to be inventive and inspired—we might even believe that they will create more delicious food if they are temperamental, imaginative, and volatile. We probably do not want our doctors to be temperamental, imaginative, or volatile.

Personality in childhood

Personality affects our lives from a very early age, and personality and cognition in very young children can be malleable. Environment has an important influence. Lex Borghans and colleagues found that children adopted by parents with high socio-economic status have larger gains in IQ points than children whose adoptive parents are from lower socio-economic groups. Children from disadvantaged backgrounds can also be helped by access to good childcare centres and home visits. These interventions are designed to help children develop good cognitive skills, but they also succeed in effectively boosting social and personality skills. Well-designed educational interventions can help children to develop complex skills requiring effort and practice. Once they have acquired these skills, then their economic success later in life will hopefully be improved too.

Personality and motivation can be as crucial to early success as cognitive ability and IQ. Economics Nobel laureate Jim Heckman and colleagues studied some of these influences using evidence from a US study of educational interventions—the HighScope Perry Preschool Study. This scheme was designed for children from disadvantaged African-American backgrounds. The curriculum focused on developing the children's cognitive and socio-emotional skills via active, open-ended learning and problem solving. Heckman and his team monitored the children's subsequent success and compared their outcomes to those of a control group (who had not had access to the HighScope intervention).

The positive impacts from this intervention declined as the children got older, and the benefits for disadvantaged children were much higher than for other groups. Heckman and his colleagues estimated that the benefits from the interventions were large. The children on the scheme went on to do much better in adulthood. They were less likely to get a criminal record or be dependent on benefits later in life. They achieved more highly in terms of their educational attainment, employability, and earnings. Heckman and his team estimated that the overall rate of return from the investment in the HighScope intervention was around 7–10 per cent. These days, most advanced economy governments can borrow at rates around 1 per cent and lower; if Heckman's figures are indicative, a government willing to borrow some money to spend on similar educational interventions, especially those targeted specifically at disadvantaged groups, will be spending public money wisely.

Emotions, moods, and visceral factors

Economist Jon Elster is one of the pioneers in the study of how moods and emotions affect economic decision-making. What is the difference between moods and emotions? Elster describes emotions as having a target, while moods are more diffuse and less directed. Moods may also be collectively experienced and in this sense moods are less affected by personality traits than emotions. We will say some more about moods in the macroeconomy in Chapter 8 because moods link to confidence and sentiment, both of which are key drivers of macroeconomic fluctuations and financial market instability.

Emotions, especially our social emotions, can be more highly evolved than our basic instincts. Even so, economists often think of emotions as an irrational element in our decision-making. Challenging this assumption, Elster and others explain how emotions and rationality can complement each other. Emotions are important 'tie-breakers' when we are feeling indecisive. Emotions often help us to decide efficiently because they can operate quickly. But in other situations they are not so helpful—for example, we often feel fear when we confront risky, uncertain situations and this can paralyse us when we need to act.

The affect heuristic

Emotions have a complicated impact on our economic and financial choices, but we can understand these complexities better by connecting emotions and heuristics. As explained in Chapter 4, heuristics are quick decision-making rules and often they guide us well, but sometimes they lead us into mistakes. Biases emerge when people use the availability heuristic, focusing on information that is easy to remember whilst ignoring less memorable, but potentially more important, objective information. Emotions play a role in this too. Emotions are more easily accessible and available to us than objective facts and figures. Emotions are often vivid and we can remember them more easily. They are also associated with quicker, more automatic responses. Emotions affect memories and so will determine what is remembered and what is forgotten. So we use emotions to guide our actions—they are integral to a type of heuristic known as the *affect heuristic*.

Emotions and the affect heuristic can also interfere with our cognitive processing. This is something that advertisers and sensationalist journalism exploit. Vivid imagery is easy to remember. When we see vivid, frightening depictions, for example of plane hijacks and crashes, it might lead us to decide to avoid plane flights when it is in fact more risky to take a train. People who have witnessed horrific car crashes may have distorted perceptions of the risk of driving, reflecting their previous emotional responses on witnessing accidents. This may lead them to decide not to drive a car, when the chances of an accident as a pedestrian are greater.

Basic instincts and visceral factors

Elster distinguishes emotions from *visceral factors*. Visceral factors link to our basic instincts, for example hunger and thirst. They are innate and often operate beyond our conscious control. Visceral factors are like emotions in that they help us to decide quickly. They are essential to human survival and basic daily functioning, but they are also powerful and can crowd out our other goals because they are more primitive and hard-wired, and less evolved than our emotions.

Amongst others, psychologist Joseph le Doux and behavioural economist George Loewenstein have done a lot of work explaining how emotions and visceral factors contribute to self-destructive behaviour. Loewenstein argues that we are more shortsighted and selfish when our visceral factors are driving us, and we are less altruistic when visceral factors are intense. They limit our capacity for empathy too: when deciding for others, we ignore/under-weight their visceral factors. We imagine that others experience our visceral factors in the same way that we experience them, yet we also under-estimate the impact of other people's visceral factors on their behaviour. Visceral factors can help to explain why we indulge in risk-taking and self-destructive behaviours, such as addiction. Partly the problem is that our visceral factors are magnified in our modern, artificial environments. Today's technologies allow us to make many of our decisions much, much more quickly than our distant ancestors could because we have computers and the Internet. For most people in advanced economies, food is abundant, and quick to buy and eat, as are many addictive substances. In the modern world, we may no longer want or need to be driven by quick, instinctive impulses. Problems are compounded when we lack insight into the role that visceral factors play in our decisions when we under-weight or ignore them.

All this means that visceral factors can have confusing and complicated impacts on our decisions and choices. They may conflict with our higher level cognitive functioning, and they may disrupt our interactions and relationships with other people. Neuroscientist Jonathan Cohen has a relatively optimistic view of this. He argues that, in evolutionary terms, we have been quite adaptable. Reason and control developed at the same time as our social and physical environments changed rapidly, and our old emotional processes became maladapted as technology developed. Impulsive, emotional responses may have played an important survival role when we were hunter-gatherers—basic resources were scarce and perishable, so quick, instinctive action was essential to avoid starvation. In a modern context these instincts may not serve a useful purpose and may in fact generate perverse behaviour such as addictions. Cohen argues that, in spite of all this maladaptation, evolution has 'vulcanized' and strengthened the brain so that reason and control can balance primitive emotional responses. As such, it has allowed humans to develop some of the pre-commitment devices mentioned in Chapter 6—for example, savings plans, smokers' nicotine gum, and e-cigarettes. In this way, our brains have evolved to moderate the influence of impulsive, self-destructive, emotional decision-making.

The somatic marker hypothesis

Neuroscientist Antonio Damasio also takes a more positive view of the role emotions play in driving our choices. Emotions are associated with important physiological cues manifested in our bodily responses—what Damasio calls *somatic markers*. Knowledge from somatic markers is communicated via our emotions, and sometimes this helps us to make better decisions faster—as noted earlier, emotions drive the affect heuristic.

Somatic markers may be the outcome of conscious thought. More often, though, they operate unconsciously. For example, if we have been burnt in a fire, when we see fires we become fearful and so we stay away. This is an example of how somatic markers translate into emotions that trigger actions. Other somatic markers are more conscious—for example, the gut feel of entrepreneurs who just 'know' intuitively that an investment will work well—in some senses gut feel represents conscious feelings about choices and plans. When experts have a hunch—for example, when a doctor suspects that their patient is suffering from a specific disease without being able to set out their reasoning clearly—they just have a feeling or intuition that represents the sum of all their knowledge and experience.

Damasio and his colleagues focus their research on patients with brain damage, including one of history's best-known lesion patients—Phineas Gage, who worked on the railroads in the USA. One day an iron rod shot into his brain. In one way, Phineas Gage was very lucky—he recovered with no obvious external physical damage. However, the accident had damaged his frontal lobe (usually associated with higher level cognitive functioning). As well as making significant changes to his personality, this brain damage impaired Phineas Gage's working ability. He eventually lost his job and suffered various other economic and emotional hardships. Antonio Damasio saw similar patterns in his own patients, including Elliot, who had suffered frontal lobe damage after an operation to remove a brain tumour. Like Phineas Gage, Elliot's basic cognitive functioning was good in many ways, but he became extremely obsessive. His emotional responses were impaired and, apart from the social consequences, this affected his economic life too because he found it very difficult to make choices when faced with a range of options. Damasio suggests that this is because emotions help us to decide between different options: Elliot's damaged emotional responses were connected with his inability to choose and decide. The constraints on his emotional responses severely impaired his productivity at work.

Attributing these behaviours to emotional influences is difficult, however, because emotions are not easy to measure and observe.

Dan Ariely and his team devised a novel way to try and capture emotional influences by giving experimental participants visual information—in colour and in black and white. Their idea was that coloured pictures are more vivid and therefore can trigger a stronger emotional response. They also manipulated their participants' perceptions via a series of 'priming' exercises: they asked the participants to recall different events in their past in which their emotions had helped them to make good decisions. The participants were also asked to recall events in their past in which their cognitive capacity had helped them to choose well. Then the participants were given a series of choices for different products. They found that when participants did not have great faith in their own cognitive capacity, they relied more on emotions; when they trusted their feelings, they also relied more on emotions; and when they had colour photos, they relied more on emotions. Ariely's team found that the participants were more likely to choose consistently when they were deciding about products eliciting a stronger emotional response. This evidence confirms some of Antonio Damasio and others' insights about emotions: they can have a positive impact and can help us to make good decisions. Emotions are not irrational.

Dual-system models

How can we reconcile all these differing views about whether or not emotions are useful? Some of the complexities and apparent contradictions are reconciled in *dual-system models*—which capture the interactions between emotion/affect versus cognition. In *Thinking, Fast and Slow*, Daniel Kahneman summarizes the work he has done in this area, and its connection with his earlier work with Amos Tversky on heuristics, bias, and prospect theory—as explored in Chapters 4 and 5. He envisages our thinking processes as a type of map, separating two main different decision-making systems—the automatic, quick, and intuitive System 1; and the cognitive, deliberative, controlled System 2.

The research on systems thinking in behavioural economics is large and growing, with many experiments designed to capture some of the influences. Following from the studies of incentives and motivations explored in Chapter 2, Dan Ariely and colleagues explored the idea that money incentives can impair our performance, because they shift our attention from effective automatic processes. For example, professional sports people tend to play better when they are not thinking too hard about how they are moving. Big prizes in high profile international sporting competitions such as Wimbledon can lead to *choking under pressure*. Ariely and his team did some experiments in the USA and India. Their experimental participants worked on different tasks and were paid according to how they performed, but those who were paid most generously did not necessarily perform the best. They postulated that participants choked under pressure when playing for large rewards because these rewards triggered perverse emotional responses and conflicts between affect and cognition, which impaired the participants' performance.

Some behavioural economists develop these ideas as an alternative to the visceral factor models of addiction, described by Loewenstein and le Doux. Both groups of theories are alternatives to the *rational addiction* models of mainstream economists including those from Gary Becker and colleagues, who argued that most of what we do, including addiction, is the outcome of a rational choice. This is hard to reconcile with our personal experiences of addiction. Dual systems models are more intuitively powerful in capturing what drives addiction. One key set of insights is seen in Bernheim and Rangel's model of *hot-cold states*. Our emotions and visceral factors are more likely to overwhelm us when we are in a 'hot' state, feeling stressed, than when we are in a 'cold' state, feeling calm. In a hot state, we are more likely to misjudge situations, and to be susceptible to temptation. For recovering addicts, this can trigger relapses into addiction. David Laibson illustrates with an example of a cocaine addict who was able to recover from his addiction whilst in prison but relapsed as soon as he was released—he was returning to places and cues that he associated with his old addictive habits.

Our emotions have wider impacts too—affecting our political as well as our economic lives. Writing in the UK newspaper *The Telegraph* in advance of the UK's 2016 referendum vote on whether or not Britain should 'Brexit' (i.e. leave the European Union), Daniel Kahneman's insights about how irritation and anger could increase the chances of a Brexit vote were prescient. In the run-up to the vote, emotions dominated the analysis. After a Brexit vote, emotions were heightened again with many 'Remainers' reporting a feeling of depression and loss at an event that did not affect themselves or their families personally, at least not immediately. Perhaps other behavioural influences such as loss aversion were driving emotional responses too.

Emotions in neuroeconomics

Measuring emotions is very complicated, even more so than measuring personality. Neuroscientists have been working on emotions for much longer than economists and some of their tools are useful when studying economic and financial decision-making, and economists and neuroscientists are coming together in an innovative branch of behavioural economics—*neuroeconomics*. Neuroeconomists combine theories and tools from economics and neuroscience. Neuroscience has a lot to offer economists, particularly in the form of new and innovative sources of data. Some experimenters link economic and financial decision-making to measurements of physiological responses—including heart rate, skin conductance and sweat rates, as well as eye tracking. For example Smith and Dickhaut used heart rate data to infer emotional states in auction experiments.

Measuring general physiological responses cannot give us very detailed information about emotional responses. Brain imaging gives richer information, but it also involves expensive and

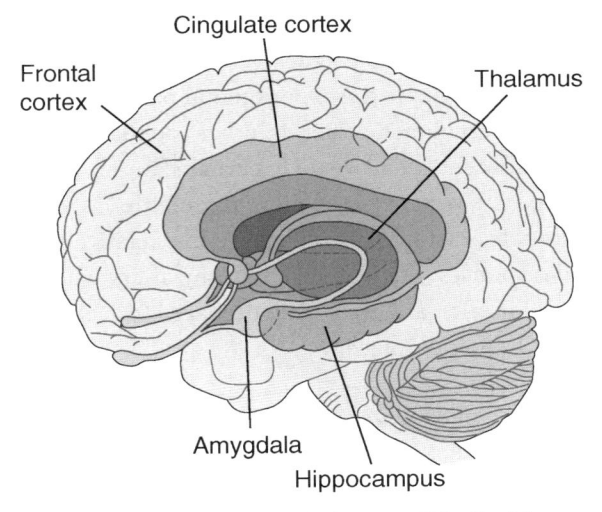

5. Some brain regions. The amygdala is part of the limbic system, a network of interconnected brain structures traditionally associated with the processing of emotion.

complicated techniques. Samples from brain-imaging experiments are usually very small, especially in comparison with the very large sample sizes used in other areas of economics. One of the most commonly used brain-imaging techniques is functional magnetic resonance imaging (fMRI). This has been used in a few neuro-finance experiments, especially to capture links between risky decision-making and emotions. Other experiments have used brain-imaging techniques to study participants' emotional and cognitive responses in social situations, a way to test the dual-systems models described earlier. These experiments are based around a loose categorization of different neural areas and their role in emotional versus cognitive processing.

A classic example is the experiments conducted by Sanfey and colleagues. They used neuroscientific techniques to capture interactions of emotion and cognition when people play the Ultimatum Game, explained in Chapter 3. To recap on the structure of the Ultimatum Game: a proposer makes an offer to a responder, if the responder rejects this offer then neither gets anything. In Sanfey and colleagues' version of this experiment, in some rounds of the game the experimental participants played with people they had met earlier. In other rounds they played against a computer. Unsurprisingly perhaps, unfair offers from human proposers were rejected more frequently than unfair offers from computers. Participants reported some relatively extreme emotional responses. They reported feeling angry when they were made an unfair offer, and they were prepared to sacrifice financial gain to punish their co-player.

The participants in Sanfey's experiments were scanned using fMRI to measure flows of oxygenated blood through different brain areas. Briefly, this sort of brain mapping approach draws on the idea that different brain areas are implicated in different types of thinking. The pre-frontal cortex is a more highly evolved area of the brain usually associated with higher cognitive functioning. Paralleling Kahneman's mapping of different thinking systems, the pre-frontal cortex is implicated in System 2 cognitive and controlled thinking. Figure 5 illustrates the frontal cortex and some of the other brain regions associated with emotional processing—in what is sometimes called the *emotional limbic system.*

Sanfey and colleagues focus on a brain region known as the insula—which is often associated with emotional processing of negative emotional states such as pain, hunger, thirst, anger, and disgust. It is a part of the limbic system but is located deep within the brain and so is not easy to illustrate here. The insula is implicated in the impulsive, automatic styles of decision-making associated with System 1 thinking. For Sanfey and colleagues' study of responses in the Ultimatum Game, they found that the insula was more strongly activated with unfair offers from humans than with those from computers, and the more unfair the offer the greater the insula response. The participants' insula activations also had predictive power: participants with stronger insula activations went on to reject a much larger proportion of the unfair offers. Sanfey and colleagues suggested that perhaps the participants were responding in the same way to unfair offers as they would to a bad smell—unfair treatment was generating a 'moral' type of disgust as well as anger.

The participants' pre-frontal cortex was more strongly activated with unfair offers that were subsequently accepted—perhaps because unfair offers are more difficult to accept and it was taking cognitive strength to overcome an emotional impulse to reject them. Another interesting finding from the Sanfey study was that there seemed to be an umpire in this conflict—an area known as the anterior cingulate cortex, commonly associated with conflict resolution. The cingulate cortex is also illustrated in Figure 5. Perhaps it was activated because it was playing a role in resolving the conflict between the cognitive versus emotional responses. Our cognitive system wants the money; the emotional system wants to punish the proposer if they are mean. The anterior cingulate cortex resolves this intraneural conflict.

Other neuroeconomic studies explore our empathetic responses. Again using brain-imaging techniques, Tania Singer and colleagues conducted some experiments showing that, when experimental participants observe their partner receiving painful electrical shocks, their empathetic responses engage automatic emotional processing circuits including the insula. Empathetic responses seem to be generated by making representations of our own internal feeling states in response to pain observed in others.

Neuroeconomic experiments on financial decision-making

Some neuroeconomic studies explore the impact of emotions on financial markets. Researchers have studied the financial decisions of lesion patients—people who have suffered brain damage. Baba Shiv and colleagues studied the behaviour of a panel of lesion patients and compared it with the decisions of healthy controls. Both groups were asked to play a financial investment game. The healthy participants quickly learnt to select less risky strategies. The lesion patients took much greater risks, but earned significantly more. Other studies have found that people experiencing intense emotional reactions behave differently in financial trading games—Andrew Lo and colleagues found that experimental participants experiencing more extreme emotional responses were less effective as financial traders.

Brain-imaging studies have also shown a relationship between emotional states and traders' behaviour. Brian Knutson and colleagues conducted some brain-scanning studies using fMRI on traders who were choosing between safe and risky stocks. Knutson and colleagues found that emotional processing played an important role in financial decisions: risky choices were associated with activations in a brain area known as the striatum—which is implicated in our processing of rewards, including rewards from risk-taking and addiction. They also found significant differentials in the activation of the insula depending on whether the traders were playing for safe versus risky options. This could reflect the insula's role in negative emotional states, including fear of loss—if fears of loss are associated with risk-avoiding mistakes.

Our hormones may also play a role. Neuroscientist Joe Herbert and economist John Coates were able to conduct a natural experiment looking at the behaviour of a group of London day-traders—traders looking to profit from fluctuations in asset prices over the course of a day.

Coates and Herbert used saliva samples to measure the traders' testosterone and cortisol levels. Testosterone is thought to be associated with greater risk-taking and anti-social behaviour; and cortisol levels are higher when we are feeling more stressed. Coates and Herbert found that the traders' testosterone levels in the morning correlated with their performance later in the day—traders with higher testosterone levels in the morning seemed to earn more profits from their trading over the day. Perhaps this suggests that risk-taking and ruthlessness are driven, at least partly, by our physiology and not by a process of rational calculation as described in standard economic analyses.

Other studies have used insights from psychoanalysis. David Tuckett is a psychoanalyst who has used some of his expertise to study traders' emotions. Tuckett suggests that the financial assets with which traders are preoccupied are not just valuable in money terms. They are what psychoanalysts call *phantastic objects*—objects that their owners believe have superlative, exceptional qualities. Emotional conflict is created when the excitement from making money is separated in time from the panic-inducing fear of losses. Traders make their profits in one phase, and lose their money in another. This might partly explain how a speculative bubble grows: traders forget quickly about past losses. They construct stories and narratives to rationalize their impulsivity. Euphoric booms are followed by emotional oscillations concluding in spectacular collapses of confidence as bubbles burst—triggered initially, according to Tuckett, by traders' emotional conflicts.

This role of emotions in trading behaviour might explain some of the financial instability that impairs macroeconomic performance. In Chapter 8 we explore some of these themes in the context of a relatively new and uncharted territory for behavioural economists—behavioural macroeconomics.

Chapter 8
Behaviour in the macroeconomy

In Chapter 7, we explored the role played by emotions in economic and financial decision-making. When we look at these emotional and psychological factors in aggregate, it has implications for the development of some new macroeconomic models designed to analyse how these socio-psychological influences drive our collective behaviours. The economic behaviour of us all together, as bit players in the macroeconomy, is a crucial issue for policy-makers but it is also the area of economics that is most misunderstood. Since the financial crises of 2007/2008, the credibility of traditional macroeconomic models has been strained. This chapter will explore how behavioural economists can contribute to the development of innovative macroeconomic theories, and to the collection of new types of behavioural macroeconomic data.

Behavioural macroeconomics is a relatively undeveloped field because it suffers from some significant constraints, partly reflecting the difficulty of bringing together the choices of lots of different types of people all with different personalities, experiencing different moods, emotions and deciding in complex ways using a wide range of heuristics generating an even wider range of biases. So behavioural economists tend to focus on the microeconomic behaviour of consumers, workers, business people or policy-makers. Even this is difficult because, as explained in

Chapter 8, it is not easy to measure personality, moods, and emotions. So the analytical task is enormous for behavioural macroeconomists because the problems of behavioural measurement are compounded by the many and complex ways in which individuals interact within a macroeconomy.

When we pull all our choices together, this has implications for headline variables usually the focus of everyday macroeconomic news stories, including employment, unemployment, output and production growth, inflation, and interest rates. Moods and emotions affect the well-being of all of us together, and policy-makers are realizing this more and more. They are designing new macroeconomic policy goals to capture some of these insights. The macroeconomy is no longer solely the territory for economists. Insights from psychology, psychiatry, sociology, medicine, and public health are showing us that the welfare of a nation is not just about the monetary circumstances of its citizens. Later in this chapter we will explore some of these themes.

The psychology of the macroeconomy

Behavioural macroeconomics focuses on how social and psychological factors, including optimism and pessimism, can help us to understand macroeconomic fluctuations. Entrepreneurs are often driven by economy-wide fluctuations in mood and business confidence, and this affects how quickly the businesses grow and whether or not business people are prepared to invest in new business projects—with implications for macroeconomic output and growth. When the business world is feeling optimistic, then this can be a self-fulfilling prophecy, driving rises in national output overall.

Attitudes towards time are important too because macroeconomic fluctuations are driven by people's decisions to consume today or save for the future. Whether consumers are generally patient or impatient determines whether or not they are inclined to spend or save today. If they are more patient and save more, then this can generate funds for entrepreneurs' new investment projects. If consumers are more impatient and consume more, this can boost economic activity in the short-term as businesses expand their production to meet consumers' demands. Business entrepreneurs must decide whether or not to invest in growing their businesses in the future. Put all these decisions together and they have significant implications for the macroeconomy as a whole.

Our psychology will interact with our attitudes towards the future too. Emotion and moods determine whether or not we are inclined to make forward-looking decisions. Hope and optimism, along with confidence, propel economies forward partly because the business entrepreneurs who play a key role in building economies' productive capacity are vulnerable to shifts in confidence and sentiment. The 2016 UK referendum vote on whether or not Britain should leave the European Union (to 'Brexit', or not to 'Brexit') was a stark illustration of this—when the voters to leave (the 'Brexiteers') won, many of those who voted to remain in the EU, amongst them a majority of UK business leaders and economists, were struck by a profound sense of pessimism. The immediate macroeconomic consequences were profound. Along with the economic, political, and financial uncertainty following the vote, the pound plummeted and many investors pulled out of the UK. The negative consequences for the UK economy were felt quickly.

Whether we are patient versus impatient and optimistic versus pessimistic will determine whether or not we feel positive about the future, which in turn will also affect how patient or impatient we are. Tali Sharot, an experimental psychologist, has shown that we seem to be naturally inclined towards optimism—we seem to have evolved a tendency to be over-optimistic with most healthy people being prone to an optimism bias. The EU Referendum also illustrated this tendency—many voters for remaining in the EU expressed surprise and shock at the result, even though many polls, for many weeks, had been predicting that the Brexiteers would win the vote, even if narrowly.

Optimism bias affects public investment in construction and infrastructure too, something recognized by the UK's Audit Office, which monitors government spending on projects. In 2013, the Audit Office conducted a study of over-optimism in the construction sector. It found that it was linked to inflated costs for government projects because planners were not always realistic about the future prospects for their projects, and so they under-estimated costs and were insufficiently realistic about potential delays.

Economists John Ifcher and Homa Zarghamee used two empirical tools to capture some of the links between optimism and patience. They analysed self-reported levels of happiness from the US General Social Survey. Respondents who were in a more positive state of mind were also more patient and reported that they were less likely to 'live for today'. Ifcher and Zarghamee also conducted an experiment to capture the impact of emotions on people's attitudes towards the future. One group was shown happy film-clips—for example, they were asked to watch a stand-up comic's routine. A second group was shown neutral films—for example, clips of wildlife and landscapes. Then all participants were asked to state how much they valued making payments today to invest in their future. The group that had watched the comedy routine exhibited more patience—they valued investments in their future more highly than did the other group, which may suggest that a happy mood makes us more interested in the future.

Early behavioural macroeconomists: Katona, Keynes, and Minsky

The focus on emotions as drivers of macroeconomies is not new. George Katona was one of the forefathers of economic psychology and many of his insights resonate with modern versions of behavioural macroeconomics. He observed that emotional factors (e.g. nervousness or euphoria) can induce shifts in consumer sentiment, investor confidence, and aggregate demand in ways not captured by standard macro economic models.

John Maynard Keynes also had a profound influence. In chapter 12 of his 1936 book *The General Theory of Employment, Interest and Money*, Keynes describes two main sets of actors driving the macroeconomy: speculators and entrepreneurs. Each group has a distinctive personality, and is affected differently by emotions. Financial speculators chase financial returns—they want to maximize their profits from buying and selling financial assets.

Keynes focused his analysis on speculators' behaviour in share and stock markets. The rapid growth of financial technologies, especially since the 1980s, has meant that stocks and shares are not the only risky financial assets available today, but Keynes's basic logic holds in modern financial markets too. Stock markets provide liquidity, which is good in the sense that it provides funds for business entrepreneurs to build their productive capacity, but this liquidity means that stocks and shares are very quick and easy to buy and sell. Financial speculators chase short-term profits and so they focus only on the very short-term fluctuations in share prices. They are also driven strongly by what other speculators are doing.

Keynes postulates that speculators will often believe that others might know more about the potential profits from a stock and so will copy others when they are buying and selling, especially if they are not very sure of market trends. Speculators are preoccupied with what others think because this determines the price they should pay for shares. Speculators are not so worried about a share's fundamental value in terms of what it could earn over its lifetime. They are more worried about the price they will get for the share in the very near future. For this, other speculators' opinions are most important because, potentially, they could be buying the shares tomorrow.

Keynes uses the metaphor of a newspaper *beauty contest* to capture this preoccupation with others' opinions. He describes a competition in which contestants are asked to examine a number of pictures of pretty women, however their task is not to select the one they think is prettiest but the one they think *others* will think is prettiest. Essentially they must second-guess the other contestants' judgements—thus creating a situation of contestants judging what others think others are thinking about others' decisions. For the macroeconomy, Keynes argues that when speculators are following these conventions and playing beauty contest games, then their valuations of shares will have no strong basis in real beliefs. This contributes to instability and volatility—with macroeconomic consequences, because an atmosphere of instability and uncertainty deters the entrepreneurs from investing to build their businesses.

Entrepreneurs are the other group of personalities in Keynes's macroeconomy. For Keynes, business and entrepreneurship are not just about making money—if you want to make money, speculation offers relatively large and predictable rewards because speculators focus their activities over the very short-term. Often speculators are most concerned about how share prices will fluctuate over a day, week, or month. Speculators are not generally focused on what happens to share prices over years and decades (though financial investment guru, Warren Buffett, is a notable exception).

Entrepreneurs face a much more tricky task than speculators. They have to think more carefully about the long-term, which is difficult because the future can be so uncertain. A perfectly rational entrepreneur would invest very little in their business if they had to rely on purely mathematical calculations to back up their investment decisions. Uncertainty about the future, especially for innovative businesses, means that it is hard to predict how well your business might be doing in a year, five years, or a decade. For entrepreneurs something else overcomes uncertainty and fears about the future: *animal spirits*. Animal spirits can be understood partly in terms of optimism bias discussed earlier, as analysed by Tali Sharot and others. Galen of Pergamon, a Greek physician to the gladiators in ancient Rome, first developed the concept of *animal spirits*. He described animal spirits as connecting our internal neurophysiology with our actions, and his ideas were the basis of Hippocrates' description of the four humours—black bile, yellow bile, blood, and phlegm—each associated with a particular temperament: melancholic, choleric, sanguine, and phlegmatic, respectively.

Keynes's animal spirits link to the sanguine temperament—they are about the desire to act and to do something positive. Making the leap from the ancient to the modern world, Galen's animal spirits may also capture a spontaneous optimism associated with the animal spirits of entrepreneurs, which propels them to feeling confident about the future and to investing in building their businesses. What has this got to do with the macroeconomy? Keynes explains that the balance between the activities of the entrepreneurs versus those of the speculators will determine the impact of the stock market on macroeconomic variables including output, employment, unemployment, and growth. Animal spirits are easily dimmed by uncertainty and instability, however. So when financial markets are volatile, entrepreneurs feel unsettled and they will be much less willing to invest in building their businesses for the future.

The financial system connects the entrepreneurs and the speculators. Entrepreneurs need funds from financial markets to build their businesses in the long-term, and financial markets can provide the funds they need. Keynes argues that all will go well when these tendencies are in balance, when speculation is just a bubble on the steady stream of enterprise. However, if speculation becomes an unstable whirlpool, then it will destabilize the macroeconomy, magnifying volatility and uncertainty.

Modern behavioural macroeconomics: the animal spirit models

As previously noted, aggregating from individuals' decisions to capture macroeconomic phenomena is particularly tricky for behavioural macroeconomists. Behavioural macroeconomists can find it difficult to bring together all the complex influences and personalities that drive individuals into a coherent aggregate macroeconomic model. Conventional macroeconomics escapes these complications by assuming that all workers and all businesses are the same, deciding in the same way. Also, everyone is perfectly rational so it is relatively easy to describe how different people interact in the macroeconomy. Standard macroeconomic theories describe one person—*a representative agent*, who makes their decisions in a relatively simple way. In many standard macroeconomic theories, the representative agent captures the behaviour of all firms or all workers. Multiply the representative agents' behaviour and you get your macroeconomic model. In this analysis the macroeconomy is strongly grounded on microeconomic principles.

Behavioural macroeconomists cannot convincingly aggregate using the device of rational representative agents in the same way because the essence of behavioural economics is to capture differences in personality and emotions, and in interactions between agents. There is no single representative agent in behavioural economics. Instead, behavioural macroeconomists tend to focus on aggregate phenomena—for example, business confidence and consumer confidence.

Another way in which modern behavioural macroeconomists build their models is by focusing on specific psychological motivators of action, often employing the concept of animal spirits, but defined in different ways from Keynes's and Galen's definitions. Akerlof and Shiller, in their book *Animal Spirits*, describe a range of animal spirits that affect the macroeconomy and financial systems. Their definition of animal spirits is much less precise than Keynes's. Essentially they equate animal spirits with a range of psychological phenomena whereas Keynes's concept was more about the gut instincts of entrepreneurs investing in building their productive capacity. For Akerlof and Shiller, animal spirits go beyond the animal spirits of entrepreneurs to include a set of five animal spirits, each with its own destabilizing influence—including confidence, preferences for fairness, corruption, money illusion, and storytelling.

Other modern behavioural macroeconomists have developed sophisticated mathematical models around animal spirits, incorporating a definition that is different again from Keynes's original macroeconomic application of Galen's concept. Macroeconomists including Roger Farmer, Paul de Grauwe, and Michael Woodford model animal spirits cycles using sophisticated mathematical techniques, essentially capturing animal spirits as random fluctuations (*random noise*) driving the macroeconomy to switch from buoyant to recessionary states of the world.

Finance and the macroeconomy

Behavioural macroeconomists also focus on the impact of finance and financial instability. Many mainstream macroeconomic theories neglect the financial sector, but since the 2007/8 financial crises and the subsequent global recessions, economists and policy-makers are being reminded how important the financial sector is to macroeconomic performance. One place to start is the psychology of speculative bubbles. Historical accounts of speculative bubbles are difficult to reconcile with the standard economic view of calmly rational agents making careful mathematical calculations when assessing the relative benefits and costs of buying an asset. Tulipmania, one of the most colourful episodes in financial history, illustrates how unstable and irrational a speculative bubble can seem. For three to four short months starting in November 1636, demand for tulip bulbs in Holland rocketed. For the rarer bulbs, price rises of up to 6,000 per cent were recorded. One bulb was particularly prized—the bulb from the exotic Semper Augustus tulip, exotically variegated, thanks to a virus, and beautiful. At the height of the mania, a Semper Augustus bulb could cost as much as a three-storey house in central Amsterdam. Bust followed boom, dramatically. By February 1637, most bulbs were impossible to sell, even at low prices, and many of the tulip speculators lost their fortunes. However, Tulipmania was not a one-off: there are many, many other examples of speculative bubbles throughout history—the South Sea Bubble of the 18th century, the rampant speculation in the US ending in the Great Crash of 1929, the dot.com bubble of the late 1990s, and the sub-prime crisis that precipitated the global financial crises in 2007/8 are just a few.

In explaining this sort of financial instability Keynes's ideas inspired a range of economists to develop richer models of financial markets, including Hyman Minsky as a notable example. Minsky developed a theory of credit cycles to capture some of the financial instability described earlier. Some of Hyman Minsky's work was particularly prescient in terms of predicting the 2007/8 financial crisis and its real impacts in terms of precipitating global recession. As with Keynes, emotional factors play an important role in Minsky's analysis of fragile financial systems and the implications of this financial fragility for the macroeconomy more widely. Minsky explained how business cycles are driven by cycles of fear and panic, with the fragility of the financial system playing a key role in driving extreme fluctuations. Minsky argued that the business cycle is driven, at first, by waves of speculative euphoria and entrepreneurs' over-optimism. Banks are lending too much. Businesses are borrowing too much. Eventually someone realizes that the boom has no stable foundation and interest rates start to rise, precipitating a bust phase as spectacular as the boom that preceded it.

Financial speculation leads to financial instability more generally, and these financial influences can have a detrimental impact on the macroeconomy. These messages have been popularized by Hollywood, most recently in the movie *The Big Short*. This tells the stories of financial traders who realized that enormous financial fragility was building up as complex new financial products were being developed, designed to make money by enabling people with poor credit ratings to take on multiple mortgages. This was the start of the *sub-prime mortgage crisis*. Even as they were making millions of dollars for themselves, the traders recognized that they were profiting on the backs of the many who would lose their homes and/or jobs because the financial instability would have such devastating impacts, not only on the US economy, but also on macroeconomic performance across the globe. As captured by Figure 6, the likely outcome was that, as people could no longer afford their mortgages, they would accumulate credit card debt and this would affect banks and other financial institutions, not only in the US but throughout the world.

Sub-prime mortgages mess

These ideas have been developed by a few economists. Robert Shiller has written much about 'irrational exuberance' (the term coined by Alan Greenspan, former chairman of the US Federal Reserve) in financial markets and its likely impact on employment, investment, output, and economic growth. Hersh Shefrin argues that irrational exuberance in bullish financial markets reflects interactions between fear, hope, and greed. A lot of what drives financial instability is about excessive risk-taking and emotions play their role in this—linking to George Loewenstein and others' insights about visceral factors, explored in Chapter 7. Loewenstein argues that the feeling of riskiness is linked to our emotional states, not to simple, stable preferences, as is usually assumed by economists.

6. Sub-prime mortgages mess.

Moods and the business cycle

Another perspective taken by behavioural macroeconomists is to analyse the impact of confidence and social mood on macroeconomic outcomes. Common factors may drive everyone's mood—for example, most of us are in a more cheerful mood when the sun is shining. Economists have used this insight to capture the connections between moods and macroeconomic and financial fluctuations at various stages of the business cycle.

Mark Kamstra and colleagues used data on seasonal depression to test their hypothesis that financial markets move differently in winter versus summer months. Seasonal depression can be measured using the incidence of Seasonal Affective Disorder (SAD). People experiencing SAD are more likely to be cautious and risk-averse. If this translates through to financial market traders too, then they will be more risk-averse in the winter and also if they live in countries with fewer hours of sunlight. Kamstra and his team found that hours of darkness, cloud cover, and temperature all had a strong impact on stock market performance. They concluded that seasonal depression was increasing traders' risk-aversion. Kamstra's evidence was confirmed in a similar study conducted by David Hirshleifer and Tyler Shumway (2003). They also found that stock market performance correlates positively with hours of sunshine.

Some analysts believe that moods collectively experienced are the key macroeconomic driver, the ultimate explanatory variable. Robert Prechter and his team from the Socionomics Institute apply this insight to the analysis of financial market fluctuations. Prechter argues that *social mood* is the ultimate causal factor and the most powerful driver of macroeconomic trends. Resonating with Keynes and his analysis of the link between financial market fluctuations and real economic performance, Prechter asserts that the stock market captures our unconscious social mood. Prechter argues that this social mood drives buoyant phases of the macroeconomic cycle. When people are feeling more buoyant and optimistic, the positive social mood has a widespread impact—music is more 'pop-y', hemlines go up, and incumbent politicians do well. A buoyant stock market is also the best time for an incumbent president to go for re-election. But when the social mood is negative and pessimistic, financial markets are unstable, fashion is conservative, and music is depressive. The macroeconomy responds to social mood because social mood drives consumers' decisions and companies' business plans. Negative social mood also feeds into government policy-making: government is insular, favouring policies such as protectionism. All these different facets of a negative social mood then feed into a recessionary macroeconomy.

Happiness and well-being

Another theme in behavioural economics takes a different perspective entirely. Behavioural economists are also developing new ways of defining and measuring macroeconomic performance. Traditionally, statisticians in government departments collect information to measure macroeconomic performance overall, often using output/income measured in money terms (e.g. prices and average wages) as well as other objective measures of performance, including numbers of employed versus unemployed people.

Rather than focusing on fluctuations in monetary measures of macroeconomic performance in terms of the monetary value of output and production as measured by gross domestic product (GDP), behavioural economists also look at the psychological aspects of happiness and well-being.

One problem with measuring happiness and well-being is that our perceptions of our own happiness are dependent on context, and this links to the ideas of reference dependence explored in Chapters 4 and 5. Most measures of happiness and well-being are based on surveys—and self-reported levels of happiness can be like a snapshot taken at an unlikely moment. Questions asked before we decide how happy we are (or not) can be used as *priming* questions. For example, students' self-reported happiness can be manipulated by asking them to think about recent events. In one set of experiments students were asked priming questions such as 'Did you have a date last night?' 'Did it go well?'—these questions were designed to prime students to feel particular emotions, depending on how they had got on the previous night. The students' self-reported happiness changed according to the ordering of the questions. Students asked to state how happy they were *after* being asked questions about how things went last night reported different happiness levels. If they had had a miserable night before, then they recorded much lower levels of happiness. If they had had a good night, then they recorded relatively high levels of happiness. On the other hand, students' stated happiness levels were affected less by last night's events if they were asked about their happiness *before* they were asked questions about how they got on the previous night. Prompts to remember recent events were changing students' perceptions of their own happiness. So, whilst policy-makers should worry more about broader definitions of well-being, using happiness surveys is problematic because our self-reported happiness levels can be distorted by ephemeral factors.

Capturing this changing focus in macroeconomics towards broader measures of macroeconomic performance, the Legatum Institute, a London-based political/economic think-tank, released a report in 2014 setting out in detail the literature exploring how our well-being, happiness, and life satisfaction are driven by a wide range of socio-psychological, as well as economic and financial factors. This report also analyses new data sources to measure happiness and well-being, as well as providing some insight into how to analyse these data using robust econometric techniques.

Behavioural economists' interest in happiness and well-being has translated across into developing these new sources of macroeconomic data around the world. Public health data can also be a useful indicator of collective mood—for example, data on suicide rates, mental illness, and stress-related illness. A wide range of national and international statistical agencies are now collecting data on happiness, well-being, and life satisfaction—for example, via household surveys including questions about subjective well-being alongside the standard labour force survey questions about employment and unemployment.

The Office of National Statistics in the UK is now including responses to questions about life satisfaction in its household surveys. Other countries from China to France are collecting similar data, and the OECD is collating international data sets. Potentially these new data can be fed into macroeconomic analyses capturing a more nuanced and wide-ranging picture of macroeconomic performance. Perhaps most influentially, the World Bank is now releasing an annual *World Happiness Report*, which should give behavioural macroeconomists some useful data to capture how macroeconomic trends in happiness shift across space and over time, as well as opportunities to connect these new happiness and well-being measures with more conventional measures of macroeconomic performance.

Technological innovations are also helpful in collecting better behavioural macroeconomic data. Behavioural researchers can now implement wide-scale online surveys and they can use text messaging and social media to collect data too (e.g. from Google searches, Twitter feeds, and Facebook 'likes'). With the growth of these types of 'Big Data', some of the gaps in the behavioural macroeconomists' data sets can potentially be filled.

Using subjective data is problematic, but with the cooperation of economists, statisticians, and government this area is increasingly gaining credibility. Capturing well-being data is also problematic, and much more research is needed to assess the pros and cons of these new statistics, as well as to explore some of the other ways in which behavioural macroeconomists can better understand and measure happiness and well-being.

Chapter 9
Economic behaviour and public policy

At its best, economics can help policy-makers to design policies to resolve a wide range of economic and financial problems, both for individual people and for economies as a whole too. Conventional economic policies focus on resolving market failures: if markets are not working well and prices are not effectively signalling information about relative supply and demand, then government policy instruments can help to resolve the problems that emerge as a consequence. In this chapter we will explore some key insights and evidence from behavioural public policy, focusing on microeconomic policy. Developing a set of coherent behavioural macroeconomic policy tools is a much more complicated challenge, which, so far at least, has not yet been properly attempted.

Microeconomic policy

Traditionally, taxes and subsidies have been the main policy instruments used by governments and policy-makers to help markets work better. A well-trodden example is smoking. If smoking imposes costs on the tax-payer in terms of strains on the public health system, then taxing cigarettes helps—not only to reduce the incentive to smoke, but also in providing governments with revenue to pay for their health systems. On the other hand, if, for example, a particular region of a country is suffering from industrial decline then subsidies can be used to encourage economic activity in that area.

Taxes and subsidies suffer from a range of practical, technical, and logistical limitations and so modern economic policy covers a wider range of economic instruments too, including instruments inspired by Nobel laureate Ronald Coase's analyses of market transactions. Coase's insights underlie the design of artificial trading systems, which can be created to address problems emerging when prices provide imperfect signals of supply and demand. These artificial markets replace 'missing markets'—markets that are missing because market prices exclude them. Pollution is a simple example. When a business pollutes the air or water, if nothing is done about that then the business is polluting for free—they do not have to compensate anyone for the negative consequences of their pollution. As such, the market for pollution is missing.

A solution based on Coase's insights is to develop an artificial market—in the last case, this could take the form of emissions trading schemes. People and businesses can buy and sell rights to pollute (or to be polluted). Creating these artificial markets is not straightforward, but overall, like taxes and subsidies, they are about resolving market and institutional failures rather than individuals' behaviours.

What is behavioural public policy? Nudging for behaviour change

Behavioural public policy looks at these problems from a different perspective. Instead of focusing on market failures, it focuses on *behaviour change*—that is, changing the way that people make their everyday decisions and choices by nudging them towards more efficient and productive decision-making.

The seminal book in the area is Thaler and Sunstein's book *Nudge*—and UK policy-makers often cite *Mindspace*, the essential insights of which are similar to those in *Nudge*. Thaler and Sunstein draw on the large literature from behavioural economics and psychology more generally, especially the ideas about choice overload, information load, heuristics, and behavioural biases, which are covered here in Chapters 4 and 5. They argue that, in designing effective policy instruments, policy-makers need to understand the heuristics and biases driving people's decisions. Then the structure of people's decision-making can be redesigned. This insight forms the foundation of what Thaler and Sunstein call our *choice architecture*. How are our choices structured? How do we process information before deciding what we want to do and buy? Can our decision-making processes be redesigned?

Thaler and Sunstein argue that if policy-makers can better understand people's choice architecture then they can design policies to help people decide more effectively. Giving people simple choices, designing prompts and nudges to lead people's decisions in more constructive and positive directions, giving frequent feedback so that 'good' decisions are reinforced and 'bad' decisions are discouraged—all these strategies form part of behavioural public policy-makers' tool-kits.

Thaler and Sunstein argue that, politically and morally, using nudges is a form of *libertarian paternalism*. People retain power over their own choices so it is libertarian, but it also incorporates *nudges* from government, and in this sense it is paternalistic. In other words, it is libertarian in the sense that people still have a choice; it is paternalistic in the sense that it is a government intervention. Thaler and Sunstein suggest that nudging combines the best of both worlds (though their critics would argue that it combines the worst of both worlds). Taxes and subsidies impose costs and benefits on different groups of people. Generally, an ordinary person cannot choose whether or not to pay taxes (though people and businesses able to pay for expensive accountants may have more control over this). We cannot easily choose whether or not we receive a subsidy, but Thaler and

Sunstein argue that nudges can be designed to allow people some choice, for example via clever design of default options.

Nudging in practice: default options

What do nudges involve in practice? Many nudges are based around the manipulation of *default options*. These are used to leverage a particular type of behavioural bias—the status quo bias—explored in Chapters 4 and 5. If a policy-maker (or business) sets up the default option (the option a person ends up with if they do nothing at all) then a surprisingly large proportion of people will stick with this default option. There is a range of reasons for this. People tend to favour the status quo. They are not always quick to move away from it because changing choices can be risky and/or involve effort. People may interpret the default option as a type of signal about what is the best choice for them. If a default option is set to match the most constructive decision, then more people are likely, albeit passively, to take that decision.

To illustrate with an example, how to encourage people to donate their organs represents a big problem in most countries. The demand for organs is much, much greater than the supply. There are policy dilemmas in this area too—for example, around the ethics of paying people to donate organs—but here we will concentrate on how a behavioural public policy-maker might respond. The policy-maker could set up the default option so that the default is to donate organs. If a person does not want to do this then they would have the option to opt out. In this way, the individual retains her freedom to choose.

Default options can also be used to help us save more for our pensions. In Chapter 4, we covered Benartzi and Thaler's 'Save More for Tomorrow' pension scheme, which also exploits default options. In order to encourage employees to save more for their retirement, the default option in this scheme is that a fixed proportion of all salary goes into an employee's pension pot, with the amount increasing alongside any salary rises. But employees are not forced to do this—they have a choice. They can opt-out. The default option is the policy-maker's tool—this is the paternalistic part of the nudge. The opt-out is the decision-maker's choice—this is the libertarian part of the nudge.

One problem with these types of nudges is that they are often exploited by commercial businesses too, to our detriment. A marketing business wanting to make some extra money from harvesting and selling our contact details to other businesses can set up their contact detail forms so that we do not notice we have given them permission to circulate our contact details. They understand our choice architecture too well.

Switching

Related to default options is the problem of infrequent switching, as also mentioned in Chapter 4. We stick with an energy supplier, a mobile phone company, or a bank for many years, even when the deal they give us is very poor value. We are slow to switch supplier. For energy switching in the UK, in 2016 Ofgem (Great Britain's energy market regulator) reported that over 60 per cent of consumers do not recall switching energy suppliers even though by doing so they could have saved £200 on their annual energy bills. The problem with our low levels of switching is that it lessens the competitive pressure on businesses: if they do not lose customers when they offer a bad value deal, what is their incentive to offer a better deal? Low levels of switching also reflect a status quo bias and, increasingly, government policy-makers are working on encouraging us to switch more frequently if we are not getting a good deal from a supplier. The tools they are designing to encourage more switching are also focused on a better understanding of choice architecture—for example, by making it easier for us to switch or by reducing the problems of choice overload and/or information load that make switching supplier a cognitive challenge. This increased emphasis by policy-makers on encouraging us to switch has had some success in the UK. There is some evidence that these policies are working with switching rates increasing. Ofgem reported that 2015 energy supplier switching rates by households were 15 per cent higher than in 2014.

Social nudges

Another powerful nudge devised by policy-makers harnesses our susceptibility to social influence, building on the ideas outlined in Chapter 3. In the energy sector, some important findings relate to household energy consumption, based on findings from a relatively large body of academic studies. For example, Wesley Schultz and colleagues analysed households in California. The householders were given two types of information. The first set of information related to the energy consumption of other households in a given neighbourhood. This gave householders a social reference point against which they could compare their own energy consumption. Harnessing Thaler and Sunstein's ideas about designing a choice architecture in which choices are simplified, social approval/disapproval for a household's consumption relative to the neighbourhood average was conveyed via a smiley face, if consumption was below the local social average—or a frowny face, if it was above the local social average. The second set of information was a set of instructions about how to reduce energy consumption.

What impact do these different types of information have? To test the differential effectiveness of the various types of information, one group of experimental participants (a control group) were only given energy saving tips. Another group (a treatment group) were given information about social averages too. The researchers found that the social nudges were powerful—the householders in the treatment group, with the social information, were more likely to adjust their energy towards the average than the householders in the control group, adjusting their consumption downwards when told that their consumption was above average for their neighbourhood. Researchers inferred that this was because householders were adjusting their choices towards a social norm or reference point. A wide range of similar studies has captured similar findings, and these insights have been incorporated into new designs for energy bills—for example the OPower bills illustrated in Figure 7.

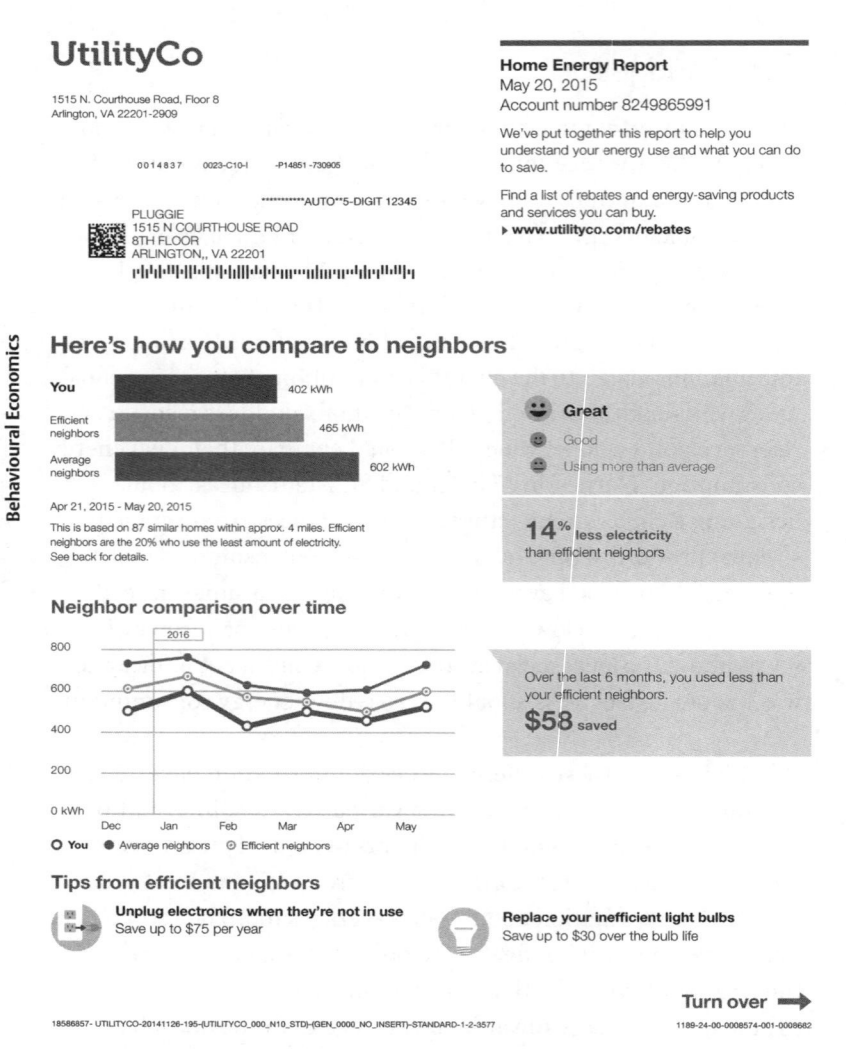

UtilityCo

1515 N. Courthouse Road, Floor 8
Arlington, VA 22201-2909

0014837   0023-C10-I   -P14851-730905

**********AUTO**5-DIGIT 12345
PLUGGIE
1515 N COURTHOUSE ROAD
8TH FLOOR
ARLINGTON,, VA 22201

Home Energy Report
May 20, 2015
Account number 8249865991

We've put together this report to help you understand your energy use and what you can do to save.

Find a list of rebates and energy-saving products and services you can buy.
▸ www.utilityco.com/rebates

Here's how you compare to neighbors

You	402 kWh
Efficient neighbors	465 kWh
Average neighbors	602 kWh

☺ **Great**
☺ Good
☹ Using more than average

Apr 21, 2015 - May 20, 2015
This is based on 87 similar homes within approx. 4 miles. Efficient neighbors are the 20% who use the least amount of electricity. See back for details.

14% less electricity than efficient neighbors

Neighbor comparison over time

2016
800
600
400
200
0 kWh
Dec Jan Feb Mar Apr May
○ You ● Average neighbors ⊙ Efficient neighbors

Over the last 6 months, you used less than your efficient neighbors.

$58 saved

Tips from efficient neighbors

Unplug electronics when they're not in use
Save up to $75 per year

Replace your inefficient light bulbs
Save up to $30 over the bulb life

Turn over ➡

7. Social nudges for saving energy.

A key lesson for policy-makers, however, is to beware the unintended consequences. Researchers identified *boomerang effects*: householders whose energy consumption was below the neighbourhood average tended to be encouraged by social information about neighbours' higher consumption to consume *more* not less. If the distribution of energy consumption across households is symmetric, then perhaps as many people will be adjusting their energy consumption upwards towards the social average as are adjusting their energy consumption downwards. If this is the case, then the average consumption will not change and the policy will have been pointless.

Other policy initiatives

More and more often, behavioural public policy principles are extending to other areas of public policy. For example, the findings about social nudges in the energy sector have spread to taxation. In Chapter 3, we noted how social influences can be harnessed by tax officials and, in the UK, Her Majesty's Revenue and Customs (HMRC) has trialled sending letters to people who are late paying their tax bills, informing them that some proportion of other people have paid their bills on time. The idea here is to use social pressure as a persuasive instrument. This type of social nudge has reportedly been successful in the UK, and in other countries too. Other policy-makers are using default options and other insights to supplement more conventional policies in areas such as competition policy and financial services too.

It is important however, that policy-makers do not lose sight of conventional economic policies—and some of the most effective policy initiatives combine standard economic policy tools with behavioural embellishments. Other policies combine behavioural insights with classic approaches to designing effective incentives. One example is the policy of charging for plastic bags—a policy implemented in Ireland many years ago, to

8. Plastic bag littering.

overcome the problem of plastic bag littering—as illustrated in Figure 8.

Plastic bag littering is a significant environmental problem and has devastating effects for wildlife, the environment, and human health. There is some evidence that our water supplies are becoming contaminated with tiny remnants of all the plastic bags which we carelessly throw away. Manufacturing plastic bags also involves negative impacts from pollution and the excessive use of scarce non-renewable resources. When the UK government introduced a 5 pence (p) plastic bag charge in 2015, stories started circulating that, in some homes, the bags were worth more than people's houses—because people had accumulated so many bags that were now worth 5p each.

More seriously, the 5p charge is an illustration of how insights from behavioural economics can inform the design of conventional economic policies while also promoting behaviour change. The 5p charge is a tax, but one designed to correct a behavioural bias not a market failure (assuming that it is not particularly rational to hoard large numbers of actually almost valueless plastic bags). Perhaps hoarding of plastic bags is a demonstration of the endowment effect—we over-value things we already own. Whatever the underlying psychological reasons may be for plastic bag hoarding, a conventional tax can be used to nudge us away from either accumulating a load of plastic bags that are useless to us or using too many and then throwing them away. But, again, there were unintended consequences and there is some evidence that the overall usage of plastic bags did not decrease. Many people were no longer re-using ordinary plastic supermarket bags as bin bags. Instead they were increasing their purchases of other, bigger plastic bags, including 'bags for life' and heavy-duty bin bags, thus negating some (possibly all) of the positive environmental impacts expected from the 5p bag charge.

The future of policy

The future for behavioural public policy is promising. Spinouts from government policy units have done well, perhaps most famously the Behavioural Insights team originally part of former UK prime minister David Cameron's Cabinet office, nicknamed the 'Nudge Unit'. The Nudge Unit is doing extremely well commercially, and is the focus of a lot of public attention, positive and negative, and on a national and international scale.

There are dangers, however. Behavioural public policy has become very fashionable but, as with all fashions, it does generate excessive hype and is vulnerable to a backlash. Also, a lot of excitement has been generated around behavioural insights and policies based around nudging. More evidence is needed about how effective and how 'sticky' these policy interventions really are. Can we establish using robust statistical analyses that these nudges are really effective, and at a large scale? Can the positive impacts identified so far be replicated across a wider range of studies? Are nudge policies just gimmicky policies with short-run impacts that quickly disappear? For those on whom nudges have been tried, do they eventually return to their old habits and choices? Or do behavioural policy nudges have stronger, more long-lasting impacts?

In ensuring that the most profound behavioural policy lessons endure, it will be important to build a robust and scientifically rigorous body of evidence that demonstrates not only when and where the policies are working, but also when and where they *do not* work. The problem for much academic research is that negative results are not easy to publish. A finding that a policy intervention has not worked is not nearly so exciting and interesting to read about as a finding that a policy intervention has had an amazingly positive benefit. Behavioural economics tells us that we tend to over-weight the information that is most memorable, and the same is true of behavioural public policy evidence.

Another pitfall for policy-makers will emerge if they are distracted away from the conventional economic policies that have been shown to work well in resolving market and institutional failures. Nudging is fashionable in policy circles, but has it led to a neglect of the traditional policy instruments that can effectively address failures in markets and other institutions? Nudges address people's biases and mistakes, but helping people to decide more effectively will not remove market and institutional failures. In the future, policy-makers need to look carefully at how policies based around behavioural insights can be used to complement rather than replace conventional economic policy instruments. In this scenario, a key policy question will be how to coordinate conventional and behavioural policies more effectively, without disproportionately favouring one over the other. If we can get this policy balance right, then behavioural economics will give us some powerful tools to resolve a much wider range of market failures and behavioural biases, with positive benefits for individuals, economies, and society.

References and further reading

Chapter 1: Economics and behaviour

There are many introductions to behavioural economics, including:

Ariely, D. (2008) *Predictably Irrational—The Hidden Forces that Shape Our Decisions*, New York: Harper Collins.

Gigerenzer, G. (2014) *Risk Savvy: How to Make Good Decisions*, London: Penguin Books.

Kahneman, D. (2011) *Thinking, Fast and Slow*, London: Allen Lane.

Thaler, R. H. (2015) *Misbehaving: The Making of Behavioural Economics*, London: Allen Lane.

For more academic introductions, which assume a background knowledge of economics, see:

Baddeley, M. (2013) *Behavioural Economics and Finance*, Routledge: Abingdon.

Earl, P. E. and Kemp, S. (1999) *The Elgar Companion to Consumer Research and Economic Psychology*, Cheltenham: Edward Elgar.

Laibson, D. and List, J. E. (2015) Principles of (behavioral) economics, *American Economic Review* 105(5): 385–90.

There is a large literature on rationality in economics, for example, see:

Simon, H. A. (1955) A behavioural model of rational choice, *Quarterly Journal of Economics* 69: 99–118.

Leibenstein, H. (1976) *Beyond Economic Man*, Cambridge, MA: Harvard University Press.

Smith, V. L. (2003) Constructivist and ecological rationality in economics, *American Economic Review* 93(3): 465–508.

Chapter 2: Motivation and incentives

For behavioural economists' analyses of incentives and motivation, see:

Ariely, D. A., Bracha, A., and Meier, S. (2009) Doing good or doing well? Image motivation and monetary incentives in behaving prosocially, *American Economic Review* 99(1): 544–55.

Bénabou, R. and Tirole, J. (2006) Incentives and prosocial behavior, *American Economic Review* 96(5): 1652–78.

Frey, B. S. and Jegen, R. (2001) How intrinsic motivation is crowded out and in, *Journal of Economic Surveys* 15(5): 589–611.

For analyses of social incentives and gift exchange in labour markets, see:

Akerlof, G. A. (1982) Labor contracts as partial gift exchange, *Quarterly Journal of Economics* 97(4): 543–69.

The nursery school study described in this chapter is explained in detail in:

Gneezy, U. and Rustichini, A. (2000) A fine is a price, *Journal of Legal Studies* 29(1): 1–17.

Chapter 3: Social lives

Some seminal papers on social preferences and related experimental studies include:

Berg, J. E., Dikhaut, J., and McCabe, K. (1995) Trust, reciprocity and social history, *Games and Economic Behavior* 10(1): 122–42.

Fehr, E. and Gächter, S. (2000) Cooperation and punishment in public goods experiments, *American Economic Review* 90(4): 980–94.

Fehr, E. and Schmidt, K. M. (1999) Theory of fairness, competition and cooperation, *Quarterly Journal of Economics* 114(3): 817–68.

Güth, W., Schmittberger, R., and Schwarze, B. (1982) An experimental analysis of ultimatum bargaining, *Journal of Economic Behavior and Organisation* 3: 367–88.

Henrich, J., Boyd, R., Bowles, S., Camerer, C., Fehr, E., Gintis, H., and McElreath, R. (2001) In search of *homo economicus*: behavioral experiments in 15 small-scale societies, *American Economic Review* 91(2): 73–8.

For more detail on neuroeconomic studies of herding, see:

Baddeley, M. (2010) Herding, social influence and economic decision-making: socio-psychological and neuroscientific analyses, *Philosophical Transactions of the Royal Society B* 365(1538): 281–90.

Singer, T. and Fehr, E. (2005) The neuroeconomics of mind reading and empathy, *American Economic Review* 95(2): 340–5.

From economics, the seminal papers on herding and social learning include:

Anderson, L. and Holt, C. (1996) Classroom games: information cascades, *Journal of Economic Perspectives* 10(4): 187–93.

Banerjee, A. (1992) A simple model of herd behavior, *Quarterly Journal of Economics* 107(3): 797–817.

Bikhchandani, S., Hirshleifer, D., and Welch, I. (1998) Learning from the behavior of others: conformity, fads, and informational cascades, *Journal of Economic Perspectives* 12(3): 151–70.

Jan Surowiecki has written an excellent lay-person's introduction:

Surowiecki, J. (2004) *The Wisdom of Crowds: Why the Many Are Smarter than the Few*, London: Abacus.

For an analysis of herding in scientific research and expert opinion, see:

Baddeley, M. (2015) Herding, social influences and behavioural bias in scientific research, *European Molecular Biology Organisation Reports* 16(8): 902–5.

Baddeley, M. (2013) Herding, social influence and expert opinion, *Journal of Economic Methodology* 20(1): 37–45.

For an early analysis of mirror neurons and imitation, see:

Rizzolati, G. and Craighero, L. (2004) The mirror neuron system, *Annual Reviews of Neuroscience* 27:169–92.

For more on identity in behavioural economics, see:

Akerlof, G. A. and Kranton, R. E. (2011) *Identity Economics—How our Identities Shape Our Work, Wages and Wellbeing*, Princeton: Princeton University Press.

Solomon Asch's original line experiments to capture group influence are described in:

Asch, S. E. (1955) Opinions and social pressure, *Scientific American* 193(5): 31–5.

Chapter 4: Quick thinking

The choice experiments from this chapter are described in:

Iyengar, S. and Lepper, M. (2000) When choice is demotivating, *Journal of Personality and Social Psychology* 79(6): 995–1006.

The evidence about choice overload is mixed, and for some meta-analyses of the evidence, see:

Chernev, A., Böckenholt, U., and Goodman, J. (2015) Choice overload: A conceptual review and meta-analysis, *Journal of Consumer Psychology* 25(2): 333–58.

Scheibehenne, B., Greifeneder, R., and Todd, P. M. (2010) Can there ever be too many options? A meta-analytic review of choice overload, *Journal of Consumer Research* 37(3): 409–25.

For Kahneman and Tversky's seminal paper on heuristics and bias, see:

Tversky, A. and Kahneman, D. (1974) Judgement under uncertainty: Heuristics and biases, *Science* 185: 1124–31.

On cognitive dissonance, see:

Akerlof, G. A. and Dickens, W. T. (1982) The economic consequences of cognitive dissonance, *American Economic Review* 72(3): 307–19.

For Thaler and Benartzi's application of default options, see:

Thaler, R. H. and Benartzi, S. (2004) Save More Tomorrow™: using behavioral economics to increase employee saving, *Journal of Political Economy* 112(1): S164–S187.

Chapter 5: Risky choices

The seminal paper on prospect theory is:

Kahneman, D. and Tversky, A. (1979) Prospect theory—an analysis of decision under risk, *Econometrica* 47(2): 263–92.

Regret theory is introduced in:

Loomes, G. and Sugden, R. (1982) Regret theory: an alternative theory of choice under uncertainty, *Economic Journal* 92(368): 805–24.

The other research on loss aversion, endowment effects, and status quo bias referred to in this chapter includes:

Kahneman, D., Knetsch, J., and Thaler, R. (1991) Anomalies: The endowment effect, loss aversion and status quo bias, *Journal of Economic Perspectives* 5(1): 193–206.

Viscusi, W. Kip, Magat, W. A., and Huber, J. (1987) An investigation of the rationality of consumer valuations of multiple health risks, *Rand Journal of Economics* 18(4): 465–79.

Chapter 6: Taking time

The seminal papers on time discounting cited in this chapter include research from neuroscience and behavioural ecology, as well as behavioural economics and economic psychology. The studies and analyses cited include:

Ainslie, G. (1974) Impulse control in pigeons, *Journal of the Experimental Analysis of Behavior* 21(3): 485–9.

Angeletos, G.-M., Laibson, D., Repetto, A., Tobacman, J., and Weinberg, S. (2001) The hyperbolic consumption model: Calibration, simulation, and empirical evaluation, *Journal of Economic Perspectives* 15(3): 47–68.

Camerer, C. F., Babcock, L., Loewenstein, G., and Thaler, R. H. (1997) Labour supply of New York City cab drivers: One day at a time, *Quarterly Journal of Economics* 112(2): 407–41.

DellaVigna, S. and Malmendier, U. (2006) Paying not to go to the gym, *American Economic Review* 96(3): 694–719.

Duflo, E., Kremer, M., and Robinson, J. (2011) Nudging farmers to use fertilizer: Theory and experimental evidence from Kenya, *American Economic Review* 101(6): 2350–90.

Glimcher, P. W., Kable, J., and Louie, K. (2007) Neuroeconomic studies of impulsivity: No or just as soon as possible, *American Economic Review* 97(2): 142–7.

Laibson, D. (1997) Golden eggs and hyperbolic discounting, *Quarterly Journal of Economics* 112: 443–78.

McClure, S. M., Laibson, D. I., Loewenstein, G., and Cohen, J. D. (2004) Separate neural systems value immediate and delayed rewards, *Science* 306: 503–7.

Mischel, W., Shoda, Y., and Rodriguez, M. L. (1989) Delay of gratification in children, *Science* 244(4907): 933–8.

Mulcahy, N. J. and Call, J. (2006) Apes save tools for future use, *Science* 312: 1038–40.

O'Donoghue, T. and Rabin, M. (2001) Choice and procrastination, *Quarterly Journal of Economics* 116(1): 121–60.

Read, D., Loewenstein, G., and Montague, M. (1999) Choice bracketing, *Journal of Risk and Uncertainty* 19(1–3): 171–97.

Rick, S. and Loewenstein, G. (2008) Intangibility in in temporal choice, *Philosophical Transactions of the Royal Society B*, 363(1511): 3813–24.

Strotz, R. H. (1955) Myopia and inconsistency in dynamic utility maximization, *Review of Economic Studies* 23: 165–80.

Thaler, R. H. (1999) Mental accounting matters, *Journal of Behavioral Decision Making* 12: 183–206.

Warner, J. T. and Pleeter, S. (2001) The personal discount rate: Evidence from military downsizing programs, *American Economic Review* 91(1): 33–53.

Chapter 7: Personalities, moods, and emotions

For an account of the Big Five personality tests and the cognitive reflexivity test (CRT), see:

Frederick, S. (2005) Cognitive reflection and decision-making, *Journal of Economic Perspectives* 19(4): 25–42.

McCrae, R. R. and Costa, P. T. (1987) Validation of the five-factor model of personality across instruments and observers, *Journal of Personality and Social Psychology* 52: 81–90.

The answer to the 'bats and balls' CRT question is that the ball costs 5 cents.

On impacts of incentives on experimental participants' responses, see:

Gneezy, U. and Rustichini, A. (2000) Pay enough or don't pay at all, *Quarterly Journal of Economics* 115(3): 791–810.

For some of David Cesarini and colleagues' research into genetics and personality, see:

Cesarini, D., Dawes, C. T., Johannesson, M., Lichtenstein, P., and Wallace, B. (2009) Genetic variation in preferences for giving and risk taking, *Quarterly Journal of Economics* 124(2): 809–42.

For other references to research on personality and economic life chances, see:

Borghans, L., Duckworth, A. L., Heckman, J. J., and Ter Weel, B. (2008) The economics and psychology of personality traits, *Journal of Human Resources* 43(4): 972–1059.

Heckman, J., Moon, S. H., Pinto, R., Savelyev, P., and Yavitz, A. (2010) The rate of return to the HighScope Perry Preschool Program, *Journal of Public Economics* 94(1–2): 114–28.

Mischel, W., Shoda, Y., and Rodriguez, M. L. (1989) Delay of gratification in children, *Science* 244(4907): 933–1038.

For the references cited relating to emotions, see:

Elster, J. (1998) Emotions and economic theory, *Journal of Economic Literature* 36(1): 47–74.

le Doux, J. E. (1996) *The Emotional Brain*, New York: Simon & Schuster.

For Dan Ariely's work with colleagues on emotions and preferences, see:

Lee, L., Amir, O., and Ariely, D. (2009) In search of homo economicus: Cognitive noise and the role of emotion in preference consistency, *Journal of Consumer Research* 36(2): 173–87.

The literature on addiction is a response to Gary Becker's rational addiction model:

Becker, G. S. and Murphy, K. M. (1988) A theory of rational addiction, *Journal of Political Economy* 96(4): 675–700.

Behavioural economists' alternative analyses of addiction include:

Baddeley, M. (2013) Bad habits, *Behavioural Economics and Finance*, Routledge: Abingdon, chapter 10.

Bernheim, B. D. and Rangel, A. (2004) Addiction and cue-triggered decision processes, *American Economic Review* 94(5): 1558–90.

Laibson, D. I. (2001) A cue-theory of consumption, *Quarterly Journal of Economics* 116(1): 81–119.

Loewenstein, G. (1996) Out of control: Visceral influences on decision making, *Organizational Behavior and Human Decision Processes* 65(3): 272–92.

Camerer et al.'s survey papers are good introductions to neuroeconomics, for example, see:

Camerer, C. F., Loewenstein, G., and Prelec, D. (2005) Neuroeconomics: How neuroscience can inform economics, *Journal of Economic Literature* 43(1): 9–64.

For introductions to dual systems models and the somatic marker hypothesis, see:

Damasio, A. R. (1994) *Descartes' Error: Emotion, Reason, and the Human Brain*, London: Vintage.

Kahneman, D. (2003) Maps of bounded rationality: Psychology for behavioral economics, *American Economic Review* 93(5): 1449–75.

Kahneman, D. (2011) *Thinking, Fast and Slow*, London: Allen Lane.

For the neuroeconomic analyses of emotions in economics and finance cited in this chapter, see:

Coates, J. M. and Herbert, J. (2008) Endogenous steroids and financial risk taking on a London trading floor, *Proceedings of the National Academy of Sciences* 105(16): 6167–72.

Cohen, J. D. (2005) The vulcanization of the human brain: A neural perspective on interactions between cognition and emotion, *Journal of Economic Perspectives* 19(4): 3–24.

Knutson, B. and Bossaerts, P. (2007) Neural antecedents of financial decisions, *Journal of Neuroscience* 27(31): 8174–7.

Kuhnen, C. and Knutson, B. (2005) The neural basis of financial risk taking, *Neuron* 47(5): 763–70.

Lo, A. W. and Repin, D. V. (2002) The psychophysiology of real-time financial risk processing, *Journal of Cognitive Neuroscience* 14(3): 323–39.

Sanfey, A. G., Rilling, J. K., Aronson, J. A., Nystrom, L. E., and Cohen, J. D. (2003) The neural basis of economic decision-making in the Ultimatum Game, *Science* 300: 1755–8.

Shiv, B., Loewenstein, G., Bechara, A., Damasio, H., and Damasio, A. R. (2005) Investment behaviour and the negative side of emotion, *Psychological Science* 16(6): 435–9.

Smith, K. and Dickhaut, J. (2005) Economics and emotions: Institutions matter, *Games and Economic Behavior* 52: 316–35.

Tuckett, D. (2011) *Minding the Markets: An Emotional Finance View of Financial Instability*, Basingstoke: Palgrave Macmillan.

Chapter 8: Behaviour in the macroeconomy

Important early writings in behavioural macroeconomics include:

Katona, G. (1975) *Psychological Economics*, New York: Elsevier.
Keynes, J. M. (1936) *The General Theory of Employment, Interest and Money*, London: Macmillan, especially chapter 12.
Minsky, H. (1986) *Stabilizing an Unstable Economy*, New Haven, CT: Yale University Press.

George Akerlof covered many of the key themes in his Nobel Prize lecture:

Akerlof, G. (2002) Behavioral macroeconomics and macroeconomic behavior, *American Economic Review* 92(3): 411-33.

Tali Sharot has done some interesting research on optimism bias, introduced in:

Sharot, T. (2011) *The Optimism Bias: Why We're Wired to Look on the Bright Side*, New York: Pantheon Books.

Other studies on optimism bias cited here include:

Ifcher, J. and Zarghamee, H. (2011) Happiness and time preference: The effect of positive affect in a random-assignment experiment, *American Economic Review* 101(7): 3109-29.
National Audit Office (2013) Over-optimism in government projects. Report by the UK's National Audit Office.

Some modern behavioural macroeconomic analyses and models include:

Akerlof, G. and Shiller, R. (2009) *Animal Spirits: How Human Psychology Drives the Economy and Why it Matters for Global Capitalism*, Princeton: Princeton University Press.
Baddeley, M. (2016) Behavioural macroeconomics: Time, optimism and animal spirits, in R. Frantz, S.-H. Chen, K. Dopfer, F. Heukelom, and S. Mousavi (eds), *Routledge Handbook of Behavioural Economics*, New York: Routledge, pp. 266-79.
de Grauwe, P. (2012) Booms and busts in economic activity: A behavioural explanation, *Journal of Economic Behavior and Organisation* 83(3): 484-501.

Farmer, R. E. A. (2012) Confidence, crashes and animal spirits, *Economic Journal* 122(559): 155–72.

Howitt, P. and McAfee, R. P. (1992) Animal spirits, *American Economic Review* 82(3): 493–507.

Woodford, M. (1990) Learning to believe in sunspots, *Econometrica* 58: 277–307.

For the analyses of financial market bubbles and instability, including the references mentioned in this chapter exploring how mood and weather might affect financial markets, see:

Hirshleifer, D. and Shumway, T. (2003) Good day sunshine: Stock returns and the weather, *Journal of Finance* 58(3): 1009–32.

Kamstra, M. J., Kramer, L. A., and Levi, M. D. (2003) Winter blues: A SAD stock market cycle, *American Economic Review* 93(1): 324–43.

Kindleberger, C. P. (2001) *Manias, Panics and Crashes: A History of Financial Crises* (4th edition), Hoboken, NJ: John Wiley.

For an introduction to Robert Prechter and others on social mood, see:

Casti, J. L. (2010) *Mood Matters: From Rising Skirt Lengths to the Collapse of World Powers*, Berlin: Springer-Verlag.

Some introductions to happiness and well-being include:

Haybron, D. M. (2013) *Happiness: A Very Short Introduction*, Oxford: Oxford University Press.

Layard, R. L. (2005) *Happiness: Lessons from a New Science*, London: Penguin.

O'Donnell, G., Deaton, A., Durand, M., Halpern, D., and Layard, R. (2014) *Wellbeing and Policy*, London: Legatum Institute.

Oswald, A. J., and Wu, S. (2010) Objective confirmation of subjective measures of human well-being: Evidence from the U.S.A., *Science* 327(5965): 576–79.

The World Bank, Happiness Report, various years, Washington, DC: World Bank. <http://worldhappiness.report>.

Chapter 9: Economic behaviour and public policy

Influential introductions to behavioural economics for policy-makers include:

Dolan, P., Hallsworth, M., Halpern, D., King, D., and Vlaev, I. (2010) *Mindspace—Influencing Behaviour Through Public Policy*, London: Cabinet Office/Institute for Government.

Schultz, P. W., Nolan, J. M., Cialdini, R. B., Goldstein, N. J., and Griskevicius, V. (2007) The constructive, destructive, and reconstructive power of social norms, *Psychological Science* 18(5): 429–34.

Thaler, R. and Sunstein, C. (2008) *Nudge—Improving Decisions about Health, Wealth and Happiness*, New Haven, CT: Yale University Press.

For a survey of behavioural economic insights around energy:

Baddeley, M. (2015) Behavioural approaches to managing household energy consumption, in F. Beckenbach and W. Kahlenborn (eds), *New Perspectives for Environmental Policies through Behavioural Economics*, Berlin: Springer, pp. 2013–235.

Also, Cass Sunstein has written deeply and thoughtfully about policy nudges built around default options:

Sunstein, C. (2015) *Choosing Not to Choose: Understanding the Value of Choice*, Oxford: Oxford University Press.

"牛津通识读本"已出书目

古典哲学的趣味	福柯	地球
人生的意义	缤纷的语言学	记忆
文学理论入门	达达和超现实主义	法律
大众经济学	佛学概论	中国文学
历史之源	维特根斯坦与哲学	托克维尔
设计,无处不在	科学哲学	休谟
生活中的心理学	印度哲学祛魅	分子
政治的历史与边界	克尔凯郭尔	法国大革命
哲学的思与惑	科学革命	民族主义
资本主义	广告	科幻作品
美国总统制	数学	罗素
海德格尔	叔本华	美国政党与选举
我们时代的伦理学	笛卡尔	美国最高法院
卡夫卡是谁	基督教神学	纪录片
考古学的过去与未来	犹太人与犹太教	大萧条与罗斯福新政
天文学简史	现代日本	领导力
社会学的意识	罗兰·巴特	无神论
康德	马基雅维里	罗马共和国
尼采	全球经济史	美国国会
亚里士多德的世界	进化	民主
西方艺术新论	性存在	英格兰文学
全球化面面观	量子理论	现代主义
简明逻辑学	牛顿新传	网络
法哲学:价值与事实	国际移民	自闭症
政治哲学与幸福根基	哈贝马斯	德里达
选择理论	医学伦理	浪漫主义
后殖民主义与世界格局	黑格尔	批判理论

德国文学	儿童心理学	电影
戏剧	时装	俄罗斯文学
腐败	现代拉丁美洲文学	古典文学
医事法	卢梭	大数据
癌症	隐私	洛克
植物	电影音乐	幸福
法语文学	抑郁症	免疫系统
微观经济学	传染病	银行学
湖泊	希腊化时代	景观设计学
拜占庭	知识	神圣罗马帝国
司法心理学	环境伦理学	大流行病
发展	美国革命	亚历山大大帝
农业	元素周期表	气候
特洛伊战争	人口学	第二次世界大战
巴比伦尼亚	社会心理学	中世纪
河流	动物	工业革命
战争与技术	项目管理	传记
品牌学	美学	公共管理
数学简史	管理学	社会语言学
物理学	卫星	物质
行为经济学		